Israel on the Road to Sinai
1949-1956

ISRAEL ON THE ROAD TO SINAI

1949-1956

BY ERNEST STOCK

With a Sequel on the Six-Day War, 1967

Cornell University Press

ITHACA, NEW YORK

First published 1967

Library of Congress Catalog Card Number: 67-23764

PRINTED IN THE UNITED STATES OF AMERICA
BY VAIL-BALLOU PRESS, INC.

To my parents

Preface

On 29 October 1956, Israeli troops crossed the demarcation line separating the territory of the Jewish state from Egypt's Sinai Peninsula in what appeared at first like another temporary foray across a frontier long troubled by raids and counterraids. But the overland move was coordinated with a paratroop drop on the Mitla Pass deep in Egyptian territory, and by now it was clear that a full-scale military campaign was underway. Soon another Israeli column set out on a hazardous trek to capture the Egyptian positions which barred the Gulf of Aqaba to Israel shipping at the Straits of Tiran. Still another element, after crossing the line into Sinai, turned toward the Mediterranean to invest and occupy the Egyptian-held Gaza Strip.

All of this occurred at a time when the world's attention was riveted to the streets of Budapest, where Russian troops were fighting rebellious Hungarians. In the United States an election campaign was in its last week, but the oratory was all but drowned out by the sound of gunfire from the two fields of battle.

The day after the Israeli operation began, Britain and France issued an ultimatum to Egypt and Israel to withdraw their forces to a line ten miles from either side of the Suez Canal. When Egypt predictably refused to comply, the two powers followed up their ultimatum with bombing attacks on Egyptian airfields and, somewhat later, with sea and airborne invasion. The world was on the brink of a conflagration.

How the fires were extinguished is part of history. In Hungary, once Soviet Russia had decided to crush the rebellion which threatened to rend the Communist system asunder, there could be no doubt about the outcome. While active intervention by the West might have saved the revolt, the stakes were not sufficiently high for the United States to provoke a direct confrontation with the Soviet Union at the almost certain risk of war.

In the Middle East, such a confrontation was averted when the United States failed to side with its NATO allies and instead joined the Soviet Union in demanding cessation of the hostilities, thereby obliging Great Britain and France to stop short of their goal and evacuate their foothold in the Canal zone. The same alignment at the United Nations forced Israel to give up most of the gains of its hundred-hour war.

In the decade that has passed, more than a dozen books have been written on the diplomatic and military aspects of the Suez affair. Some attempts to assess the blame for the West's debacle find that either inept statesmanship or poor planning of the Anglo-French military operation, or both, were at fault. The roles of France, Great Britain, and the United States have been analyzed. Several of the books conjecture about the degree of collusion between the two European allies and Israel. One study traces the course of relations between Israel and France which culminated in the supply of weapons and of French air and naval cover for Israel's campaign. A revealing and authoritative publication on the Israel side is General Moshe Dayan's *Diary of the Sinai Campaign*. While leaving no doubt on the score of coordination of the actual battle plans, the *Diary* also points up some of the earlier books' fallacy of viewing Israel's campaign as a mere diversionary action in a drama the main parts of which were enacted by other protagonists. For although the interests and objectives of the two Western powers and of Israel overlapped temporarily in their opposition to Egypt, the antecedents of Sinai were altogether different from those which produced the crisis over the Canal and the Anglo-French intervention. The present study explores the antecedents of Israel's campaign.

This calls, in effect, for an analysis of the nature of the Israel-Arab confrontation, which proved so intractable to the ordinary means of settling disputes; and of the objectives of Israel's foreign policy and the means by which Israel tried to attain them before deciding to march into Sinai.

Foreign policy, it has been said, is made on the basis of subjective truths as perceived by men acting in their country's interests. The perspective in this study is that of an observer viewing Israeli policy in order to arrive at an understanding of the subjective truths by which it was motivated. This is obviously a partial view. The historian of the period will require a perspective which includes also the subjective truths of the other side. What follows, however, is not a historical account but an analysis of a political process. In it, salient and characteristic events are selected to illustrate how a small and new state, disposing of limited resources and power, faced a most serious challenge to its integrity and perhaps its existence.

In the writing of this book I was greatly aided by the advice, assistance, and encouragement of numerous individuals on both sides of the ocean. In the United States, I am particularly grateful to my teacher and friend, Professor J. C. Hurewitz of Columbia University, for his careful guidance and consistent encouragement throughout the various stages of the project. Professors William T. R. Fox and Charles Issawi made many cogent suggestions after reading the doctoral dissertation upon which this book is based. In Israel, I owe thanks to those officials, colleagues, and friends who took the time to read all or portions of the manuscript and who gave me the benefit of their ideas and friendly criticism. An interview granted to me by the late Moshe Sharrett, former Prime Minister and Foreign Minister, will always remain a cherished memory.

PREFACE

A portion of this study is based on research conducted during a previous stay in Israel on a fellowship grant from the Ford Foundation; I am indebted to the Foundation for its support, but of course it is in no way responsible for the result, and, in general, any errors or misjudgments which the book may contain are my own.

My wife and son have contributed to the fruition of this project in their own, manifold ways.

ERNEST STOCK

Brandeis University
Waltham, Massachusetts,
and Jerusalem, Israel
January 1967

After this book had gone to press, the Arab-Israeli confrontation once again erupted into crisis and war, and the Sinai Peninsula again became the arena in which Egypt and Israel tested each other's strength. To relate the Six-Day War to the Sinai Campaign and its political consequences, a new chapter, "The Sequel: 1967," has been added to the book.

E. S.

Jerusalem
August 1967

Contents

Israel on the Road to Sinai

1949-1956

INTRODUCTION ≺≺≺≺

Israel's Foreign Policy

Israel as a Small State

In territory and in population, Israel emerged on the international scene as one of the smallest states in existence. The Jewish state that was to have come into being under the terms of the 1947 Partition Resolution of the U.N. General Assembly would have had a territory of 5,729 square miles and less than 900,000 inhabitants. After the signing of the armistice agreements in 1949 the territory at Israel's disposal comprised 7,977 square miles; the population was 1,200,000. The only Middle East state smaller in area, though slightly larger in population at the time, was Israel's northern neighbor, Lebanon.

Size and population are not in themselves indices of power. But they are basic among the resources the availability of which places constraints on the action of states and thereby limits their role in international politics. It is not surprising, therefore, that the foreign policy of small states was long an untilled field in the study of interstate relations: from the Congress of Vienna, which first distinguished formally between great powers and lesser powers, until after World War II, the course of world affairs was determined undisputedly by the former. But in the postwar era two developments occurred which enhanced the role of the smaller states within the state system, and indirectly served as a backdrop to the Arab-Israel conflict and the Sinai

Campaign. One was the gravitation of power from a multi-national balance, such as prevailed under the European Concert, to two distinct poles. With the harnessing of nuclear energy into weapons of mass destruction, the United States and Soviet Russia emerged as superpowers opposing one another, while the rest of the former great powers, either defeated in the war or exhausted by it, were no longer in a position to bring decisive influence to the course of events. The second development was the attainment of sovereignty by a large number of ex-colonial territories.

In the shadow of the two power blocs competing for influence in the Cold War, small states were able to pursue their own paths relatively undisturbed, as the restraints previously imposed by the great powers acting in concert ceased to be effective. Some of the new small states began probing the limits of their freedom of action, usually with little regard to their relative strength. In their relations with great powers, they tended to ignore the power discrepancy, acting instead on the assumption that the sovereign equality of states was an immutable fact of international life.[1] The bipolar concentration of power facilitated this, and the active role assigned to the small powers in the United Nations opened up for them an entirely new field of diplomatic activity. While many of the older small states tended—voluntarily or forcibly—to join one of the power blocs, and their foreign policies became dependent upon the policies of the superpowers, most of the new states of Asia and Africa refused to be similarly inhibited. Their location outside the European state system caused them to be insensitive to the balance-of-power aspect of international politics, in which they had never participated. The leaders of these states were as a rule too bemused by their own struggle for independence to pay close attention to the larger political scene. The power against which their struggle was waged appeared to them, first of all, as an imperialist power, and only secondarily as a Western democracy.

2

Although sometimes vaguely socialist or even dogmatically Marxist, leaders in the new states generally did not view the capitalist-communist dichotomy with inordinate interest. The democracy versus totalitarianism issue also did not appear of major relevance to them; a number of the new states have become military dictatorships. As far as most new states were concerned, the Cold War was not fought over moral issues—only the Cold War itself was immoral. Since neither of the opposing sides represented to them a superior morality, the new states were able to preserve a cool detachment, and to take sides on specific issues in the light of their own self-interest.

Small and new states frequently define their foreign policy in terms of peace, international understanding, and other high-minded abstractions. But since these are the international versions of being "against sin" and are worded in such general fashion that they can be subscribed to by every state, they do not express specific policy goals. Nor could they, since an individual small state's contribution to international peace must necessarily be proportionate to its power—that is, it must be quite limited.

An understanding of the disproportion between these aims and the limited resources which the small state can marshal for their realization on a global scale is needed in order to drive home the point that these broad general aims do not qualify as foreign policy goals. A small state could, it is true, make an effective contribution at the expense of its own interest where the latter conflicts with the interests of another state and therefore leads to friction on the international scene. But instances of such sacrificial behavior on the part of states are so rare as to be excluded from the list of probabilities in interstate relations. When the small state does endeavor to play a role in the deliberations of international bodies outside its own sphere of interest, it is generally motivated by reasons of prestige. The intense competition over a seat on the Security Council, for

3

example, points to the prestige value of such a seat to the small state. Similarly motivated is the participation of small-state spokesmen in debates where their position has no power-relevance to the matter under discussion; the prestige value of an appearance in this forum causes few small states to pass up an opportunity for registering their views.

Foreign policy has been described as being primarily directed toward achievement of decisions based on internally generated conceptions of the national interest over foreign opposition.[2] This formulation is particularly apt when applied to the foreign policy of the small state. It implies that the degree of foreign policy activity by the small state stands in direct relationship to the degree of opposition its national interest—as subjectively conceived by it—evokes among other states. If there is no opposition to these interests, the small state has no need of an active foreign policy. The example that comes to mind is Switzerland: the conflict situations that do arise from time to time can be dealt with on an *ad hoc* basis.

In Israel's case, it was precisely the degree of opposition to its vital interests which distinguished its foreign policy from that of the "normal" small state. Faced with an implacable kind of opposition, Israel was bound to engage in diplomatic activity of appropriate intensity. Since the hostility of the states in the area precluded diplomatic interchange on a regional level, Israel pursued its objectives outside the region, attempting to enlist great-power support for the furtherance of its interests.[3]

What were these interests?

Security and economic well-being are interests common to all sovereign states, large and small, and their foreign policies seek ways to safeguard and maximize both. This was also true for Israel, but with a difference: the very legitimacy of its survival as a state was being challenged, so that security meant securing survival in the face of that challenge. Economic prosperity also became a corollary of survival, on the reasoning that

4

an economically weak and dependent state could easily succumb to renewed hostilities or to other pressures.

The preservation of territorial integrity, again in the face of designs by the neighboring states, was also a direct extension of the survival motif: the demarcation lines of the armistice agreements came to be regarded as encompassing the minimum territory required for maintaining a viable polity.

Still another interest linked up with survival was the preservation of the ethnic integrity of the Israeli population—preservation, that is, of a Jewish majority sufficiently large to exclude the possibility of its being outnumbered by citizens of Arab descent.

The foreign policy objectives which grew out of this core of vital interests may be described, in their broadest terms, as follows: (1) to obtain ratification of the territorial *status quo;* (2) to obtain foreign aid in the attainment of economic self-support and in the defeat of Arab obstacles to economic well-being, such as the boycott and the obstruction of navigation in Arab-controlled waterways; (3) to prevent the return of large numbers of Arab refugees from Palestine.

The pursuit of these objectives was complicated by the fact that they were being presented to the world as a "package." The legitimacy of survival had been endorsed by the United Nations and was accepted by the great powers, and the quest for economic prosperity also found sympathy. But the two other interests deemed vital by Israel, territorial integrity and ethnic homogeneity, on the basis of the *status quo,* met with opposition not only within but outside the region as well.

The integrity of the territory claimed by Israel, while not openly challenged by the powers outside the area, was described as subject to compromise,[4] and Israel's position on the return of the Arab refugees was never endorsed by the international community. These circumstances distinguished Israel's problem from that of the "normal" *status quo* state which defends interests long

5

validated or simply tries to maximize its citizens' welfare through obtaining the advantages that may be gained by manipulating great-power rivalries.

While the powers, and the West in particular, wished to ensure Israel's survival as a state, they were averse to recognizing its borders as permanent until the Arab states had also recognized them, and also to accepting the Israeli position on the Arab refugees in the face of adamant Arab opposition. This ambivalent attitude of the powers toward Israel's basic foreign policy objectives further accentuated the global nature of its diplomacy. Former Prime Minister David Ben-Gurion has written:

Israel always faced an array of forces in two spheres: in the small sphere of our own area . . . and the large sphere, which comprises the entire globe. . . . If we existed only in the first sphere, and had no contact with the wider one, or if the wide sphere did not interfere in the affairs of the small one, then the military factor alone would be decisive. . . . But there were two reasons why Israel could not ignore the wider sphere:

(1) It contains the great majority of the Jewish people, from which we draw manpower, material and cultural resources, and moral and political support;

(2) the forces at work in the wider sphere will not lightly accept all the decisions secured by the Israel forces, *if these decisions are in opposition to their true or imagined interests*.[5]

Israel as an Ideological State

Ben-Gurion here put his finger also on that other element which distinguished Israel's international relations from those of "normal" small states: its character as a Jewish state, and its relationship to world Jewry. It has just been pointed out how Israel's character as a state with a population predominantly of a single religio-ethnic group desiring to preserve its homogeneity

6

shaped one of its vital interests and thereby influenced its foreign policy objectives. But there were additional ways in which foreign policy was affected.

The existence of a state of and for a particular ethnic group is not unusual in itself. The doctrine of national self-determination, which led to the establishment of small as well as large states in the present era, is frequently based on ethnically homogeneous groups (religion has also been a determinant, as in the case of India and Pakistan). What is *exceptional* about the Jewish state is its relationship to other Jews. Here again, the fact that large numbers of coreligionists (or members of the same ethnic group) live outside its borders is not a unique circumstance: the state system knows several similar instances. The unique feature in Israel's case is the specific nature of Jewishness, with its interwoven elements of religion and nationhood, which, shaped by a history of several millenia, do not fit readily into modern political categories. Zionism, the Jewish nationalist movement which fathered the state, offered a specific ideology concerning the nature of Jewishness in the modern world, in which the existence of a Jewish nation-state played a key role. Both the internal character of the Israeli state and its foreign policy continued to be affected by the ideological heritage of the Zionist movement. This made Israel a rarity among small powers—an ideological state.

The meaning of that term can be best elucidated by using as a reference the modern ideological state *par excellence,* the Soviet Union.

As an ideological state the Soviet Union seeks to achieve not only the orthodox ends of the sovereign state (security, prosperity, maximalization of power) but also professes an ideological aim. As long as the ideology is centered in the internal structure of the society and economy, it need not affect the state's foreign relations. But when it has its corollary on the outside, it is likely to bring on friction on the international scene as when, for a period, the Soviets refused to be bound by international law on the ground that it was an instrument of the ruling classes in capitalist countries.

For it is quite apparent that the admixture of ideology to the national interest tends to make foreign policy more unpredictable, and this is detrimental to the smooth functioning of the state system. Although national interest is necessarily a subjective concept, the common denominators of security and prosperity lend the system a necessary element of predictability.

Zionism as a Nationalist Ideology

A small state, however, would find it difficult to be the protagonist, or at any rate the exclusive protagonist, of a world-wide ideological movement whose basic premise is detrimental to the smooth functioning of the state system. Indeed, Zionism differed fundamentally from communism in that its purpose was the creation of a nation-state which would take its place among the other members of the state system, and thereby create the conditions for a normal national life for its Jewish population.

But if the main purpose of Zionism was the creation of a state, what was the content of the ideology once the state was achieved, and how did it affect foreign policy? Surely, the ancillary goals of the Zionist ideology as a nationalist movement concerning the quality of the group's existence within the state, such as the religious, cultural, or economic forms it should take, were of no direct international import and therefore of little interest to the other members of the state system. "Zionism's real significance lies in the fact that twenty centuries of self-distortion, self-estrangement and self-blame have ended for a people which is now free to live its own life at every level of emotional and cultural experience," writes an American rabbi.[6] Zionism, however, differed from most other nationalist movements aspiring to sovereignty in that its subjects were originally scattered rather than concentrated in a particular place. Therefore, concurrent with the pursuit of the territorial goal went the process of "ingathering." This process was not terminated with the achievement of sovereignty. It continued after the claim to the territory was validated, actively encouraged by the state, and remained operative as a kind of open-ended policy directed not only at homeless Jews but also at Jewish citizens of other countries.

Immigration—Interest or Ideology?

It would seem, therefore, that a tenet of ideology had become an objective of foreign policy. It must be noted, however, that immigration is also regarded as being in the national interest, quite apart from its ideological import, though it is usually cited in close juxtaposition with it. The following quotations from an article written by Ben-Gurion for the 1951 *Israel Government Year Book* are examples: "The cardinal aim of our state is the redemption of the people of Israel, the ingathering of the Exiles." "A primary and deciding factor in our security is mass immigration in swift tempo. . . . No economic or such-like considerations can be allowed to slow down the rate of immigration." [7] Eight years later, Ben-Gurion still expressed the same thought in nearly identical words: "Israel can have no security without immigration. The population of Egypt alone numbers 23 million. Israel's is only about two million. Aliyah (immigration) is not only the redemption of Jews from physical or spiritual extinction in the Diaspora and the supreme historic mission of the State of Israel; it is of paramount importance for our security." [8]

The establishment of the state in 1948 had opened the sluice gates to a flood of immigration generated by the tragic fate of European Jewry on the one hand (its candidates having been dammed up not only in the DP camps on the Continent but also in the British-run detention camps of Cyprus); and by the quasi-messianic impact of the state on certain Jewish populations in the Arab world. The latter process then generated its own

9

momentum as the hostility of the Arab states to Israel placed Jewish populations in a precarious position and stimulated the desire to emigrate.

This process would not have been stemmed, or interfered with, by any Israel government no matter what the consequences. The influx of immigrants represented visible proof of the correctness of a main premise on which the state rested—namely that a Jewish state was required to receive the homeless, the persecuted. the insecure among the world's Jews. However, immigration not only did not run counter to national interest but became an adjunct of its most important aspect—security. The small size of the Jewish population—650,000 on 15 May 1948—was a critical weakness which had to be remedied, and the only remedy was mass immigration. The military motivations are obvious; to hold its own on an extended front the Israeli high command was obliged to send some of the young men freshly arrived from the Cyprus detention camps into battle.[9] And the military necessity for manpower continued after the signing of the armistice agreements and is likely to remain until the *status quo* is finally ratified. Aside from the strength of the armed forces, manpower was needed to settle the country more evenly and therefore make it both militarily and politically defensible. From the economic point of view it was widely believed that immigration brought prosperity and economic activity. And from a general political viewpoint, it was felt that Israel needed a larger Jewish population to make its voice heard and to speak with authority.

The criterion of economic absorptive capacity which had been upheld by the mandatory government was abandoned in favor of a policy of unlimited immigration, and this policy was crystallized in the Law of the Return, which conferred the right of immigration and citizenship upon every Jew of good moral character.[10] Nevertheless, at about the same time that this legislation manifestly made the policy of unlimited immigration a fundamental tenet and removed it from the realm of controversy, some

10

administrative measures were taken to curb the influx of sick, aged, and handicapped migrants without means of support—categories which constituted the most visible drain on the state's resources and contributed nothing to its security. This was the policy of selective immigration.[11] By that time the mass influx which lasted from 1948 to 1951 had come to an end, not to be resumed again in the same proportions. Despite large-scale aid from American Jewry designed to help pay for the cost of immigrant settlement, Israel's international payments position was critical. Housing construction could not keep up with the need; after abandoned Arab housing was fully utilized, tent cities and tin huts dotted the landscape.

This indicates that economic prosperity had a higher priority in the hierarchy of goals than unlimited migration where that immigration did not serve another high-priority end, namely security. As long as the state itself was the main instrument for the fulfillment of the Zionist mission, it could easily be rationalized that the welfare of the state must not be jeopardized, though it might temporarily conflict with the mission itself, since without the state the mission would be totally inoperative. Even where ideology and interest converge in a single policy, there comes a time when the policy no longer serves the national interest.

The World Zionist Organization

In Israel, the duality in the motivation for immigration was symbolized by passage in 1952 of the Status Law for the World Zionist Organization, which charged that body and its executive arm, the Jewish Agency for Israel, with implementing immigration and settlement policy. Although the Knesset debate on the draft law indicates that there were misgivings among the Israelis, and that the principal pressure for adoption came from the non-Israeli Zionist leadership who were eager to have their role forti-

11

fied by legal sanction, the fact that the government was willing to delegate this function to a nongovernmental ideological body points to the ideological wellsprings of the immigration policy.

It must be noted, however, that Ben-Gurion himself remained consistently on the side opposing special status for the Zionist movement in Israel; he kept up what amounted to a vendetta against the organized Zionist movement and its role, proposing its abolition and seeking instead formal acknowledgment of the broad base of support for Israel among the Jews of the world.

Attempts to provide an unambiguous definition of the role of Zionism after the establishment of the state have indeed been unsuccessful, and many Israelis have shared Ben-Gurion's impatience with the desire of the Zionist organization to perpetuate itself after its primary aim—the acquisition of a territorial base which Jews require for their survival as a group, physical and spiritual—was accomplished.

Is it justifiable, then, to contend that the only way in which the Zionist origin of the state affected foreign policy was through the policy of immigration, which would be pursued in any event as a vital national interest? Not quite. The force of the ideology which brought the state into being had not spent itself in the consciousness of the men who implemented the ideology, though it began to lose its hold on the generation born in Israel. Like any nationalist movement, Zionism created a strong social cohesion in the group through a common myth: in this case, identification with the religio-historical Jewish heritage and the belief in a revived Jewish creativity in Palestine. The consciousness of "mission" which the Zionist ideology imparted to the group and to individuals was bound to affect the style of Israel's diplomacy; the sense of destiny which attended Israel's rebirth as a state was reflected at times in the conduct of foreign affairs. Thus in November 1953 a Tel Aviv daily said of certain policy-makers that

their actions were guided by the spell of the vision, not by reality, both internally and externally. They acted in the U.N. and elsewhere as if they were already speaking for the heavenly and not for the earthly Israel. . . . It is obviously impossible to reconcile a belief in the greatness of the state, in its legitimacy which is equal to that of the greatest powers, and in its capacity to bring a message of salvation to the world, and at the same time act within the framework of reality, of dependence on neighbors and on other powers.[12]

Moreover, the support which Israel found among Jews throughout the world was based, at least initially, on a sharing of the myth, or at least certain aspects or modifications of it. This then evolved into general economic and political support of the Israel state, and it is for this reason that Ben-Gurion and others felt that they could dispense with the sectarian Zionist ideology and its organizational apparatus. They were convinced that the support of Jews for Israel was no longer a matter of particularist interpretation of Jewish existence which the ideology, in its pure form, would impose on them. Thus Israel's character as a Jewish state has had continuing influence on its foreign policy, while the importance of its origins in the Zionist movement lies mainly in the past. With time, its ideology tends to become more assimilated to the national interest. This is true not only of the immigration policy, but also of the sense of "mission" in general. In Ben-Gurion's words:

Two basic aspirations underlie all our work in this country: to be like all the nations, and to be different from all the nations. . . . This (latter) aspiration is not the outcome of a feeling that we are a chosen people, but an imperative necessity for our survival, because we are few, and our position is different from that of all other nations: the great majority of our people is still scattered abroad, and only by spiritual superiority can we win hearts and friends and attract the best of the Jewish youth to come forward and settle in Israel.[13]

With all its ideological-messianic overtones (Zionism), the statement ends on a pragmatic-political note (national interest).

13

World Jewry as a Power Reservoir

But unlike the ephemeral ideological nature of Zionism, Israel's character as a Jewish state was a more permanent part of Israel's geopolitical configuration and was likely to remain a determinant of its foreign policy for much longer. It may be compared to England's insular position and its effect on the United Kingdom's policy toward Europe, or to the United States' geographic isolation from Europe and its frontage on two oceans. But just as technological and other changes were able to affect these at one time seemingly immutable factors in the two powers' foreign policy, so the relationship of Israel to world Jewry may also eventually diminish in importance. Among young people born in Israel, there was noted not only a reaction against Zionism but against close ties with world Jewry as well. Although the ideological movement (Canaanism) which embodied these ideas never made much headway, the ideas themselves continued to find expression in various forms.[14] Traditional religious Judaism was being practiced by only a minority of Jews both within Israel and outside of it, and therefore was not likely to constitute a universally acceptable bond. On the other hand, statehood may yet turn out to be a divisive factor for, as Elie Kedourie has observed, "In Zionism, Judaism ceases to be the *raison d'être* of the Jew, and becomes, instead, a product of Jewish national consciousness." [15] And an Israeli political journalist called Israel's attachment to world Jewry a "substitute for a place in the area," which must be sustained, presumably until that place is secured.[16]

Israel government leaders have repeatedly declared that Jews outside Israel owe undivided loyalty only to the countries of their citizenship,[17] though occasional demands by party spokesmen in the Knesset and the press for active support of Israel's policies indicate that there is no unanimity in Israel as to what is

14

meant.[18] Moshe Sharett, no longer a cabinet minister but speaking as a private Israel citizen to a Jewish gathering in 1959, gave voice to this ambivalence:

From the standpoint of constitutional law and formal sovereignty Israel does not differ from any normal state in the world. It claims political loyalty only from its own nationals. . . . [But] in a deep historic sense—which, however, receives a most tangible expression both in long-term policy and in day-to-day life—Israel is a common possession of the entire Jewish people, that is to say of all the Jews of the world. Every Jew can claim a share in it. . . . They can, as Jews, no longer imagine their own existence without it. . . . Therefore, they must do everything they can—materially, politically, whatever and whichever way is practical, effective and legitimate—to preserve it, to strengthen it.[19]

Influence of the Parties on Foreign Policy

Along with the Zionist ideology itself, the several subgroups within that ideological framework exerted their separate influence on foreign policy.

Zionism was never a monolithic movement. Its history is replete with schisms, parties, and splinters of parties, differing not only in the way the goal should be reached but also as to the shape the Jewish society in Palestine should take, once created.[20] These ideological submovements were extrapolated into the state, where they became political parties appealing to the electorate with their various doctrines.[21]

The particularist ideological doctrines of the parties had foreign policy implications especially on the left and the right— much less so in the center and among the religious group. The left's views were affected by its close ideological ties to the Soviet Union. The major difference with the Soviets was over the latter's rejection of Zionism as "bourgeois nationalism," incompatible with communism. Here, the Israeli leftists believed the Soviets would eventually recognize their error, and that the Russian's disdain for the Israeli agricultural communes as "utopian" was based on misinformation and misconception. But as long as the error persisted, there was a wide gulf between the left-socialist Mapam (United Workers party) and the Communists. For if the choice had to be made, most of Mapam's members were Zionists first, and when Israel and Soviet interests appeared irreconcilable, they reluctantly took the consequences. In the process, a small group broke away from Mapam to the left to form Si'at Smol (Left Faction) and later to merge with the Communists; a larger group, representing a somewhat more radical disillusionment with Soviet policy, separated off to the right to form Ahdut ha-'Avodah (Unity of Labor). The process of disillusionment began with the Prague trials in 1952; was exacerbated by the disclosure of the Moscow Doctors' Plot the following spring; was halted temporarily with Khrushchev's exposure and condemnation of Stalin's anti-Semitism, but picked up momentum again with Russia's support of the Arab states in the United Nations and elsewhere and culminated with the Czech arms deal with Egypt in September 1955.

Before this process set in, Mapam's ideological affinity with the Soviet Union caused it to advocate a foreign policy line of strict neutrality between the East and West. In actuality, this line had an edge against the West, as it constantly attempted to counteract the tendency of Israel's diplomacy to incline toward the West, from which it received vital economic assistance, and to point it eastward instead. The speeches by Mapam's foreign policy spokesman in the First Knesset, where the party—still undivided —was the second largest with nineteen seats, contain many passages of sharp anti-American animus.[22]

Because the foreign policy it advocated was too far to the left of that pursued by Mapai (Palestine Workers party), the labor party which dominated the political scene from the beginning and rolled up decisive pluralities in each election, Mapam remained outside the government during most of the period. There were no irreconcilable internal conflicts between the two (later three) non-Communist labor parties, and they frequently professed a desire for a government based on a united labor front. It was only after disillusionment with Russian policy caused Mapam and its offshoot, Ahdut ha-'Avodah, to mitigate their rabid anti-Americanism and to realize the futility of a policy of rigid neutrality, that they became eligible to join the government and eventually did so. They stipulated some reservations about their participation in foreign policy decisions, but in effect tacitly endorsed a pro-Western position.[23]

On the right, Herut (Freedom party) never formed part of the Government; the views and personalities of its leaders clashed with those of the Mapai leadership so vehemently that the party was in effect relegated to permanent opposition.

The personality clashes had their roots in the bitter pre-state struggles between the Revisionists, precursors of Herut, and the Jewish Agency-Haganah leaders—particularly Ben-Gurion— who later formed the nucleus of the government. While the temporary participation in the government of the "bourgeois" General Zionists showed that broadly based coalitions are possible and that doctrinaire differences over internal policies can be held in abeyance; in the case of Herut, Mapai was unwilling to pay the price of cooperation. In foreign policy Herut's extremist doctrine was better suited to opposition politics than to being a party to policies that must take account of realities.

Zionist diplomacy before statehood as carried out by the Jewish Agency on behalf of the World Zionist Movement and the Jewish population of Palestine was a dynamic diplomacy. Its goal—formally since the adoption of the Biltmore Program in 1942 and informally among major factions long before that— was the establishment of a Jewish state in Palestine.[24] When the goal was achieved, the policy of the parties in control of the Israel government became one of defending the *status quo*. However,

17

the goal that was achieved represented a compromise from the maximum desideratum, which was a Jewish state in all of Palestine. This gave the right-wing opposition a ready-made issue: to continue to demand the maximum which had been officially renounced. Its position was facilitated by the refusal of the Arab states to agree even to the partition compromise (as expanded by the Israeli victories in 1948–1949). The opposition was thus able to retain the ideology which had been its stock in trade from the days when it claimed Transjordan as part of the Jewish homeland—rejection of compromise and revision of the *status quo.*

Although Herut's approach could be described as *Realpolitik,* it was too self-centered to take account of *all* the realities that governed Israel's position. Thus a Herut spokesman declared that Israel could obtain better treatment at the hands of the United States by pursuing a policy of militancy toward the Arabs —the United States would then be impressed by the evidence that Israel was the factor of strength in the area and would base its Middle East policy on support of Israel.[25] The Sinai Campaign was to be enthusiastically endorsed by Herut, but Herut again was in violent opposition when the decision was taken to evacuate the Sinai Peninsula and, eventually, the Gaza Strip.

The religious parties, or some faction of them, formed part of most government coalitions. There were no major disagreements between Mapai and these groups over foreign policy; their religious outlook did not commit them to a distinctive foreign policy position. Even if their maximal demand—a Jewish state governed by Jewish law—were ever met, it would not necessarily affect foreign policy. Judaism is not a political religion in the same sense as Islam; its dynamic is sociolegal, directed inward toward the group, and it has no conversionist drive. Pakistan, as a professed Islamic state, made close relations with other states where Islam was the dominant religion a basic tenet of its foreign policy; Israel's appeal could be directed only at Jewish individuals and communities. In brief, the religious parties acted like centrist rather than extremist parties on foreign policy issues; moreover, they were content to follow the lead set by the majority party in the government.

The Opposition as Pressure Group

The opposition ideologies inevitably influenced government policy. They were expressed with vigor and consistency in the party press [26] as well as in the foreign policy debates which regularly took place in the Knesset. On any particular foreign policy issue, the opposition parties generally took a more extreme position than was adopted by the government, which had to reconcile its own policies with the interests of other powers. Thus Herut pressed for the transfer of the Foreign Ministry to Jerusalem long before the government felt it prudent to do so. Both right and left urged the government to stand pat against American and U.N. pressure and were quick to castigate the government for any inclination to make concessions.[27] The most effective pressure on the government, of course, was the parties' appeal to the voters at election time. The fact that the percentage of votes cast for Herut rose from 6.6 to 12.6 between the elections to the Second Knesset (1951) and those to the Third (1955) represented a vindication of their advocacy of an activist policy, and the lesson was driven home even more emphatically by the decline in Mapai's share from 37.3 to 32.2 per cent of the vote in the latter elections.

In spite of these divergencies, the common Zionist ideology as well as the requirements of the state that grew out of the unratified *status quo* provided enough common ground among the Zionist parties to make the orderly conduct of foreign policy possible.

In terms of the choices pursued in regional and great-power relations, three distinct phases may be discerned in Israel's diplomacy during the early period, which came to an end with the

19

Soviet-Egyptian arms transaction in September 1955. The phases may be roughly defined as follows.

(1) *In hopes of peace.* This theme was dominant from the signing of the armistice agreements to the Tripartite Declaration of May 1950. In this phase, regional objectives were paramount: ratification of the *status quo* was sought above all on the regional level (through a peace policy), and the approach to the great powers was based on the assumption that Israel's interests could best be served by not identifying with a particular bloc.

(2) *The search for alliances* was the dominant characteristic from the issuing of the Tripartite Declaration until early in 1952. Chief emphasis now turned from the area to great-power relations. This phase evolved when it was realized that peace was not to be attained through direct effort on the regional level and that security must come first. But it was felt that security could best be achieved by participating in the Western plans for the area's defense, which would simultaneously bring acknowledgment of the *status quo* and alleviate economic hardship. (There was overlapping between the first and the second phases, as the alliance policy was in the making while peace negotiations were still being carried on. The dates are, therefore, approximations.)

(3) *Isolation.* This phase began when it was perceived that the Western powers were not receptive to Israel's alliance policy. It lasted—for the purpose of this analysis—until the Soviet-Egyptian arms deal in September 1955. During the same period, the Soviet bloc also cooled toward Israel, so that there was no going back to neutrality. On the regional level, tangible manifestations of the lack of security—physical encroachments on the *status quo* through infiltration and border raids—were met by a clearcut security policy culminating in a tangible demonstration of power: retaliation. This phase saw diminished concern for global and regional matters except where Israel's own security was affected, and a tendency to rely on world Jewry for support to compensate for internal weaknesses.

It is legitimate to ask whether and to what extent these approaches were consciously followed by Israel's policy-makers, whether the various alternatives were carefully considered before decisions were made, whether one course was then deliberately abandoned in favor of another, and so on.

Certainly, at the earliest stage of Israel's independence, the model Israel's leaders saw before them for the future of their state in international relations encompassed little more than being established as a sovereign state in a region at peace, and preserving a stance of detachment toward great-power politics. This combination promised to afford the optimum conditions for the attainment of the internal goals, for which much more elaborate models existed in line with party ideologies. In the first of the three phases just described, Israel's diplomacy was oriented toward this simple model. The Israelis reluctantly came to acknowledge that it was too simple for Israel's position in the particular circumstances, but no coherent substitute model was to take its place. The global alliance policy left open the type of regional organization desired by Israel aside from the military organization which the allies' interests required. A security policy begs the question of a model. The best illustration of this is the Cold War; its only peaceful termination envisaged by the antagonists is "peaceful coexistence," which says nothing about the type of structure required to maintain it. Israel's security policy had peace as its ultimate goal, but it offered no clue as to the type or regional organization needed to preserve it and to assure a peaceful *modus vivendi* in the future. In the phase of isolation particularly, Israel's concern for security on a day-to-day basis was detrimental to the kind of thinking which could produce such a model. This means simply that conditions were not ripe for the ideal process of making foreign policy: the "systematic formulation of national interests in which inconsistent interests have been weeded out, the interests have been judged against one another in terms of priorities, and the interests as a whole have been budgeted against the power of the state to achieve those interests." [28]

21

Part One

POLICY IN ACTION

CHAPTER I ≺≺≺≺

The Early Phase

Area Relations: In Hopes of Peace

The Jewish leadership accepted the Partition Resolution of 29 November 1947 because it appeared to embody the maximum territorial limits for a Jewish state that could be attained by political means. Implicit in the acceptance was the belief that the international sanction conferred on partition by the United Nations' action would be enforced by the international community if it proved necessary. The sanction, however, was not respected by Israel's adversaries, and enforcement was not forthcoming. In the fighting that ensued, Israel extended the partition boundaries by force of arms.[1] At the end of the fighting, Israel held not only all of the territory assigned to it by the resolution, but also 4,912 additional square kilometers which were to have been part of the new Arab state. These territorial gains over the Partition Plan were incorporated, together with 467 square kilometers added by peaceful means in the negotiations with Jordan, in the armistice agreements concluded with Egypt, Lebanon, Jordan, and Syria between 24 February and 20 July 1949.

The armistice agreements, however, failed to bring about permanent acceptance on the part of the Arab states of Israel's existence, or of the armistice lines as final boundaries. Israel's military successes did not result in political settlement or, more precisely, no political agreement was reached to ratify the military successes. Not only was it apparent from the start that the armistice agreements in themselves did not provide final validation of Israel's claim, but it later turned out that there was no agreement among the parties on whether they signified the end of the state of war or merely its temporary interruption. The opposing points of view on the nature of the armistice agreements far transcended their technical and legal scope: while Israel regarded them as a prelude to an overall peace settlement,[2] the Arab states soon demonstrated that they considered them a means for obtaining a breathing-space in the hostilities in which they had engaged with the intention of destroying Israel.

The conclusion of a peace treaty became the stated objective of Israel's foreign policy even before the armistice agreements had been signed. The program of the first regular government (which succeeded the earlier provisional government) as submitted by the Prime Minister for approval to the seventh meeting of the First Knesset on 8 March 1949, enunciated these goals of foreign policy: [3]

(1) Loyalty to the principles of the U.N. Charter.

(2) Striving toward a Jewish-Arab alliance providing for economic, social, cultural, and political cooperation with the neighboring countries within the framework of the United Nations, and without this alliance being directed against any state in the United Nations.

(3) Support of every step which strengthens peace.

(4) Assurance of the right of exit to Jews in every country who wish to come to their historic fatherland.

(5) Active watch over the independence and full sovereignty of Israel.

This program, with the desire for regional cooperation which it contained, was general enough to elicit the support of all parties in the Knesset with the exception of Herut, which declared that it "was not enough to say we want peace with our neighbors, follow the principles of the U.N., etc." Herut wanted peace

26

through victory rather than through negotiation. Said party leader Menahem Begin: "Foreign policy must tell us how we can achieve victory over our enemies who threaten us from day to day, and how it plans to bring us real peace, which will enable us to achieve our historic mission of absorbing millions of returners to Zion and making our state a true home for them." [4] Mapai disavowed this approach. One of its members, Pinhas Lubianiker (his name changed to Lavon, he became minister of defense during Ben-Gurion's temporary retirement on 24 November 1953), acknowledged the Arabs' right to a part of Palestine and at the same time stressed the record of compromise on the Jewish side:

I should like to tell Mr. Begin something he may find it hard to hear: in the reality of this country, Palestine, there are two peoples and there were two peoples. These two peoples have had two different political methods. . . . Ours, represented by that of the provisional government preceded by the Jewish Agency, is one method. That of the Arabs, represented by the Grand Mufti is opposed to our method but it has characteristics well known to Mr. Begin: unwillingness to make any concessions, unconcern with any international situation; insistence on dotting the i's in every demand, on total demands, on negation of every compromise. . . . If we are today in the situation where we find ourselves, it is because the Jewish people is not given to this method. . . . We have followed another line: dynamic, realistic and revolutionary at once, which took into consideration changes in circumstances, held back and advanced both, which knew how to explore new approaches, to adapt to change, to the discovery of new power. Only because we refused to adopt Mr. Begin's methods for 25 years did we arrive where we are.[5]

Three months later, in a debate on the future of central Palestine, Moshe Sharett replied to Herut's question: "Why shouldn't it belong to Israel?" by saying: "Our face is turned to peace. I know there is a concrete plan to conquer this territory—I reject it." [6] And in May 1950 Ben-Gurion told Ya'qov Meridor of

Herut: "We won't give up our illusion of peace with the Arabs—with every one of the Arab peoples. We will do everything to attain peace." [7]

Israel wished to negotiate a peace settlement with each of the Arab states separately, just as it had negotiated separate armistice agreements (though under U.N. auspices). It favored direct negotiations, without great-power or U.N. intervention, fearing on the basis of its experience that the great powers would put pressure on Israel for concessions.[8] But Israel responded to the invitation of the Palestine Conciliation Commission, after some prodding by the United States, to attend a conference in Lausanne under the Commission's auspices, even though the secret talks with Jordan which were taking place at about the same time seemed to bear out the view that the direct individual approach was the more fruitful one. In 1960, a veteran Israeli diplomat said of the peace negotiations between King Abdallah and representatives of the Israel government: "The atmosphere was one of give and take. Territorial adjustments were made and there was provision even for a Jordanian corridor to the sea through Israeli territory. Progress was made to the point where the heads of agreement were actually initialed by both sides. Before final signature, however, the fact of the negotiations began to be known, and the counterpressure of the other Arab States began to assert itself." [9] It was the fatal error of the Conciliation Commission in 1949, in the Israeli view, to treat the Arab states as a single party to the dispute with Israel and so to buttress their intransigence.[10]

But since the signing of the Armistice Agreements there had been an intensification of the inter-Arab rivalries which would have been a serious obstacle to a separate settlement even if the delegates of other states were not present at the negotiating table.[11] In particular, the increasing rivalry between the Hashimi kingdoms (Jordan and Iraq) on the one hand, and Egypt, Syria, and Saudi Arabia on the other, made it difficult for either of the

two sides to advocate peace. Abdallah, whose army was undefeated, hoped to realize his dreams of a Greater Hashimi kingdom, which his rivals were determined to prevent. Egypt was
afraid that the annexation of Western Palestine would constitute
a step toward this goal and its own isolation. Abdallah was
attacked in the Egyptian press, and the Jordan prime minister,
unwilling to sign a peace treaty with Israel, submitted his resignation.[12] Later the King's assassination made it clear to Israel that
Jordan, though undefeated and having most to gain from the
ratification of the *status quo,* was yet too weak to take the initiative for peace. Henceforth Israel's overtures, while directed to
all comers, were more specifically aimed at Egypt. Ironically, at
a particular moment in early 1950 chances for an Israeli-
Egyptian understanding had appeared bright, and Egypt's
minister of war had actually predicted that a peace treaty would
be signed. But then the progress of the negotiations with Jordan
appeared to make Israel more obstinate in its attitude toward
Egypt, and the opportunity was lost.[13]

Test of the Peace Policy

The instability which manifested itself in Egypt and Syria was
rightly interpreted by Israel as a sign of Arab weakness. But
there is no evidence that the conclusion was reached that this
was directly attributable to popular unrest and economic difficulties stemming from the Arabs' defeat in the Palestine war, and
that if they were to be in a position to make peace, these governments needed propping up. One way to prop them up, of course,
would have been to permit them to come away from Lausanne
with a victory. The Arab leaders had indeed come to Lausanne
in hopes of political gains—most of them were in no position to
survive a political defeat on top of the military one.

Here Israel was faced with a dilemma peculiar to its position:
Israel's existence contributed to instability in the Arab countries,

29

yet only stable Arab governments were in a position to make peace. Should Israel therefore offer major concessions in order to promote stability in the Arab countries, hoping that this might lead to peace? Or should it weigh against this the likelihood that stable Arab governments would be in a better position to resume their hostility and then present a far greater threat to Israel?

In this the peace policy was put to the test: how great a sacrifice was Israel willing to make for the sake of peace? The answer, as it is to be found in the record of the P.C.C.,[14] is that Israel was not willing to jeopardize its present vital interests in order to enjoy the as yet doubtful benefits of peace. Under these circumstances, peace had a lower priority than security. It had a lower priority than territorial integrity, and the ethnic balance which would be upset by the return of large numbers of refugees. Although Israel was never given any certainty on that point, it is possible that a substantial revision of Israel's stand on either point might have brought peace. Sharett in his report to the Knesset on 15 June 1949 reflected the essence of Israel's position: the borders were a main point at issue in the Lausanne talks, he declared. In Paris, at the third U.N. General Assembly in December 1948, an attempt was made to get Israel to renounce part of the Negev in return for Western Galilee (which was already in Israel's possession as a result of the fighting). But the attempt failed. However, the door was left open to an agreement by both sides, and the attitude of Israel therefore did not contradict Resolution 194 (III/1) of 11 December 1948, which had called on the parties to "seek agreement by negotiations conducted either with the Conciliation Commission or directly, with a view to the final settlement of all questions outstanding between them."

Sharett set forth as Israel's bargaining position the borders of the British Mandate where they were contiguous with Egypt, Lebanon, and Syria; whereas special considerations would apply to Jordan and to what was then referred to as the Rafa-Gaza area. "If corrections are desired benefiting both sides, they must be made by negotiations." As against this, the Arab states now wanted to return to Resolution 181 (II) of 29 November 1947, Sharett reported. He said it would be strange if these states received the support of the United States in their attempt to "obtain by political pressure what they were not able to obtain through military operations." (The U.S. had already called for an exchange of territory on the basis of the 29 November resolution in Paris, an approach Sharett now called "unrealistic, illusory and complicating.") He went on to say that the Arabs, having been unable to cut down the tree, were now trying to rob it of its fruit. "Everything which wittingly or unwittingly encourages the Arab states to believe they will squeeze territorial concessions out of Israel . . . does not serve the cause of peace in the Middle East." The solution, Israel insisted, was to be left to the two sides, "free from previously determined principles and without encouragement or warning to either side." [15]

This meant in effect that Israel wished to negotiate a final settlement on the basis of its military superiority as demonstrated in the fighting, and feared that great power intervention would upset the chances for such a settlement by introducing extraneous political factors. The 29 November Resolution was no longer operative because the Arabs had tried to destroy it; had they succeeded, they would have created a *status quo* in disregard of the resolution, and it was unfair to resurrect the resolution merely because they failed, this argument went. "The conquests of the Israel Defense Army . . . serve as the basis for our dynamic foreign policy since 29 November 1947 until today," a Mapai deputy told the Knesset in debate on the first government's program.[16] This was no unreasonable attitude. The conquests of armies have served as the basis for peace settlements since time immemorial, and Israel appeared in an especially strong position because most of its victories were won as a

31

result of defensive operations. Abd al-Rahman Azzam Pasha, then Secretary-General of the Arab League, is himself reported to have told two representatives of Palestinian Jewry in the course of the U.N. debate preceding partition that "the claim of the Jews should be established in the way history has dealt with all such claims: by victory and defeat." [17]

The Refugee Issue at the P.C.C.

The refugee issue, Sharett told the Knesset, was the second rock on which the Lausanne talks had foundered.

They (other states pressing Israel for concessions) forget the mortal danger we were in. . . . Those who tried to massacre us fell into the hole they dug with their own hands. Now they try to hold us responsible.

We were ready to establish a state under an arrangement which would have provided that 45 percent of the population were Arabs. But the Arabs rebelled against that decision . . . there was an Arab exodus. These things happened several times in the last decades. What never happened is that a population uprooted under these circumstances returned to its soil.

Security is our first consideration. Such a wave of returnees can undermine the state from within. A return without peace is suicidal for Israel; it would mean driving the knife into our breast by our own hands. Even with peace, the possibilities of return are small in view of the second consideration, the economic factor. If they had remained here, all our processes and methods for internal stabilization would have been adapted to this reality. The vast Arab minority would necessarily have impressed its stamp on the state. . . . Without them, other processes came into being; another face was put on the state . . . through the mass immigration of Jews.

Nevertheless, we have said, and we say today, this is not a problem which we can avoid dealing with. We want peace . . . human suffering hurts us. . . . We shall pay compensation for abandoned land. . . . We also will not decree in advance that none can return. . . .

We have already agreed to the reunion of families. And we may make an additional contribution by permitting the return of a certain number. . . . But . . . the war created the problem, only peace can solve it. We will not put the refugees' return before peace.[18]

As this statement implies, Israel's position on the number of refugees to be readmitted was by no means uncompromising, at least as long as there was a possibility that the P.C.C. proceedings—or the separate negotiations with King Abdallah—might bring about a formal settlement. But Sharett also made it clear, as did Israel's delegation at Lausanne, that in Israel's view a partial return of the refugees was conditional on the Arabs' agreeing to sign treaties of peace and would therefore have to be part of an overall settlement. Partial repatriation was to be a concession in return for ratification of the *status quo* in regard to territory, and acceptance of the nonreturn of the majority of the refugees. The Arabs, however, were not ready for this. They insisted on a prior commitment for the refugees' return, feeling that only Israel's acknowledgment of the moral right to repatriation could pave the way for a possible final settlement in the future. They felt they were supported in this position both by the late U.N. Mediator, Count Bernadotte, who had declared that the refugees had every right to return to their homes "at the earliest practical date," [19] and by the 11 December 1948 General Assembly Resolution 194 (III/1), which called for the return, "as soon as practicable," of those refugees who were willing to live in peace with their neighbors. Israel, in turn, pointed to the two qualifying phrases in the text to justify its refusal to implement the resolution.[20]

As the chances of an overall settlement grew more remote—by January 1951 Sharett was saying it would be a miracle if the P.C.C. succeeded [21]—Israel's position on the refugees hardened.[22] The offer made on 3 August 1949 to take back 75,000 refugees in addition to the 25,000 which Israel claimed already to have repatriated under the reunion-of-families project [23] was

33

declared lapsed. Total resettlement in the Arab countries became the official policy, with Israel ready to pay compensation for abandoned property "in the framework of a peace treaty." However, Israel would be ready to contribute to a resettlement fund on account of future compensation payments even before a treaty would be signed. In the United Nations, the Israel delegation embarked on a wearisome struggle against the Arab clamor for repatriation, which, Sharett conceded in his account of the work of the Fifth General Assembly, "found many sympathizers." Israel, he reported, "had to go again over the entire history (of the refugee problem) and to put the blame where it belonged." As a result, "the recognition that their return is impossible was shared by a majority of U.N. members. The slogan of repatriation received a setback in this Assembly, but it is not defeated yet. The struggle may last for years." [24]

Concessions

Although determined not to surrender the territorial *status quo* in any major respect, Israel did announce various concessions it was willing to make in order to get negotiations under way. Apart from the offer of partial repatriation, these included free port zones, transit rights, and right of access to Holy Places. They were made in response to strong American pressure and against the view of those who held that concessions announced in advance would be considered a sign of weakness and cause the Arabs to use them as a starting point when it came to real bargaining.[25] In particular, Israel felt that prior concessions on return of the refugees would destroy the Arabs' incentive to seek peace. When Israel had attempted to establish direct contact with Egypt, Arab newspapers had interpreted the peace feelers as a sign of weakness.[26] Nor did Israel's readiness to give in on certain procedural issues, such as agreeing to discuss the refugees first and the territorial arrangements later, produce a

34

change in attitude. Not only the Arabs but the P.C.C. itself found the offer to take in a total of 100,000 refugees inadequate.[27] On top of this Israel was exposed to criticism at home for making the concession.

Although the P.C.C.'s efforts were to continue, off and on, for more than two years, Paul Porter, one among the succession of U.S. delegates, summed up the probable outcome at an early stage: in view of the extreme position adopted by both sides at Lausanne, it became clear to him that a settlement negotiated on a purely political basis was not possible at present.[28] However, the economic approach presaged by this statement turned out to be hardly more fruitful, nor did the group's initiative to get the parties together in Paris in September 1951 to settle specific causes of friction prove successful.

Without detailing the convolutions of the P.C.C. conferences, which never even saw the two sides negotiating around the same table, it will be seen that Israel's desire for an overall agreement which would settle both the territorial and refugee questions in a manner not unfavorable to it was not capable of achievement in this setting. Israel was not willing to follow the P.C.C.'s call to take the first step to "counteract the dislocations caused by its own establishment among the Arabs" or to recognize that the refugees were the "foremost problem" and to permit the return of that number "which would be consistent with their own best interests." [29] Israel soon became convinced that the Arabs did not want to make peace, certainly not on the terms which Israel was offering. Israel interpreted the reference to peace in General Assembly Resolution 194 (III/1) of 11 December 1948 as meaning peace should come first,[30] even though the terms of reference of the P.C.C. itself did not call for an overall peace settlement. Possibly the signing of a working protocol at the Lausanne Conference in which both sides agreed that outstanding problems be settled by political and peaceful negotiations in accordance with the 11 December 1948 resolution and with

35

the 29 November plan as the basis for discussion [31] misled both parties as to the other's intentions. While the Arabs claimed that by signing this protocol Israel had committed itself to acceptance of the partition frontiers, Israel asserted that neither it nor the Arabs ever accepted the protocol as anything but a basis for discussions with the Commission.[32] As it turned out, this protocol did not constitute the basis for true negotiations, which are "an attempt at reconciling divergent interests through a process of give-and-take in which both sides either concede minor points while leaving the substance of their interests intact, or else in which one side receives through compensations from the other at least the equivalent of what it concedes." [33]

Nor did the objective relationship between the two sides at the time the Lausanne meeting was convened make it likely that such a process would take place.

Negotiations require first of all the objective conditions conducive to a negotiated settlement; there must be room for maneuver, for retreat, advance and side-stepping, for mutual concessions. When neither side can afford to yield an inch, negotiations are *a priori* impossible. Given the objective conditions conducive to a negotiated settlement, both sides, in order to negotiate successfully, must be strong enough to support their negotiating positions with promises of benefits and threats of disadvantages. In other words, they must be able, in Dean Acheson's famous phrase, to negotiate from strength.[34]

Although this was said about negotiations between the United States and Soviet Russia, the general principles set forth are of equal relevance to the negotiations—abortive, in the event— which the P.C.C. tried to foster between Israel and the Arab states.

Great-Power Relations: Security through Alliance

Israel began its career as a member of the family of nations with the support of both sides in the Cold War. Both the Western powers (with the exception of Great Britain) and the Soviet bloc had voted for the Partition Resolution in the General Assembly. Because the support of either side was indispensable to obtain the required two-thirds majority, it would be difficult to say which side played the more significant role in bringing the state into being. While the United States, with its long history of Zionist sympathy, took an active part in rounding up votes at the crucial time and was the first to grant *de facto* recognition to the new state on 14 May 1948, Russia's support was the more dramatic as it represented a sudden switch in the Soviet attitude to Jewish nationalism and was one of the few times since the start of the Cold War that the East and the West were on the same side of an issue. Subsequently, Czechoslovakia, by then already a Soviet satellite, supplied Israel with modern armaments to help it win the fight for independence at a time when the United States was having second thoughts about partition and advocated a U.N. Trusteeship for Palestine.[35]

It was logical, therefore, that Israel should wish to adopt a neutral attitude in the Cold War in order to retain the support of both sides. Although Israel took pride in being a Western democracy, needed economic aid from the West, and was dependent on the support it derived from the Jews of the free world, there were good reasons for avoiding all-out identification with the Western camp. Being faced with absorbing internal tasks on the one hand, and with the need to keep up its defenses against Arab hostility on the other, there was little inclination to get involved in ideological conflicts between communism and Western democracy. Israel's goal, a Mapai deputy declared, was the fulfillment of the Jewish Revolution; Israel was one of the few small states which was not a satellite.[36] With the United States applying strong pressure for concessions to the Arabs, the Soviet Union might be needed as a counterweight. The thought that the great powers might eventually have to coerce the Arabs into making peace was also sometimes expressed,[37] in which case the Soviet Union's attitude would be a factor.

Israel's left-socialist party, Mapam, was strongly pro-Soviet and exerted every effort to create a neutralist climate of opinion within the country. Its actual voting strength in the 1949 general elections had been 14.7 per cent, while the Communists polled an additional 3.5 per cent of the vote. As early as June 1949, in foreign policy resolutions tabled as substitutes for the government-sponsored resolution concluding the debate on Israel's admission to the United Nations, both Mapam and the Communists had the State of Israel "oppose a Middle East Defense Organization or any connection with NATO." [38] Sharett was able to give assurances then that there was no danger on that score. Mapam not only insisted on neutrality as a condition for joining the government, but also objected to an alliance with the Arab states as advocated in the first government's program because it feared that a regional alliance would become the tool of the West.[39]

All the parties at the time still shared a hearty dislike of the British—another reason identification with the West was unlikely. The right-wing Herut was particularly virulent in its denunciation of the erstwhile British foe, its spokesman asserting that the United States and France were "caught in the net of Britain's plans" for regional defense, which was a fiction, in view of the weakness of the states in the region. "Bevin and his Foreign Office can't be so naive as to think that his arms will really be used for the defense of the area—they are to be used for an attack on Israel. . . . We mustn't fall for the Bevinite tricks, and the nonsense about regional defense." [40] Even the General Zionists, traditionally the most Western-oriented of all the parties, called for non-identification as the first principle in their foreign policy plank.[41] Izhar Harari, foreign policy spokesman for the Progressives, the middle-of-the-road liberal group, insisted that Israel's task as a small state was to remain independent and neutral insofar as possible. "We don't know who will win the cold or hot war," he said. "It is better not to be dependent." The fate of the Jews of Eastern Europe also weighed heavily with Harari, as it did with other speakers. "As long as there are millions of our people on both sides, we must guard our independence." [42] On another occasion he said, "We cannot identify with the various interests of the several blocs, because their interests are more important to them than ours. As long as East or West are not ready to defend us as they do their own territory, we are not ready to identify with their interests." [43]

As for Ben-Gurion, it was clear already from his pronouncements in these early foreign policy debates that he had no illusions about Israel's ability to maintain a rigid neutrality between the two camps. Reacting to Mapam's ceaseless prodding for neutrality, and to their declaration that "our people will never forget the help from the Soviet Union in establishing the State," [44] the Prime Minister said: "We received aid from both sides and we say thanks, and go our own way. We needn't be satellites of either side." He revealed that a Western state had helped Palestinian Jewry found their war industry in 1945, and that in the war against the Arabs, Israel got help from both an Eastern and a Western state. "Our heavy arms we received from the West. But we paid both of them for their arms. They both wanted dollars from us—and dollars are only to be had in one certain country. We got many millions of dollars from the U.S." Thus he indicated Israel's ultimate reliance on financial help from American sources.[45] He cited one more reason why Israel could not afford to be rigidly neutral as between the United States and Soviet Russia: "Neither the United States nor the Soviet governments gave us arms. But when the Soviet Government says No, that goes for everybody in Russia. It isn't so in America."

However, the Foreign Minister strove to arrive at a formulation of Israel's position somewhere between neutrality and commitment. It was designed to preserve Israel's liberty of action in specific situations without tying her to one side (meaning the West, since there was never any serious thought given to supporting the Soviet bloc). Sharett told the Knesset it was one of the government's basic principles "in no case to become identified with one great bloc in the world against the other." But this line, he added, does not release us from taking a stand on various matters.[46]

The Shift toward the West

The Mapam group continued to maintain that Israel would prosper under the benign regard of Soviet Russia provided nothing were done to give aid and comfort to the West in it efforts to build "aggressive bases" against the "world of progress." But the majority which did not share Mapam's kinship to the "world of socialism" gradually realized that Israel's vital interests could best be served through close association with the West, in particular the United States; that Israel needed the help of the Western powers more than these powers needed Israel; and that this was a poor premise on which to build a policy of non-identification. Lack of commitment in the Cold War, Israel was soon to learn, was permitted only to the self-reliant, the secure, or to those who were being wooed by both sides. Israel was none of these. It was not self-reliant, but needed economic support which was available only in the West. It was not secure: the Arabs were threatening a second round—and it needed military supplies. And it was not being wooed: whatever it had to offer was compromised by the antagonism of the Arabs, whose resources, strategic position, and numbers weighed far more heavily in the scale.

"Non-identification" was, therefore, an ephemeral concept which had to be abandoned almost as soon as it was conceived; an ideal in small-state–great-power relations which Israel could not even adumbrate, much less attain.

Michael Comay, a senior Foreign Ministry official, viewed the experiment in retrospect in 1953 when, with the diplomatic rupture with Russia, the last traces of it had been swept away:

Even if our non-identification policy was more flexible than the formal neutrality of Switzerland or the neutralism of a country like India, it became increasingly difficult to steer the small craft in stormy seas. The Korean war (on which Israel took a clear pro-U.N. stand), the changes in the Soviet attitude toward us, our economic difficulties, the search for physical security, our way of life which made Israel a natural part of the free world—these were amongst the influences which produced a shift towards the West—a shift which has recently become more defined, with the breaking-off of relations by Russia.[47]

Of the factors cited by Comay, the most compelling was the search for physical security, with its corollary, relief from economic difficulty.

The attitude of the Israel government toward regional peace, when it became clear that the Conciliation Commission would fail in securing ratification of the *status quo,* was perhaps best summed up in the words of the Progressive party's foreign policy spokesman: "If one wants peace, one mustn't run after peace. Peace will come with the resignation of the Arabs to our reality." [48] The new attitude was that peace could not be the primary aim but the end result; it would come when a prior condition was met: when Israel would be sufficiently strong to make the Arabs realize that a military solution through a "second round" would be unsuccessful. This, in brief, meant a policy of security first. The new attitude was reflected in policy statements of successive governments, such as the one with which Moshe Sharett presented his government to the Knesset following Ben-Gurion's resignation as Prime Minister. It spoke of

increasing immigration, safeguarding Israel's independence and security and repressing any attack against its vital rights and interests. . . . The Government . . . will strive untiringly to advance Israel materially, as well as spiritually; to enhance its international position, to enable it to fulfill its historic mission in Jewish history and to make of it an agent of peace and progress in the Middle East and the world beyond.[49]

Still later, Sharett said: "Without security there is no peace— and the effort for peace must not lead to the neglect of security. That is our policy." [50]

To help it achieve that security, Israel now turned to the Western powers. Specifically, its objectives were (1) to obtain economic support which would enable it to receive and integrate immigrants and to achieve a viable economic structure; (2) to obtain equipment for its armed forces; (3) to prevent the Arab states from obtaining armaments which would lead to their superiority.

At the same time, having been unsuccessful in its attempt to obtain ratification of the *status quo* within the area through permanent treaties of peace, Israel turned outside the area for assurance that the *status quo* would not be upset. The United Nations could not qualify as an adequate guarantor: not only had it been unable to enforce its own Partition Resolution, but it was now pressing Israel for implementation of those aspects of it and of subsequent resolutions which Israel considered forfeit by the outcome of the hostilities initiated by the Arabs. Foremost among these was the dogged pursuit by United Nations bodies of the internationalization of Jerusalem in the face of Israel's determination to make the new city its capital. The United Nations had also demonstrated its impotence in connection with Egypt's interference with passage of goods bound for Israel in the Suez Canal. The Chief of Staff of the U.N. Truce Supervision Organization, General Riley, in a report to the Security Council, called Egypt's action a "hostile act" but not in the meaning defined by the Armistice Agreement, and therefore outside the competence of the Mixed Armistice Commission; [51] the Security Council's resolution of 1 September 1951 calling on Egypt to end its interference remained unimplemented.[52]

The Tripartite Declaration of May 1950

The request for a guarantee of the *status quo* was, therefore, directed primarily at the Western powers, as was the request for armaments. The original demand for arms came as a reaction to Britain's resumption of its traditional arms supplies to the Arab countries with which it had treaty relations, whereas the arms embargo which the Security Council had imposed during the Arab-Israel war formally remained in force as far as Israel was concerned. Israel's insistence that the arms balance in the area was being disturbed by the shipments to the Arabs elicited a policy statement by the United Kingdom, the United States, and France which became known as the Tripartite Declaration of 25 May 1950.[53] Like the armistice agreements, which it was intended to reinforce, the Tripartite Declaration was expected to be a stop-gap and a stabilizing factor facilitating transition to permanent peace. Yet it was made to serve as the principal instrument of Western policy in the area, hovering somewhat nebulously over the precarious balance between the two sides, its exact scope and meaning never clearly defined.

The Declaration pledged joint action by the three powers to prevent any alteration of the armistice borders by force. It opposed arms deliveries to the area which would result in an arms race, while not precluding supply of arms for local security needs and for defense of the area as a whole. The three powers left no doubt, however, that they considered Israel well enough supplied for the first purpose, while the second was subject to specific arrangements still to be worked out. No new avenues for arms acquisition were thus opened up under its provisions.

No wonder that the reception the Declaration was accorded in Israel was less than enthusiastic. Ben-Gurion told the Knesset that he regarded it as a unilateral declaration which was not binding on Israel, though he welcomed it "to the extent that it was designed to increase security and peace." [54]

If this was ambiguous language, it was probably because the Israelis found the Declaration to be an ambiguous document. They were never quite sure whether it was a territorial guarantee and, if so, whether the signatories meant what they said. In the absence of proof, the Israelis preferred to "rely on our own strength." Intermittent attempts to pin the three powers down on the extent of their commitment were inconclusive. Subsequent developments tended to vindicate Israel's skepticism. Although the British government reaffirmed its validity twenty-five times between October 1951 and October 1955,[55] Prime Minister Eden did not mention it in his famous Guildhall speech of 9 November 1955, when he urged Israel to make territorial concessions as a step toward peace. In his memoirs, Eden writes that only after the Czech-Egyptian arms deal of 1955 were the United States and Britain "anxious to put teeth into the Tripartite Declaration of 1950." [56] Almost as soon as this was attempted, differences developed among the three powers as to the extent. While Britain urged the United States to make it clear that they would stand together in opposing any act of aggression by force, Washington placed the primary emphasis on the United Nations, and a White House statement expressed readiness to act "within constitutional means"—after the Security Council had identified the aggressor.[57] This meant that any action would be subject to the Soviet veto, and that no armed forces would be committed without approval of Congress. When Eden was asked in Commons, at the time of the Sinai Campaign, about his government's obligation under the Declaration, he pointed out that "the Egyptian Government had never accepted this declaration," implying that it had been futile from the beginning.[58]

In Israel, Herut considered the Declaration as having a deleterious effect by neutralizing the superiority of Israel's armed force. As a result, the party's foreign policy spokesman declared, the Tripartite Declaration put an end to the efforts of the Israel government to come to terms with the Arabs—for why should they make peace with Israel? "For the Arabs, a declaration on borders suffices—but not for us. The Declaration doesn't solve the problems of infiltration, of economic warfare and of boycott. We are not afraid of an armed attack; we can withstand it. . . . What if we react to infiltration? Who will determine who the aggressor is?"

The spokesman, Ya'qov Meridor, called the Declaration a legalization of arms shipments to the Arabs. Had not the United Kingdom supplied much heavy armament to the Arabs under its treaties in spite of the 4 August 1949 declaration of the three powers in the Security Council opposing a Middle East arms race? Were jet planes, warships, and heavy tanks needed for internal security? "They are to be used for an attack on Israel." [59] This theme recurred in statements on arms shipments to the Arabs among spokesmen of virtually all parties in the years to come.

Mapai's Meir Grabovsky (later Argov), chairman of the Knesset's foreign affairs committee, thought Herut's approach illogical: why should the Arabs be prevented from tampering with the borders and not we? We cannot have it both ways. And he recalled graphically that the Declaration was issued partly in response to Israel's pressure on the West about arms:

The declaration was given after much shouting by the Yishuv and American Jewry about the arms race, and about the danger of the second round against Israel. I was in the U.S. when the press there did not stop writing about the Blitzkrieg that was threatening Israel. Jewish delegates visited all the high government officials. And now we have left our isolated position and a declaration was issued. . . . We have been shouting: why are we being discriminated against? In the declaration, there is a passage which has all the Arab parliaments ranting against it: Israel also has the right to buy arms, like the Arabs. . . .

Of course, the declaration was given against a certain background.

But it's not up to us to intervene in the great quarrel which divides the world today.[60]

While Ben-Gurion in his statement did not mention this aspect of the Declaration at all, speaking as though it was intended solely to affect the Arab-Israeli dispute, Mapam fairly jumped on the text's reference to "defending the area as a whole." The party saw in this "aggressive tendencies against the Soviet Union" which it denounced vigorously. "We will not take any regional responsibility on ourselves . . . if anybody wants to make a Western base of Israel, all lovers of peace will nullify this intention. We need arms . . . we hope that Jews the world over, and above all American Jewry, will insist on this right: to obtain defensive arms without obligations and without a program of military adventure." [61]

Thus the effect of the Tripartite Declaration was to remind the states of the area, and the Soviet Union as well, that the Middle East was still in the Western security zone, and that the West intended to be the custodian of its internal peace as well as its guardian against outside attack. Since the powers had expressed the view that Israel had sufficient arms for internal needs and legitimate self-defense, the only way of acquiring them would be for the purpose of "defending the region as a whole." At this period, when plans for a Middle East Command were ripening in the minds of allied military staffs, there was no reason to doubt the sincerity of the West's intention of letting Israel carry its share in such a defensive arrangement. The Mapam leadership was therefore not far off the mark when it feared that the Tripartite Declaration would give the *coup de grâce* to Israel's policy of non-identification.

In spite of its silence on this aspect, the government appears to have had no illusions about the meaning of the Declaration in the Cold War. Eytan writes: " 'Defense of the area as a whole,' in the language of the Western Powers, meant defense against Soviet attack. The Soviet Union, for its part, has always seen

Western plans for defense of the Middle East as the beginning of aggression against itself. The global struggle between East and West was now superimposed on the local tug of war between the Arab states and Israel, and the two were never again to be disentangled." [62]

The U.N. Vote on Korea

Shortly after the debate on the Tripartite Declaration, there came the crucial vote in the U.N. General Assembly on Communist aggression in Korea. While true neutrality (or even "neutralism" such as practiced by India) would have called for absention, "non-identification" was not meant to preclude Israel from voting its conscience in a specific case, without definite commitment to either bloc. This is what Israel did, joining the forty-five nations who responded to the Security Council's call for sanctions against the aggressors and assistance to the forces of the United Nations. Israel did not go as far as to send troops, pleading its own security needs, but it did send a token supply of medicines and foodstuffs. The Soviets were not impressed by this kind of "non-identification" and classified Israel as a member of the Western camp. The record of previous votes in the United Nations against American interests, as when Israel had been the sole non-Communist member to vote with the Soviet bloc against a Nationalist Chinese resolution to censure the Soviet Union for intervening in the Chinese Civil War at the fourth General Assembly in 1949, did not weigh in the scale. [63]

It would hardly be correct, however, to consider the stand on Korea as the principal factor in the decline of Israel's "non-identification" and the subsequent worsening of Israel's relations with Russia; it was more a symptom of a process already under way than a cause. The reasoning behind Israel's U.N. vote illustrates how a small state must calculate its own interest even

47

in a situation that, on the surface, does not appear to be of direct concern to it.

A semiofficial chronicler of Israel's foreign policy during its first five years describes the reasons leading to the decision as follows:

This was the first time in its history that the state stood before a grave and far-reaching decision in the relation between the blocs, and in a problem which to all appearances did not directly concern her. Israel felt that by becoming a member of the U.N. she joined a system which guaranteed mutual defense to its members—she had hoped through it to secure herself against aggression. This time she had to fulfill the obligation which was connected with this privilege.

Can one say, then, that there was in the problem of her position toward aggression in Korea no direct connection with the vital interests of Israel? If the U.N. had failed to push back the invader to his starting point at the 38th parallel, would this not have created an opening for further armed aggression along other borders which divide a people into two parts on the basis of an agreement among the powers of the world? It was clear that an attempt to unite by force of arms the people of Azerbaijan, or East and West Germany, was apt to plunge the world into global war, to divide the Jewish people, to separate Israel from the sources of its supplies and of immigration, and to put her very existence in jeopardy. More than that: the neighbors of Israel, who are planning to attack her in a second round, would also learn their lesson from the precedent which the U.N. would set against aggression all over the world.[64]

The simple thought underlying this reasoning is that Israel found its own interest coinciding with the cause of the West. Only a few weeks earlier, the Tripartite Declaration had made it clear that it was to the West Israel must look for security. With the Cold War reaching its zenith, peace with the Arabs remote, and economic difficulties intensifying, the feeling was rapidly gaining ground that it might be wisest for Israel to follow the example of other small nations and entrust its security in greater degree to others, more powerful than itself. The influential newspaper *Ha-Arez* put it succinctly: "In view of the decision of the West to remain the determining factor in the Middle East, we have no alternative but to adapt ourselves to it." [65]

Middle Eastern Defense

On 13 October 1951, the Western powers informed Israel of their decision to establish an Allied Middle East Command, "in which countries able and willing to contribute to the defense of the area should participate." They conveyed the opinion of NATO that the defense of the Middle East, which was vital to the security of the free world, could be secured only through the cooperation of the interested powers, including those not territorially part of the area. In view of "the paramount importance to the Command of bases in Egypt," the Egyptian Government was being invited to participate as a founder member "on a basis of equality and partnership with the other founder members." [66]

This, Eytan writes, put Israel into a delicate and ambivalent position:

On the one hand, Israel could not afford to be left out of a scheme which must vastly increase Egypt's military strength. She believed that Egypt would never, in practice, use this strength for the 'defense of the area as a whole,' but only, as soon as there was enough of it, against herself. . . . But if Israel could not afford to be left out of a scheme which, as she saw it, was going to strengthen Egypt at her expense, she was not eager, on the other hand, to be dragged into political conflict with the Soviet Union. Even if she joined only a defense organization, the Soviet Union would see her as one of the powers conspiring for aggression.[67]

But Sharett's report to the Knesset on 4 November indicated that the government had overcome its hesitations.[68] The Foreign Minister skilfully wove together the themes of American aid (which helped Israel out of the serious economic crisis into which the effects of mass immigration had plunged it), the failure of the P.C.C.'s latest initiative, the exposed position of the region in the Cold War, and Israel's own security needs, to pave the way for a sharp turn toward the West. U.S. economic assistance had, he declared, entered a new stage—after two Export-Import Bank loans totaling $135 million and $20 million in surplus food and technical assistance (Point IV), Israel was just receiving a $65-million grant-in-aid, out of a total of $160 million made available for the entire Middle East and Africa.

The Arabs were to blame for the P.C.C.'s failure in Paris, Sharett told the Knesset; they had turned down the Commission's proposal for a proclamation of peaceful intent, which they wanted limited to action by the armed forces only. They saw the armistice agreements as instruments prohibiting armed conflict only, whereas Israel wanted every kind of hostile action pro-scribed. Until the Arabs accepted the original preamble to the proclamation, Israel would not discuss the specific disputes on the Commission's agenda.

While stating Israel's readiness to compensate the refugees being resettled in Arab countries, Sharett hedged it with several provisions, including the demand that assets of Iraqi Jews who emigrated to Israel be deducted from the sum owed.

The preservation of world peace, he then said, is a vital need for Israel, and it continues to be "our most ardent desire." In the concern for our security, he added, we cannot overlook the fate of the region around us. "The absense of peace and of democracy in the area has aggravated anxieties for the fate of the entire area in the event of a world war, and impels us to do everything to strengthen our position in the region, to explore all possible sources of economic and military assistance, and to broaden the concept of our security and our future."

Israel, Sharett continued, must therefore address itself to the plans for overall defense being mooted among the Western

50

powers. Though not invited to participate, the government had been provided with general information about the preliminary stages in the setting up of a regional command; it had confidence that the powers regarded Israel as a Middle Eastern power vitally concerned in anything affecting the entire region. The question of Israel's participation had not arisen. Yet the government was devoting every effort to strengthening the country's economic and defense potential. "The government," Sharett concluded, "will strive as before to maintain relations of friendship with every peace-loving state well disposed toward Israel. Its vital interests, however, demand that, above all, its relations be close with those countries where Jewish communities are free to further the fulfillment of Israel's historic mission, and whose governments render practical assistance to enable it to stand up to the trials of today and those which lie ahead tomorrow."

If there was still any doubt that Israel had entered a new stage in its policy, Ben-Gurion's statement the following day officially buried non-identification. He divided the nations into three categories: those who refused relations with Israel, those who maintained contacts on the governmental level only (the Soviet Union and its satellites), and those who maintained governmental and other relations and permitted free intercourse between Israel and their Jewish populations.[69]

The debate which accompanied these pronouncements showed that "the overwhelming majority of the House favored closer alignment with the West." [70] The General Zionists and Herut in particular now favored regional defense, while Mapam's Ya'qov Riftin appealed to the army "not to submit to this reactionary and anti-national policy." [71] However, Mapam's motion asking for rejection of the $65-million U.S. grant was roundly defeated.

Israel replied to a Soviet warning of November 21 against joining a Middle East Command with a good deal of nonchalance, and Sharett told the Knesset that, "if Israel needs these arms and if, in order to acquire them, it will be necessary to enter certain commitments, she will enter into these commitments." [72]

The plan for a Middle East Command as originally conceived was shelved as a result of Egypt's refusal to join.[73] But the three powers and Turkey informed the Arab states that their own plans could not be delayed. While the Arab states were not being asked to join immediately, hope was expressed that they would do so eventually. Israel was told that its views would be sought later, "when the sponsoring powers have proceeded further in the organization" of the Command.[74] The meaning of this phrase was made plain to the Israel government by the Turkish minister, who explained that in his government's view the "tense relations" prevailing between the Arab states and Israel were a "retarding factor" in the plan for Middle Eastern defense. Turkey, he said, hoped that Israel would adopt a "realistic attitude" about the matter, which meant that Israel should stand aside, at least until all the Arab states had been signed up. To Israel, this meant that the Middle East Command would be organized without it, and that the Arab states would be supplied with arms while Israel would not.[75]

Israel vigorously opposed this point of view, trying to impress the Western allies with the futility of relying on Arab strength and proposing instead that they start their defense set-up with countries willing to cooperate—meaning Turkey, Israel, and Iran—while at the same time effecting by a firm attitude the Arab *rapprochement* with Israel which was necessary if a regional security plan was to make sense.

This reasoning did not have any visible effects on the allies' procedure. In the 1951 and 1952 Mutual Security Acts, Congress had earmarked $396 million and $499 million respectively for direct military aid to Greece, Turkey, Iran, and the rest of the Middle East. The President was authorized to allocate up to 10 per cent of these amounts to Israel and the Arab countries, and Israel had made formal application for arms and equipment. In spite of repeated inquiries by Israel about the delay, no allocation materialized (although in July of 1952 the United States did authorize sale to Israel of certain "reimbursable" military equipment from surplus stocks).[76] The West's plans for a Middle Eastern Command were modified to provide for a Middle East Defense Organization, with emphasis at first on planning and consultation rather than on a full-fledged integrated command. The Arab states were to be given an opportunity to join this framework gradually, but until such time as they had joined up Israel would have to wait.

The eventual fruit of this planning was the Baghdad Pact, from which Israel was entirely excluded.

CHAPTER II ≺≺≺≺

Isolation and Retaliation

The realization that an alliance with the Western powers as a short cut to security was not in the offing—certainly not for the short-term future—ushered in a phase of diplomatic isolation as both the West and the Soviet bloc showed mounting coolness in their relations with Israel. At the same time, stepped-up activity in the area itself was designed to produce conditions promoting security. Israel's diplomacy, leaving behind its active quest for peace in the area and for alliances outside of it, now became preoccupied with defending the situation created by local actions. And from the diplomatic effort to obtain ratification of the *status quo,* Israel turned to military measures designed to halt incursions by marauders which it regarded as piecemeal attempts against its territorial integrity and a challenge to its ability to maintain security on a day-to-day basis.

Soviet Relations

On the global level, the deterioration of relations with the Soviet Union was the more spectacular development. Relations with the United States never reached the same crisis stage; they followed a fever-chart course in which peaks and valleys were marked by actions and reactions by either side.

The early Western initiative toward formation of a Middle East Command had elicited Soviet warnings, presaging a sharp

54

reaction if these plans were to be implemented. Once the new Russian Middle East policy was determined upon, it was probably unavoidable that Israel should feel the backwash of Russian wooing of the Arabs. But it is noteworthy that the most violent clash, resulting in a break of diplomatic relations, was brought on not by Russia's Middle East policy but by her policy toward her own Jewish population.

As a Jewish state, Israel was bound to be painfully affected by the wave of anti-Semitism which swept over the Soviet area during the final period of Stalin's life. In a prelude to events in Russia itself, an Israeli and leading Mapam party functionary, Mordecai Oren, was arrested in Prague on 23 March 1952 and charged with complicity in the activities which led to the trial and execution of former Communist party chief Rudolf Slansky. Oren's arrest, trial and subsequent conviction on 3 November 1952 caused much indignation among all political circles in Israel (excepting the Communists) and led to a crisis of confidence within his own party. That indignation was heightened further when Moscow announced the discovery of the "Doctors' Plot" on 13 January 1953, emphasizing the fact that out of the nine accused no less than six were Jews. The announcement was followed by virulent attacks on Zionism.

On 9 February unidentified persons exploded a bomb on the premises of the Soviet embassy in Tel Aviv, and the Soviet government reacted by breaking off diplomatic relations. In its note, the Soviet government charged Israel's policy with "obvious connivance" in the engineering of the explosion and also accused Foreign Minister Sharett of open incitement to hostility in his Knesset speech of 19 January. Ben-Gurion's apologies were dismissed as "hypocrisy."

Press comment about the Soviet action was characterized by unprecedented ire and acerbity, and the speeches of Israeli diplomats at the United Nations also contained bitter denunciations of Soviet policy. The advocates of a neutralist or Soviet-oriented policy had to take cover. After the exoneration of the doctors, not long after Stalin's death on 3 April, the way was cleared for normal relations to be resumed, as they were on 20 July. The initiative had been taken by Israel, notwithstanding the Foreign Minister's statement in the Knesset on 17 February that it was up to Russia to reconsider its action. Sharett's declaration of 21 July in which he promised that Israel would not support "the execution or preparation of acts of aggression against the Soviet Union or any other peace-loving state" sounded to some observers much like a commitment to stay out of the Western alliance structure.

As for Soviet Russia, the imbroglio with the Jewish state over the treatment of Soviet Jewish citizens was not enough justification for an active pro-Arab policy, but it was certainly not likely to raise scruples in the Soviet leaders' minds when the time did come to chart a new Middle East course.

Since the unsuccessful attempt to encroach on Iranian territory in 1946 and the equally abortive tiff with Turkey over the border areas of Kars and Ardahan in the following year, the Soviet Union had pursued no active policy in the Middle East. Its support of partition in Palestine was interpreted not as an ideological about-face regarding Jewish nationalism, but as an opportunistic move designed to benefit Soviet aims in the area by hastening British withdrawal from Palestine, to exploit Anglo-American differences on the implementation of the UNSCOP report, and possibly to bring about Soviet participation in the eventual resolution of the conflict through the Security Council.[1] Now, with the West striving for an alliance structure in the area, a change in Soviet attitudes toward the Middle East was about to crystallize. On 15 February 1952 Turkey joined the North Atlantic Treaty Organization, and at the other end Pakistan became a partner in the South East Asia Treaty Organization early in 1954. The two alliance systems were joined by a Turkish-Pakistan Friendship Pact on 2 April 1954, while the

Turkish-Iraqi Pact of 24 February 1955 was expanded into the Central Treaty Organization (Baghdad Pact) when it was joined by Pakistan, Iran, and Great Britain. This structure was supported by bilateral military aid agreements between the United States and Iraq and Pakistan, and subsequently by American participation in the "military committee" of the organization itself. This was apart from existing air base agreements between the United States and Libya and Saudi Arabia, and the close ties between Great Britain and Jordan.

It became the aim of Soviet policy to break through this cordon, and at the same time to offer a challenge to the West's favored position in the Middle East. This policy was officially articulated in a policy declaration on 16 April 1955, in which the Soviet Foreign Ministry charged that the Western powers were trying to turn the Middle East into a battlefield and reduce the peoples of the region to colonial enslavement. It warned that the Soviet Union would not remain indifferent to Western military alliances in the region.[2] The various means used by Soviet diplomacy in implementing this policy have been described elsewhere;[3] suffice it here to point out that the split among the Arab states caused by Iraq's adherence to the Western Alliance system and the consequent downgrading of the Arab League's ambition to have the Arab world as a whole play a neutral role was skillfully exploited by the Soviet Union when it concentrated its economic offensive and efforts at political *rapprochement* on Cairo. Soviet support of Egypt has been compared with support of Israel in 1948 in that it focussed on the one element most likely to upset the political balance in the area and to produce conditions unfavorable to Western hegemony.[4]

Of direct concern to Israel's foreign policy in this phase was Moscow's realization that an effective way to appear as a friend of the Arabs was to support them in their quarrel with Israel. This called for no radical turnabout in Soviet policy; the anti-Zionist line of the last period of the Stalin regime and the break in relations had prepared the stage for more permanent abandonment of neutrality in the Arab-Israel conflict. Moreover, Israel's continued dependence on American aid, lately supplemented by reparations from West Germany, made it easy to depict it as a creature of the West and of Western imperialism, a description which fitted in well with the Arabs' own image of Israel's role.

Relations with the United States

The same Western policy which caused this reaction in the Soviet Union also was a source of conflict between the interests of Israel—as it saw them—and those of the United States. This was in some ways ironic, for the break with the Soviet Union had at last brought about a general conviction among the Israeli public that the Rubicon had been crossed, that Israel's lot was now thrown in irrevocably with the Western camp.

A major address by Sharett before the National Press Club in Washington on 10 April 1953 reads like a paean to Israel-American friendship. Sharett even lent his endorsement to President Eisenhower's announced intention to pursue a policy of impartiality between Arabs and Israelis, by declaring that "friendship towards one side is fully compatible with friendship towards another." [5]

But this sanguine mood was dissipated by the address which Secretary of State Dulles delivered to the American people on June 1 following his return from a survey tour of the Middle East, and which embodied the main lines of the Eisenhower Administration's policy for the area. [6] Dulles admitted frankly that the earlier concept of a Middle East Defense Organization had to be shelved, and that instead the United States should help "to strengthen the interrelated defenses of these countries if they want strength" so that a security system could "grow from within." To the Israelis, this meant just one thing: the United States was determined to back the Arab League. This particular passage in the speech also dashed two specific hopes that had been quietly nurtured in Israel: that the United States could persuade the Arabs to make peace with Israel in the interests of common defense, and that Israel's military potential would so impress the Western allies that they would decide on a skeleton Mediterranean defense plan based on Turkey and Israel, the only two countries with effective armies in the Eastern Mediterranean. Then the Arab states, though left out in the beginning, would eventually see the light and join up.

Another part of the speech which caused shocked surprise in Israel contained Dulles' call for a return of some Arab refugees to "the area presently controlled by Israel"—a phrase which was interpreted as a thinly veiled attack on Israel's territorial integrity—and his somewhat oblique appeal for the internationalization of Jerusalem.[7] Knesset discussions on Dulles' tour and speech were uncommonly vehement. The left-wing parties, abashed since the break in relations with Moscow, took the opportunity to get in some licks of their own at last. A Mapam spokesman referred to Dulles as "Hitler's helper to power," [8] and the same party's Ya'qov Riftin taunted the government for not even being able to show American friendship for the deterioration of its relations with Russia.[9] The *Si'at Smol's* Dr. Moshe Sneh called Dulles the chief warmonger, responsible for blood and tears in Korea,[10] while the Communists continued to proclaim that the Secretary of State's real mission was to establish an aggressive bloc against the Soviet Union. At the other end of the political spectrum, Arieh Altman of Herut said the Dulles speech showed America's anti-Israel policy to be a fact.[11]

The Foreign Minister himself preferred to wait and see: for the time being, he said, there was only a speech and not yet a policy. But at the same time, he told the parliament, "we stand before demands, whether enunciated clearly or not, which we cannot fulfill." [12]

He did not spell out at the time what these demands were, but three months later he elaborated: a few years ago, the State Department had shown a tendency toward adopting definite attitudes on Arab-Israel issues. The United States then sought a short cut to peace and, confronted with Arab stubbornness, it attempted to get there through concessions from Israel. Israel regarded this as fatal to its interests. The situation later changed; but now the State Department was reverting to the same approach. Israel, Sharett concluded, must always face the possibility of complications in its relations with the United States as long as relations with the neighboring states were not solved.[13]

That the Dulles visit represented a turning point in Israel-American relations could also be gauged from the tenor of newspaper comment. A content analysis of nine daily papers over a two-week period prior to the Dulles speech and a similar period thereafter shows that, while before the speech editorial comment was predominantly favorable to the United States (65 per cent positive and 35 per cent negative), the proportion became reversed during the second time span. Even the papers that had been consistently friendly now became critical.[14] It was now taken for granted by the press as a whole that the United States was bent on a policy of "appeasement" of the Arab states, and public opinion braced itself for a struggle to resist implementation of such a policy. Though leading Israelis did not doubt that the United States was sincere in its desire to bring peace to the area, they were convinced that it was choosing the wrong means to that end.[15]

It was in the light of this attitude that Israelis viewed a series of developments in relations with the United States during the second half of 1953. These included the following:

(1) Assistant Secretary of State Henry A. Byroade's statement to a Congressional committee on 20 July that the United States meant to supply larger quantities of arms to the Arab states than to Israel.

(2) Rejection, on 25 July, of an Israeli request for a $75 mil-

lion loan for consolidation of short and medium term debts.

(3) Secretary Dulles' sharp reaction, on 28 July, to the transfer of the Israeli Foreign Ministry to Jerusalem.

(4) The supposed slighting of Israel in various speeches and messages by American government officials to Jewish bodies.[16]

(5) The severe condemnation by the United States of the raid on Qibya in October.

(6) The suspension of American aid, on 20 October, as a result of Israel's refusal to comply with the request of the U.N.T.S.O. Chief of Staff to suspend work on its hydroelectric project on the upper Jordan.

Some details on the most important of these incidents are pertinent here. The move of the Foreign Ministry to Jerusalem was a prime example of the policy of the *fait accompli,* which lends itself especially well to small-state diplomacy when it is thought likely that the great power, in spite of its opposition to the move, will not find it worth while to apply its superior power to force a return to the *status quo ante.* While pressure for territorial concessions in the Negev was, for all practical purposes, suspended by the United States with the demise of the Bernadotte Plan, the American government's insistence on the international status of Jerusalem or at least its urging that Israel do nothing to prejudice the city's status for as long as the United Nations' resolution remained on the books, was a continuing source of friction between the two governments. From the time Washington forbade Ambassador James McDonald to attend the first meeting of the Constituent Assembly in Jerusalem in January 1949, the issue became a recurring subject of notes and *démarches,* until Ben-Gurion ordered the seat of the government moved to Jerusalem and proclaimed the city as Israel's capital. It remained dormant for a while, only to be revived again on 10 July 1953, when the Premier ordered the Foreign Ministry moved to Jerusalem from Tel Aviv. The government seemed to expect that the diplomatic missions in Tel Aviv would follow suit, but these stubbornly refused to move and thereby recognize Israel's suzerainty over part of Jerusalem.

In his 28 July press conference, Dulles regretted the move. It was likely to increase tension in the area, he said, adding that the American Embassy would not follow the Ministry to Jerusalem for as long as the U.N. internationalization resolution remained in force.

The issue was clearly one of those controversies which Sharett later characterized as being "the result of our own initiative." [17]

The same can be said of the retaliation policy and its effect on relations with the United States. While the details of the policy fall properly into the category of area relations, the policy also had global repercussions. The Qibya incident [18] was the high-water mark both in the number of victims and in the effect on Israel's foreign relations. In rapid succession, Israel's action was condemned by the Mixed Armistice Commission, by the State Department and other Western chancelleries, and by the Security Council.

On 19 October, Dulles announced that financial aid to Israel was being suspended, declaring that the decision had been taken because of Israel's defiance of the United Nations in the matter of the Jordan hydroelectric project and not as a reaction to Qibya. It is true that Israel had been warned as early as 9 October, when Dulles had met with Ambassador Eban in Washington, that the United States might take this drastic step if Israel failed to comply with the order to cease work on the project. But it is likely that the Qibya raid precipitated the suspension of aid.

The clash with the United Nations had come about in the following manner. Israel's master plan for diversion to the south of a portion of the Jordan's waters called for construction of a hydroelectric installation to exploit the drop in the river's flow between the Huleh and Lake Tiberias (Kinneret). The site of the project, near the bridge of B'not Ya'qov, was in the demilitarized zone in close proximity to the Syrian border, and the Syrians objected to it on the grounds that it would give Israel a military advantage.

General Vagn Bennike, the U.N.T.S.O. Chief of Staff, sustained Syria's objections and ordered Israel to stop its activities until Syria gave its consent.[19] This, to the Israelis, indicated either incredible naïveté or overt espousal of the Arab side. They refused to comply and continued digging the disputed channel; Syria lodged a renewed complaint with the Security Council and the United States reacted in the manner indicated above. On 28 October, Ambassador Eban told the Security Council that Israel had agreed to suspend the work, pending a decision by the Council itself. On the following day the United States released $26 million in grant-in-aid funds which had been blocked.[20] President Eisenhower told his news conference that American aid had been resumed because Israel had accepted the findings of the U.N. Truce Supervision Organization.

The reinstatement of the grant marked the beginning of a slackening of the tension in relations with the United States, but a good deal of bitterness remained over what was generally considered the blatant use of economic assistance for political ends. Only three days before Ambassador Eban's announcement of compliance, Ben-Gurion had vowed that "we will never bow to the golden ring of Caesar, however powerful." [21] The editorial writers were outraged. *Ha-Zofeh,* the Mizrahi daily, said that the suspension of the grant was a greater blow to American moral standing than to Israel. "Mr. Dulles makes a mockery of the grant's moral value," the paper declared. At the same time, it hoped that the suspension might lead to a "gradual elimination of overdependence on American and foreign aid." [22] In the event, this expectation proved somewhat premature. The loss of more than $50 million would have left a gaping hole in Israel's foreign currency income for 1953–1954, with the minimum requirements set at $270 million, of which only $40 million was covered by exports.

The Mapam daily saw in the suspension of aid a confirmation of its persistent cry of "economic enslavement," and opposed acceptance of further grants. Only *Ha-Arez* dissented from the general mood. The independent daily advocated making every effort to regain the confidence of the United States and the United Nations, since "without them Israel's irrigation projects cannot be carried out in any event." The paper's editorialist said that the United States had thus far been Israel's best friend and had made considerable sacrifices on Israel's behalf, even though everyone in the country was taking this for granted. "In order to keep allies, one must occasionally make some concessions to them," the article continued. "In the past months, Israel has given the U.S. one cause for annoyance after another." [23]

The Security Council's deliberations on the Syrian complaint ended without a resolution being adopted, the Soviet Union having vetoed a Western draft which would have left the task of proposing a settlement to the Chief of Staff. Thus the "urgent examination" which the Council by its own resolution of 27 October had promised to undertake was never completed, and Israel was effectively prevented from completing the work.

Johnston and Byroade

On the day after the Qibya raid, President Eisenhower appointed Eric Johnston as his special envoy to the Middle East to "sell" Israel and the Arab states a joint Jordan River irrigation project.[24] The move was a token of the stubborn American faith in the efficacy of economic remedies for political ills which, in this instance, failed of vindication by a quite narrow margin. In his optimistic report to the President at the conclusion of his initial survey tour on 17 December, Johnston proposed a $121-

million project to irrigate 250,000 acres of land capable of sustaining 300,000 refugees and requiring the cooperation of Lebanon, Syria, Jordan, and Israel. The Arab countries, persisting in their refusal to have any direct dealings with Israel, suggested that the project be based on bilateral agreements between the United Nations and the states concerned. The United States, which had expressed its readiness to foot most of the bill, accepted this condition, and Johnston started out on a series of visits to the riparian states as well as to Egypt to negotiate agreement on the details. Israel adopted an attitude of cautious cooperation, though there was a good deal of opposition to the plan on the ground that it would allot less water to Israel than it had intended to exploit in its master plan.

While the Johnston plan brought an element of constructive cooperation into American-Israel relations in early 1954, two other developments again beclouded the picture. On 14 April it was announced that the United States grant-in-aid for fiscal year 1955 would be pared to $52.5 million because Israel was nearer to self-support and no longer required the large sums that had been made available in the previous three years. The implied compliment was appreciated, but the announcement nevertheless was unwelcome because it upset the calculation on which current economic planning was based: that the development of the economy could be predicated on a more or less constant flow of American aid.[25]

The second contretempts was Byroade's speech of 10 April and a sequel which he delivered on 1 May.[26] In retrospect, the furore which Byroade stirred up in Israel seems disproportionate to his utterances, which were rather well-reasoned and temperate. Byroade, after presenting a summation of the views held by an imaginary Israeli and his Arab counterpart, advised Israel to cease thinking of itself as the center of world Jewry and the Arabs to accept Israel as a reality in their midst. He also pointed to the beneficial effect which a limitation on immigration would have on Arab attitudes. Yet the two speeches apparently epitomized to the Israeli public the new direction of American policy. The press branded Byroade as anti-Israel by emphasizing those sections which expressed views running counter to Israeli policy, without always identifying them as being held by the imaginary Arab of Byroade's discourse. Eban lodged a protest with the State Department; and Sharett, in opening the foreign policy debate on 10 May accused Byroade of a "lack of insight into the way Israel was born." He ascribed the "greater leniency" shown by the United States to the Arabs, as exemplified in Byroade's attitude, to the Soviet wooing of the Arab states which was by then in full swing. But the Foreign Minister was realistic enough not to oversimplify and hold the Soviet attitude alone responsible for American policy. The United States, he said, had been engaged in a basic reappraisal of its Middle Eastern policy independent of Soviet moves. Sharett also conceded that the Byroade speeches were not consistently opposed to Israel: "He told the Arabs some home truths too. But he did not tell them to cease being themselves, as he did to Israel." And most injurious of all, the Arabs heard a great-power spokesman justify their fears of Israel expansionism.[27]

Israel's isolation in its relations with the great powers became further aggravated during 1954 and 1955. Great Britain's agreement on 13 October 1954 with Egypt on evacuation of the Suez Canal base, the various treaties culminating in the Baghdad Pact, prospective and actual arms shipments by both Britain and the United States to Egypt and Iraq, and finally the Czech Egyptian arms deal in September 1955, all contributed to Israel's feeling that it stood alone. Before reverting to these developments, it is necessary to review relations within the Arab-Israel area during this period.

Area Relations: Security through Force

The dominant manifestation of policy within the area was retaliation for border crossings and acts of violence perpetrated by infiltrators. Retaliation was a major facet of the security policy, which was intended to furnish protection against revision of the *status quo* by force. It could hardly forestall an all-out attack on Israel's territory, or "second round," but it was conceived as an answer to partial, piecemeal encroachment on the land area, and accompanying crimes against persons and property, while at the same time demonstrating Israel's military superiority.

The tactic of retaliation goes back to the Arab-Jewish partisan warfare of prestate days. After a long period of restraint (*havlagah*) in the face of Arab attacks on villages, road traffic, and individuals, the philosophy of striking back eventually gained the upper hand among the leadership of Haganah, the underground military organization of the Jewish community. After 1948, the pattern of marauding, cattle rustling and other thefts, and ultimately murder of Jewish farmers, was not unlike the experience of the *Yishuv* in 1936 and 1937, when Arab villages such as Ein Zeitun and Sasa had become nests of guerrilla activity and were raided by Jewish forces in retribution.

With the founding of the state, the conflict which until then had the character of an intercommunal struggle within the same polity turned into a conflict between states, but the first phase of the retaliation policy in the period of sovereignty was not dissimilar in character to the prestate pattern. The Israeli raids followed closely upon incursions from Jordan-held territory in which Jewish lives were lost, with the reprisal related directly to a particular incident.[28]

The tempo of the raids and counterraids mounted but gradually in frequency and intensity. During 1951 there were still only isolated incidents. Both sides cooperated willingly in the investigations of the Mixed Armistice Commission, and at one point even expressed their regret over a series of fatal incidents.[29] Israel appeared to credit Jordan's desire to exercise control. But the year 1952 started out less auspiciously. A major reprisal raid occurred on 6 January, when Israeli forces entered the village of Bet Jallah near Bethlehem in retaliation for a rape-murder on Israeli territory. They destroyed several houses in which seven inhabitants died. Israel complained of ten instances of infiltration, in which two of its citizens were murdered, and six Arabs from Jordan were intercepted and shot on Israeli territory within one week. Jordan alleged that Israeli forces had fired across the border and killed five more Jordanians. The curve dropped again after 1 February, when an agreement among the local commanders went into effect by the terms of which complaints by both sides were handled with dispatch by the commanders themselves.[30] The agreement was allowed to lapse, however, after Israel felt it was ineffective in preventing infiltration.

Thereafter, serious incidents occurred with increasing frequency. Yet such names as Falamah, Rantis, and Qalqilya, highlighting the series of raids and counterraids in late 1952 and early 1953, were soon overshadowed by the bloodier and more widely publicized incidents of Qibya, Maaleh Aqravim, and Nahalin, which marked the second phase of the cycle of violence in late 1953 and early 1954.

By this time a mood of anger and frustration over the almost nightly violence had taken hold in Israel, fanned by detailed press reports on each incident. A sense of insecurity pervaded the border areas and made inroads into the settlers' morale. Against this setting, there exploded the news of the murder of a mother and her two children by infiltrators from Jordan in the village of Yahud, just ten miles from Tel Aviv, on 14 October 1953.

On the night of 15 October armed forces from Israel retaliated with an attack on the Jordanian village of Qibya in the "Little Triangle," killing 66 persons, most of them civilians. Demonstrations took place in Amman and elsewhere in Jordan protesting the Arab Legion's failure to intervene; the Israel-Jordan M.A.C. condemned the action as "cold-blooded murder"; and the Security Council, called into session at the initiative of the Western powers, censured Israel and asked its government to "bring those responsible to account." [31] Eban told the Council that Israel had suffered 421 killed and wounded in Jordanian infiltration raids since 1950 and that Jordan had been found guilty 159 times by the M.A.C. against Israel's 25 times, but his impassioned speech could not stave off the censure.[32]

After a period of relative quiet the infiltration-retaliation cycle received a new impetus on 17 March 1954 when an Israeli bus driving from Beersheba to Eilat was attacked by an Arab band at Maaleh Aqravim (Scorpions' Pass) and nine of its occupants massacred. This was the largest number of Israelis killed in a single operation; public indignation ran high, yet there was no reprisal raid while the M.A.C. investigated the killings. But the truce team's search for evidence as to the gang's origin was inconclusive. The tracks disappeared some distance from the Jordanian border. As a result, the chairman refused to cast the deciding vote which would have declared Jordan guilty, reasoning that the perpetrators might have been Arabs from Egypt or even from Israel itself.[33] This infuriated the Israelis, who launched a bitter press campaign against the M.A.C. chairman, Commander Elmo Hutchison, and decided to boycott the M.A.C. for as long as he was in charge. When the Commission subsequently met without the Israeli delegate, the papers referred to it as the "Hutchison Commission" or the "Rump Armistice Commission." The Histadrut daily said the Jordanians were encouraged in their guerrilla warfare by the role of the U.N. observers in the Scorpions' Pass investigation.[34]

When infiltrators killed an Israeli farmer at Qisalon on 26

March, Israel refused to cooperate with the M.A.C. in the investigation and once again took matters into its own hands. In a raid on the village of Nahalin two days later, nine Arabs were killed. Sharett called it a "local reaction" to Jordan's provocation, maintaining, as Ben-Gurion had done after Qibya, that regular troops were not involved.[35]

Nevertheless, Qibya had been a watershed as far as retaliation against Jordan was concerned. Though the Nahalin raid was also a major operation, it was characterized by the fact that the number of victims was in proportion to the number of Israelis killed at Scorpions' Pass. Furthermore, the dead at Nahalin were members of the Jordan National Guard and the building picked for the attack could be considered a military objective. Walter Eytan writes that women and children had been killed at Qibya "contrary to intention," and that there was never another Qibya. "Care was taken later to attack only police forces, military posts and other such bases from which the raiders operated." [36] This meant that there was no thought of abandoning the retaliation policy, but to rationalize it and to restrict its application. For the defenders of the policy could claim that it was effective in compelling the Jordanian authorities to take stronger measures against infiltration.

The record of Israelis killed in the areas bordering on Jordan seemed to support this, although not conclusively. According to the Israeli figures, 44 citizens were killed in 1951, 46 in 1952, and 57 in 1953. The number dropped to 34 in 1954 and to 11 in 1955.[37]

Clashes with Egypt

The focus of major border violence now shifted southward to the armistice line with Egypt, as shown by this U.N. tabulation of casualties for the year 1955: [38]

Casualties	Jordan-Israel Front	Egypt-Israel Front
Israelis killed	8	47
Israelis wounded	30	118
Arabs killed	18	216
Arabs wounded	7	188

It should be mentioned that the motivation of the retaliation policy vis-à-vis Egypt was considerably more complex than it was with regard to Jordan (see Chapter III, below). Here a brief sketch of the violence along the Israel-Egypt line of demarcation is in order.

The armistice line along the Gaza Strip had been the scene of sporadic marauding, murder, theft, blowing up of pipelines, and some Israeli counteractivity in the fall of 1954. But in a report to the Security Council on 11 November, General Burns felt the respective Israeli and Egyptian complaints and the decisions of the M.A.C. for the past several months did not reflect a critical situation. However, on 21 January 1955 an Egyptian army unit crossed the line and attacked an Israeli military post, killing or wounding its three occupants. In condemning the attack, the Israel-Egyptain M.A.C. noted that the "armistice demarcation line was clearly marked near the place of the attack," and that the "aggressive action" was carried out by an Egyptian military patrol commanded by an officer. Three days later, an Egyptian armed band attacked the settlement of 'Ein Hashlosha and ambushed its farmers, and in February Egyptian raiders penetrated as far as thirty miles into Israel territory, killing a cyclist near Rehovot. The M.A.C. called upon the Egyptian authorities to "terminate immediately these aggressive actions by Egyptian military patrols and the continuous infiltration into Israel." [39]

On 28 February 1955 Israel mounted its major raid against Gaza in which 37 Egyptians were killed and 39 wounded. Beyond its retaliatory character, the raid should be viewed in conjunction with Egyptian actions in other spheres: the hanging of

71

two Egyptian Jews convicted of sabotage on behalf of Israel in January, and the detention of the Bat Galim. In justifying their continued interdiction of the Suez Canal against ships flying the Israeli flag, Egypt had once again used the argument that a state of war still existed, and that the Constantinople Convention gave it the right to protect the Canal in time of war.[40] After the Gaza raid, Sharett said that if Egypt wished to maintain a state of war it must take the consequences.[41] Thus a new element was injected into the relationship: Israel served notice that it not only would meet violence with violence, but warlike acts with other warlike acts. Prime Minister Gamal Abdel Nasser countered by saying that Egypt would no longer depend on the United Nations but would meet force with force.[42]

As was to be expected, the Security Council unanimously censured Israel for the Gaza raid.[43] Before doing so, it heard a plea by Eban for Egypt to renounce useless hostility and join Israel in a code for peace in the Middle East. He declared that his government stood ready to give an assurance that if no hostile act was carried out by Egypt against Israel, then no hostile act of any kind would be carried out by Israel against Egypt.[44] But the hostilities continued. On 25 March infiltrators from the Gaza Strip bombed a wedding party in the village of Patish, killing one and wounding eighteen of the guests. For this the M.A.C. promptly found Egypt guilty of a "brutal and murderous act of aggression." On 29 March, the day the Security Council adopted its resolution on the Gaza raid, two Israeli soldiers died of wounds suffered when their car struck a mine. On 31 March the M.A.C. again took note of the "aggravation caused by repeated acts of aggression by Egypt against Israel," and on the same day an Israeli patrol car in the Gaza border area was blown up by a land mine. On 6 April the Security Council convened once more, at Israel's request, to hear Eban charge that Egypt had "embarked on a relentless siege of border violence" and list Egyptian attacks on ten Negev villages as well as repeated assaults on

72

Israeli border patrols. He told the Council that there had been a significant shift in Egyptian tactics: from border violations by Arab marauders to overt acts by Egyptian troops, from which a new and purposeful military design was emerging.[45]

During postponement of the debate, further bloody incidents took place for which both sides were censured by the M.A.C. On 15 April General Burns reported that both sides were ready to work out an agreement whereby local commanders would cooperate to check infiltration, and had pledged to keep only disciplined regular troops in the vicinity of the demarcation line. At the same time, his report pointed to Egyptian mining of roads used by Israeli patrols as the "most important factor contributing to increased tension." It added that these minings were probably reprisals for the 28 February Gaza raid.[46]

The Security Council took no action beyond appealing to both sides to avoid future clashes.[47] Israel then advanced proposals, through General Burns, for a high-level conference to discuss the means of improving security. But Egypt rejected the idea, suspecting an Israeli plan to lead up to peace talks.[48]

There was another serious incident on 30 May, when an Israeli jeep was fired on from an Egyptian post, and in the exchange of fire there were casualties on both sides. General Burns's diligent diplomacy, which included a visit to Cairo to tell Nasser that his side was now responsible for the tension and that the Israelis might once more retaliate, may have prevented a more serious flare-up. Low-level negotiations for a new security arrangement continued at snail's pace until 22 August, when an Israeli patrol was fired upon once again. This time the Israelis drove into the nearby Egyptian position with their armored cars, killing and wounding some of the garrison.

Nasser now decided to suspend the negotiations for a local commanders' agreement. Before the efforts of the U.N. Secretary General to get them going again had any effect, a new wave of violence broke out. There began a series of raids into Israeli territory by Egyptian-trained *fidayun*—guerrilla attacks against civilian population and installations deep inside Israel. The raiders were refugees from the Gaza area who knew the Palestine countryside intimately, as was apparent from those captured or killed by the Israelis, including some who were interrogated by members of the U.N.T.S.O. Israel complained to the Security Council on 29, 30 and 31 August of successive attacks, the most serious of which was the wounding of a family of five persons—one of whom later died—by small-arms fire near Rehovot. Shortly thereafter, four unarmed workmen were massacred in an orange grove near Rishon le-Zion. General Burns reports being "deeply shocked" by the extent and character of the Egyptian campaign. He appealed to both parties to observe a strict cease-fire and to issue the most positive orders to prevent anyone's crossing the demarcation line. While Egypt was willing, Israel demanded that Egypt accept responsibility for the previous incidents, a condition which General Burns found unreasonable. He assumed that a decision to retaliate had by this time been taken, and indeed during the night of 31 August–1 September the reprisal raid on the police station of Khan Yunis took place. In Israel newspaper reports of the attack, the station was described as the headquarters from which the *fidayun* camp was directed. The Egyptians reported casualties of 36 killed and 13 wounded, including soldiers, policemen, and civilians.[49]

This time the Security Council resolution did not condemn Israel,[50] a fact which General Burns ascribes to the revulsion which the *fidayun* campaign had created, and possibly also to the feeling that the Egyptians were as much to blame as the Israelis for the breakdown of the negotiations which had been conducted in accordance with the Council's 28 March resolution.

After the *fidayun* raids subsided, there arose a new focus of conflict: the demilitarized zone of al-Awja. Because of its strategic importance as a junction on one of the two principal invasion routes between Egypt and Palestine, the area had been

74

given special status in the Israel-Egyptian General Armistice Agreement. General Burns writes:

It was from this general area that the decisive attack by the Israeli forces on the Egyptian forces had been launched in December 1948, and that another was to erupt again in October–November 1956. If, indeed, the zone had remained demilitarized—that is to say, if it could not have been traversed or occupied by the armed forces of either side—it would have been almost impossible for either to have carried out an offensive successfully, the balance of forces being as they were.[51]

There had been previous contention about both the status of the zone and its use by Israel, centering around the establishment of a kibbutz in the territory, which the Egyptians considered a prohibited military organization, whereas Israel insisted it was a pioneering farming endeavor which it was entitled to maintain by virtue of the fact that the zone was Israeli territory. The M.A.C. had sided with Egypt in this dispute, but pending the outcome of an appeal of the decision by Israel, the kibbutz had stayed put.[52] Now a new quarrel developed over Israel's stationing of civilian police in the zone—to which General Burns had given his consent—and Egypt's determination to maintain border checkposts which the Israelis insisted were defensive positions, and therefore prohibited.

On 27 September 1955, while the al-Awja controversy was still in its nonviolent stage, Nasser announced the signing of his agreement with Czechoslovakia for the sale to Egypt of substantial quantities of arms. The Israel-Egyptian conflict had now entered a new and decisive phase.

Part Two

THE MEANS OF POLICY

CHAPTER III ≺≺≺≺
The Arab-Israel
Power Balance

During all of the period discussed in the preceding part, the notion that the military strength of Israel must remain superior to that of any combination of its Arab foes was an underlying assumption of Israeli foreign policy. Yet the term "balance of power" rarely occurred in Knesset debates, newspaper editorials, or utterances by public figures. Two reasons may account for its absence: (1) no serious threat to the existing power relationship was felt to exist; and (2) as long as a preponderance of power appeared assured, power was not considered an end of policy in itself. Peace, alliances, *status quo*—these were policy goals. It was only when peace appeared unrealizable, alliances unobtainable, and the *status quo* endangered by a build-up of countervailing power that the maintenance of the balance emerged as a concrete policy goal.

Arms Supplies and the Suez Treaty

In 1954 two events occurred which for Israel signaled a threat to the prevailing power position. One was the arming of Iraq by the United States, a concomitant of the Northern Tier concept pursued by the Republican administration; the other was the Anglo-Egyptian agreement for the evacuation of the Suez Canal zone.

The Tripartite Declaration had done little to allay Israel's apprehension over the continuing supply of Western arms to the Arab states, and expressions of concern over this issue had become a regular feature of Israeli policy pronouncements. In a press conference in December 1952 Sharett protested sharply that the continuing Western arms shipments were incompatible with the Declaration and menaced the region's security. Since the Arabs were not participating in any scheme beyond regional defense, he declared, they obviously planned to use the arms against Israel.[1]

Throughout 1953 there continued to be growing concern over the intentions of both the American and British governments with regard to arms sales to the Arab states. Along with diplomatic warnings and protests, the Israel press vigorously condemned the projected arms shipments, going so far as to say that the situation created by them was more dangerous than it had been in 1948.[2]

These alarms, however, receded into the background when it became clear that the United States would become a regular supplier of modern armaments to Iraq as part of the treaty arrangements it was promoting.

On 3 January 1954, the *Jerusalem Post* carried a report from Washington to the effect that the United States was planning to extend arms aid to Pakistan, Iraq, and Saudi Arabia. Israel, Egypt, Lebanon, and Syria were not to benefit from the deliveries because they were not in the immediate path of a possible Russian invasion. The report served as a signal for a full-scale diplomatic offensive against the new prospect. But the United States was determined to go through with its policy,[3] and on 21 April Ambassador Eban was forced to protest the conclusion of the arms agreement with Iraq, while the Foreign Minister himself published a sharply worded statement the following day.[4] In the Knesset, on 12 May, Sharett said Israel put no faith in Iraq's guaranties to use the arms only for regional defense.[5] A week later the Knesset adopted a government-sponsored resolution expressing concern over the armament of Iraq, the majority having defeated more extremist versions of both the right and the left.[6]

Israel had been following with some anxiety the course of the Anglo-Egyptian negotiations over evacuation of the Suez Canal base zone, but the news on 27 July that an agreement had been initialed which would leave the Canal and the military installations on its shores in Egyptian hands came as a shock nevertheless. Because of the protracted and complex nature of the negotiations it had been widely assumed that the views and interests of the two parties remained far apart; few Israelis appreciated the full extent of the waning of British power in the area which the agreement symbolized. For those on the left, in particular, Britain had remained the *bête noire* of Middle Eastern politics, hatching its imperialistic designs even while pretending to withdraw. Now the agreement raised the specter of an unfettered Egypt, militarily well equipped, and no longer subject to the restraining hand of the British. Adding to the disquiet were two specific clauses in the treaty: one providing for British re-entry in case of war in the area, from which contingency a conflict involving Israel was pointedly omitted; and another, recognizing the Arab League security pact, which Sharett called "an instrument for waging war against Israel." [7] In a press conference on 20 August, Sharett said that Britain should have made the Suez agreement conditional on peace with Israel, or at least give Israel assistance to counterbalance the advantage gained by Egypt. At the same time he condemned the military aid granted by the United States to Egypt and Iraq.[8]

In the debate which followed a policy statement by Mr. Sharett on 30 August, the Knesset heard these sentiments expressed over and over again, with variations along party lines.[9] The resolution voted on 1 September declared that "Israel will not reconcile itself to the policy of the United States and Great

Britain with regard to the arming of the Arab states, and their lack of concern for Israel's security problem." The upsetting of the balance of military strength, the resolution warned, would undermine the security of the area.[10]

While the Knesset resounded to talk of equilibrium and balance of power, Arab statesmen also began to speak the language of geopolitics. In a joint note to British Foreign Secretary Selwyn Lloyd, the Arabs said on 16 September that they rejected the idea of an equilibrium between a state comprising 1.5 million and a group of states with many times that number. Israel would like to see sixty million Arabs weak and powerless because it is "imperative for Israel to keep the Arab states weak and divided," the note declared.[11]

Meaning of the "Power Balance" in the Arab-Israel Area

The term "balance of power" had thus become by late 1954 part of the political vocabulary of Israel and also of its opponents. What was its meaning in the Arab-Israel area?

Most writers on international relations who deal with the concept point out that it has more than one application. As it is most frequently used, the term "balance of power" no longer reflects its literal meaning, namely an equilibrium among forces, but rather a slight superiority by one party. The tendency is to use it in the former sense, equality, in peacetime and in the latter sense, superiority, during a time of diplomatic crisis or of warfare.[12]

Some writers use the phrase "distribution of power" to characterize what is otherwise called a "balance of power" among several states. When the "balance of power has shifted," the opponent has become more powerful than he was previously. To redress the balance, then, does not mean to restore an equilibrium but to gain an advantage for oneself. A distribution of power is also involved in the third definition of the power balance, sometimes called the "balancer theory." Here the distribution in a multistate system is such that no single state would be able to overawe other states. In practice this describes a condition in which any state attempting aggression would find itself faced by such a powerful coalition that it could not succeed. A balance of power policy, in this sense, means that each state in the system, in addition to preparing directly for its own defence, would indirectly also act for its defense by joining with other states in preventing any state from becoming so powerful that it can ignore any other.

The post-World War II bipolar system was not an inclusive state system, and in its shadow subsystems arose which, while subject to the pulls generated by the two poles and their interaction, yet managed to preserve some freedom of action in internal conflict situations. The India-Pakistan constellation has been described as one example; the Middle East, with the Arab-Israeli area at its core, another. It is precisely because a situation of mutual deterrence obstructed great-power intervention that the smaller states in the subsystem remained relatively free to act.

In comparing the Middle East as a power system to the classical balance-of-power situation, Leonard Binder sees Israel as a stabilizer, a kind of balancer, preventing important shifts in the system's internal structure. This it did in two ways: "unconsciously," by diverting energies from internal differences and disagreements and drawing them on to itself; and "consciously," by moderating Egyptian pressure on Jordan and on Iraq.[13]

But Israel could hardly have played the role of a balancer in a classical balance-of-power situation, not being in a position to conclude an alliance with either side. Moreover, the balance-of-power situation which dominated the politics of the Middle East during the period was not primarily between the two principal Arab states—Egypt and Iraq—but between the Arab states as a group on the one hand and Israel on the other. The Egyptian-

Iraqi rivalry, with its struggle over Jordan as a subordinate theme, did not enter the stage of acute conflict where power was brought into play. For Israel that rivalry was of concern only inasmuch as it affected its own interest and its strength relative to the potential foe.[14] That interest was the maintenance of a balance of power in its most elementary sense, namely, to prevent any combination of foes and certainly any single foe from gaining sufficient power to match or overwhelm it.

The thought was clearly expressed by a Mapai deputy in a Knesset foreign policy debate in 1951: "What is the basic line of our policy in this region? Not to let an Arab coalition arise; a coalition which builds on the tension in the world, a coalition which will coalesce by the strength of the great powers, and will create a force of one-sided aggressiveness directed against us. We will remain in isolation in this process. The danger exists, and we must be on guard against any such attempt to form a permanent Arab coalition which has not yet accepted Israel's existence." [15]

This brief discussion on the balance-of-power concept as it related to Israel may be summed up in the words of a veteran theoretician of international politics: "States are interested only in a balance which is in their favor. . . . There is security only in being a little stronger. . . . There is a chance for a positive foreign policy only if there is a margin of force which can be freely used. . . . Whatever the theory and the rationalization, the practical objective is the constant improvement of the state's own relative power position." [16]

To Israel's policy-makers the margin of force meant more than a chance for a positive foreign policy—it meant survival as a sovereign entity.

Components of the Power Inventory

The report of a scholarly symposium on the subject of the New Egypt, held early in 1956, provides some insight into how the

Israelis themselves classified their country's war potential in relation to that of their principal foe. In his address to the symposium, an intelligence expert defined the power potential of a state as the sum of geography, demography, and economic values, the latter two being made up of quality and quantity. Demography is translated into military capacity in terms of the number of soldiers the population can furnish; their morale, technical proficiency, and battle-worthiness; the level and quality of the officer corps; and the like.

The economic potential expresses itself first in the quantity and quality of equipment and ammunition that can be supplied to the war machine and second in terms of the food and fuel the economy can produce and its financial capacity.[17]

Geography

The geographical environment was favorable to Israel in the event of attack by a single foe in that the strongest enemy power was separated from, and the weakest closest to Israel; but it was unfavorable in the event of a coordinated attck by a combination of foes. Then the whole of Israel and its population would be closely accessible to the effect of Arab hostility, while the bulk of the Arab area would be inaccessible to Israel.

This would apply in a conflict initiated by the Arab side. In the event of an offensive by Israel, the territorial advantage would be reversed: Egypt's heartland would be protected by the intervening Sinai Peninsula, whereas the part of Jordan situated on the Western side of the Jordan River would be entirely vulnerable to attack.

Israeli strategists had to regard an offensive action as an eventuality because of the nature of Israel's territory which, because of its narrowness at the "waist," permitted only a minimum of maneuverability in defense.[18]

This was the reason the first item in every inventory of national power—geography—continued to be of supreme importance in determining Israel's strategy. The fundamental geographic fact of Israel's position was that the country was surrounded on all of its land borders by hostile powers, and the memory that all four contiguous states—plus two noncontiguous ones—had made war simultaneously left an indelible imprint on subsequent strategic thought.

The war of 1948 was conducted successfully by Israel through the shifting of forces from one front to another, from the Syrian front in the north, to the Jordanian sector in the center, and lastly to the south. This defensive strategy was successful because of the weakness of the opposing forces and because of the absence of a unified command which could have coordinated the enemies' operations. The necessity to avoid a war on multiple fronts against an enemy operating under an effective unified command motivated the planners of Israel's defense in the ensuing period as well, and their great concern was that they would not be able to do this a second time. Israel was thus able to feel relatively secure as long as there was no radical development in the direction of a joint Arab command which would effectively coordinate the fighting forces of several contiguous states and make war on two or three fronts a possibility. The military force at Israel's disposal was deemed sufficient for coping with its enemies one by one, but there were doubts about its adequacy in dealing with a genuine invasion.

In fact, the threat from the north was not viewed as serious following the 1948 experience except in conjunction with an attack from the east and/or the south. The Lebanese occupying the western sector of the northern frontier maintained a fighting force whose dimensions were negligible compared with Israel's. The Syrians, occupying the strategic heights overlooking the Huleh valley and the eastern side of the Galilee had come close to reaching their objective of overrunning Jewish defensive positions to the south and southwest of the Sea of Galilee, but only because of the greatly inferior strength in men and equipment on the Jewish side. The arrival of two field artillery pieces turned the tide, after a well-placed Molotov cocktail had stopped the Syrian armor in its tracks inside the key village of Degania. The Syrian capture of the border village of Mishmar ha-Yarden, further north, on 10 June was also ascribed to the shortage of arms, ammunition and manpower in the area. "Except for relatively minor tactical offensives . . . the initiative on the northern front as elsewhere in the country had been in Arab hands during the weeks following May 15; nevertheless, their initiative had failed to yield victories." [19]

Jordan came to be the best placed of Israel's enemies after the armistice, its newly acquired cis-Jordanian area jutting as a vast bulge into Israel's waist with the Hebron area and the Old City of Jerusalem forming smaller wedges that could be potential springboards for a surprise attack. The armistice demarcation line is 333 miles in length, of which 65 miles border on Israel territory that is no more than 15 miles in width. Yet Jordan's fighting force, while eminently suited to defense in the hills, as shown in the battles for Latrun and Jerusalem in 1948, was not well adapted for attack in the plain, where Israel was most vulnerable.[20] Poor in resources though Israel was, Jordan was even poorer and unable to sustain prolonged fighting without foreign aid.

Egypt was not well placed for an attack since the Sinai desert effectively separated its main base from Israel's borders. But Egypt under the revolutionary regime was both more powerful militarily than Jordan and more dangerous politically because of its pan-Arab ambitions. However, the geographic separation fostered a feeling in Israel that there was no fundamental conflict of vital interests between Egypt and Israel. This resulted in periodic peace overtures to Egypt long after the attempts to reach an agreement with Jordan had collapsed. These proclamations of Israel's willingness to come to terms with Egypt were, however, invariably coupled with a warning that Israel was ready to fight if Egypt so willed it.

Economic Factors

Regarding conversion of economic resources into military power, Israel was bound to view the situation of the Arab states against its own meager potential. Israel was heavily dependent on foreign aid during the first half of the 1950's and had no assets of its own to convert into military power in the absence of such aid. Having neither oil nor metallic ore among its natural resources for the establishment of an arms manufacture and the running of a war machine, it was dependent on supplies from abroad. Stock piles of essential commodities had to be accumulated with foreign aid.

If this decription of Israel's economic war-potential characterized the position after statehood, it was even more characteristic of the prestate Jewish community. Yet the Arabs failed to inflict a military defeat on the Jews of Palestine-Israel because their own position was not much different. Indeed, neither Israel nor Egypt (and certainly none of the other Arab states) could have made war on the basis of their own organic power—in other words, without the import of foreign arms their military power would have been zero. There was no evidence that any substantial change had occurred in any of the Arab states to alter the situation in Israel's disfavor. Jordan was even more dependent on foreign aid than Israel, not only for its military needs but also for essential civilian requirements. The influx of a large Arab refugee population had diluted whatever resources it possessed. Neither in Egypt nor in any of the other Arab states had national income risen sufficiently to permit the creation of a "war chest," or margin of resources, which could be spared from the need to feed, clothe, and find jobs for the population.

Until 1956, there were only three small metal plants in Egypt which were equipped with steel-melting furnaces using scrap as raw material. For most of its steel, Egypt depended on other countries. The country had neither coal nor coke. Electric power for industry was short and depended on fuel for steam generation.[21]

The advent of the Egyptian revolution had been welcomed by Israel, not only because President Muhammad Nagib had expressed himself in moderate terms about the Palestine War and about Israel, but also because the junta's determination to bring about internal reforms and to raise living standards was expected to turn attention away from "foreign adventures." And in effect, the regime's short-range projects were designed, first of all, to improve the balance of trade through expansion of production of high-quality cotton thread, to grow more food for home consumption, and to mobilize savings and direct investment into productive channels so as to overcome the critical shortage of capital.[22]

Although it was understood in Israel that success of these programs would inevitably increase Egypt's power, prestige, and ultimately its military capacity as well, it was expected that Egypt would find a natural sphere of influence in the African sphere, a tendency which Israel had no reason to oppose.

As for Iraq, that country underwent remarkable growth annually between 1951 and 1956, but even in the latter year per capita income was only $103.00. Of the rate of growth, two thirds were due to soaring oil earnings, and one third to general economic expansion. While Iraq did not face Egypt's population problems, which had a treadmill effect on the latter's economic development, Iraq's ambitious programs for irrigation and other infrastructure development made a major military expansion out of these resources improbable. Iraq's industry was considerably more backward than Egypt's.

Iraq's territory was not contiguous with Israel's, and therefore accretion of economic or military strength to Iraq offered no direct threat to Israel for as long as ambitions for a Fertile Crescent or similar scheme for union with one or the other of the contiguous states remained in abeyance. Iraq's close association with the West under Premier Nuri es-Said had dual political consequences, both of which had the short-run effect of further diminishing a potential Iraqi threat to Israel: it placed Iraq's military force within a Western-directed framework and thereby made action in Israel's direction less likely, and it led to a deterioration of relations with Egypt, thereby also diminishing the chances of joint action against Israel by the two key Arab states.

Iraq's oil resources, while a prime source of wealth, did not have the same effect on the war potential that oil in large quantities would have in a highly developed industrial state. For the presence of crude oil as such, without the corresponding industrial capacity, does not add to the war potential except in a most indirect way. It may even have a negative effect: if the oil economy of the country is dependent for exploitation, transportation, refining, and markets on foreign interests, this tends to make the national economy highly vulnerable.

The same applied to an even greater extent to Saudi Arabia, where oil revenues did not even contribute to development in any appreciable measure.

None of these other Arab states registered any change in its economic potential significant enough to affect its power relationship toward Israel. However, if both sides were unable to make war without foreign armaments, Israel's lack of resources made it vulnerable in the economic sphere quite apart from its military capacity. Israel disposed of almost no natural resources of use to its industries, nor was food grown in sufficient quantities to support the population. Oil—later discovered in amounts roughly equivalent to 10 per cent of the local demand—had to be imported over extended sea lanes, not only to drive transport but also as a source of electrical energy. Stock-piling of critical materials was resorted to, and the early 1950's saw shortages in many lines of consumer goods as well as raw materials. Nuclear energy was still only a distant dream, and despite the use of advanced agricultural methods, the farming sector produced less than 50 per cent of the food basket of the population. Such staples as cereals and meat had to be largely imported.

Israel was vulnerable to two contingencies in the event of hostilities: interruption of vital imports on the part of the great powers, either through blockade by an enemy or the imposition of sanctions by the powers themselves; and overall attrition which would strain the economy beyond endurance. Military strength therefore had to aim at forcing a quick decision in the event of war. Such strategy could not be content with a vague overall "balance of power" but called for clear military superiority able to inflict a decisive blow within a minimum period. And through its influence base, Israel had to strive to prevent any threat to the life line of imported supplies.

After it had been demonstrated to the Arab states that their military power was inadequate for defeating Israel, they resorted to measures not specifically prohibited by the armistice agreements because they were in the twilight zone between war and diplomacy. These included such measures of economic warfare as boycott of firms dealing with Israel, interdiction of Israeli shipping on waterways under Arab control, and blacklisting of vessels calling on Israeli ports—all designed to weaken Israel and eventually compel it to make political concessions out of economic necessity. Israel could not legitimately apply military power in return until economic measures turned into openly warlike acts. But by using its influence on another front, Israel was able to obtain the foreign aid necessary to overcome its payments deficit, which these hostile measures tended to aggravate.

From the beginning of statehood to 1957, about $1,970,000,-

000 in private and governmental gifts and loans from abroad poured into the economy. Of this amount, about $1,350,000,000 came from the United States, including $630,000,000 in philanthropic contributions; $270,000,000 in Israel government bonds purchased by the public in America; and $450,000,000 in grants, loans and surplus commodities from the U.S. government.[23]

Next to philanthropic income, the largest single source of "unrequited" foreign revenue was West Germany whose government had contracted, in September 1952, to pay Israel the equivalent of $822 million in goods and services over a period of twelve to fourteen years toward the cost of integrating refugees from territories formerly under German rule. By 1957, a million tons of goods worth $275 million had been shipped under the agreement.[24] The signing of the Reparations Agreement was not, strictly speaking, a result of Israeli influence upon the German Federal Republic in the sense the word is being used here, as a facet of national power. Rather, it grew out of Israel's role as a haven for survivors of German persecution and death camps that provided the emotional and even the legal basis for the agreement, which the West German government entered into as a gesture of atonement for these crimes, and only tangentially as a political act. In that sense, Israel may be said to have disposed of a reservoir of power in the stark suffering of so many of its inhabitants, since the German government's readiness to compensate the victims made this past suffering convertible into economic value. In addition to collective compensation, in the form of Reparations payments to the Israel government, Germany later also agreed to compensate its victims individually for material, physical, and moral damages suffered, and these indemnification payments to individual Israeli residents had reached an annual level of $102 million by 1961.[25]

The signing of the reparations draft agreement caused strong resentment in the Arab capitals on the ground that the projected deliveries would raise Israel's war potential and alter the power balance. A protest delegation was sent to Bonn, and General Nagib at one point threatened that the Arab states might break off economic ties with West Germany if the agreement were implemented. However, the Adenauer government stood firm and in a note of 9 November 1952 "finally and flatly" refused to accept the Arab demand that it delay ratification.[26]

The Demographic Factor

If the old rule of thumb for measuring power—square miles and population—had applied to the Middle East, Israel would have stood no chance of resisting Arab pressure. Its territory of slightly less than 8,000 square miles compared with an aggregate 1,300,000 for the seven states opposing Israel, and its population of 1,700,000 in 1953 was less than one-twelfth that of Egypt alone. But where population is concerned, the quality of the manpower is at least an equal determinant with quantity. This was demonstrated by the experience of 1948–1949 when the population ratio was even less favorable. Moreover, out of a population of some 22 million in the mid-fifties, Israel estimated that Egypt was able to mobilize no more than 200,000 men,[27] or approximately one per cent of the population, in the place of two million which a fully developed country with a like number of inhabitants should be able to field. Israel was able to match the number of men Egypt could put into uniform: every male eighteen years old and every immigrant under thirty was obliged to serve two and a half years in the armed forces; women served for two years except for mothers and those claiming exemption on religious grounds. After military service, men were called to reserve duty for about a month each year plus one day each month until age thirty-nine. From age forty to forty-nine, reserve duty consisted of fourteen days for enlisted men and twenty-one days for officers. Israel's citizens have been described as soldiers on leave eleven months of the year.

But while quantity is easily measurable, the measurement of quality presents difficulties. One method is inferential: the Jewish population of Palestine-Israel was mainly of European stock at the time of the Arab-Israel war, products of European education, with Western habits of thought and action, familiar with the processes of modern technology and science, and above all almost wholly literate. There was a high standard of hygiene and of health. While there were cultural and educational gradations in the population, its cultural level as a whole was of a different order than that prevailing in all the Arab states, where Western standards of education had been the privilege of a mere elite (the proportions of which varied with each country) and were only now gradually introduced on a broader level.

The general educational level of the population is, naturally, reflected in the quality of the military as well. A high proportion of technical and managerial skills among the general population is directly utilizable, just as their absence is a detriment. The presence of organizational and leadership qualities, which are the "enzymes" in the metabolism of resources into power, help determine the quality of the military establishment no less than quantities of equipment and manpower.

But the educational level of the population was one aspect of the power inventory which did not remain static. In Egypt especially, education on all levels made rapid strides under the impetus of the revolutionary regime. At the same time, the Western component of the Israeli population became diluted through mass immigration from non-European countries.

Ben-Gurion was wont to express a certain disdain for economists and their careful estimates of Israel's economic prospects, his credo being that the human spirit was stronger than economics. Translated into our terms, this might mean that the power inventory was not the limiting factor in a nation's achievement when the *élan* of fresh nationalism was at work against apathy or inertia.

But Israeli leaders were also aware that Arab nationalism, particularly the kind symbolized by Nasser, might well be capable of producing a similar effect. Israel's demographic advantage was bound to diminish to the extent that the Arab world reaped the benefit of dynamic leadership and education.

CHAPTER IV ≺≺≺≺
Policy Based on Power: Area Relations

The Absence of Diplomacy

The basic tool of foreign policy is diplomacy, which seeks to settle conflicting interests through negotiations, backed up by power or influence. But Arab opposition to Israel's primary foreign policy goals was so intense that it excluded ordinary diplomatic interchange. Such interchange, in addition to providing channels for negotiating conflict situations, is in itself a means for preventing incipient interstate differences from assuming major proportions. And where the regular diplomatic and direct "people to people" contact might serve to alleviate hostility between states, the absence of such relations allows it to harden. Finally, states that maintain normal relations are able to obtain concessions from one another even without the threat of force or economic or military pressure.

The intensity of the Arab states' negative attitude toward Israel, their intransigence when it came to normalizing relations, transcended ordinary interstate animosity, partly because it was not based on ordinary conceptions of national interest. It is notable that Arab spokesmen were wont to describe Israel as a threat to the Arab world as a whole rather than to the security or to the economic well-being of a particular Arab state. In other words, it was not a particularist Arab national interest,

96

but rather a pan-Arab nationalist sentiment which found the notion of peaceful coexistence with Israel unacceptable. Neither of the two principal demands relating to Israel which were enunciated from time to time by Arab spokesmen could be defined in terms of the national interest of the states most directly concerned. A return to the boundaries of the 1947 Partition Resolution (presumably accompanied by establishment of a Palestine Arab state) would oblige Jordan to relinquish a major part of its territory; return of the refugees would deprive it of much of its population. Nor is it apparent how the interest of any of the other Arab states would be served by implementation of these demands. Opposition to Israel, therefore, was more in the nature of an ideology, or what one writer has called an "abstraction," [1] as contrasted to a vital interest from an objective point of view.

A common abstraction, particularly in new states having but recently achieved independence, is prestige. Prestige may take on the role otherwise reserved to a vital interest, either because a realistic conception of the national interest has not as yet crystallized, or because the leadership and politically conscious population see in prestige a substitute for the ideological void that comes about in national liberation movements once independence has been achieved.[2]

For the Arab states, the establishment of Israel was a major blow to their prestige which, in resisting the emergence of the Jewish state, was engaged on several levels: toward their own populations, the world at large, and one another. Hence there existed a certain rivalry in their hostility to Israel, and a corresponding sensitivity on the part of public opinion in one state toward actions that could be interpreted as *rapprochement* on the part of another.

The presence of the Palestine refugees in the surrounding states also involved a question of prestige for the host governments, since the refugees were a visible symbol of defeat and frus-

97

tration. Israel's desire to see a solution of the refugee problem linked to a general peace settlement ignored the psychological barrier toward such a settlement which the presence of the refugees created. Aside from the immediate effect of their presence on the policy of the host governments, the problem of the refugees also brought an extraneous factor into the conflict with Israel; extraneous, that is, to the working of the state system. For while physically under the jurisdiction of the respective host governments, the refugees also constituted an autonomous political factor of some consequence. The sporadic and unsuccessful efforts to confer a political shape upon this amorphous force, such as the attempt to breathe life into the stillborn government of the Arab area of Palestine provided for in the Partition Resolution, did not fully reflect the extent of the pressure which the existence of the refugees exerted on Arab politics. Albert Hourani wrote, "The most urgent problem of Palestine is not that of the existence of Israel. . . . It is not that of 'settling the refugees.' It is that of a whole community which wishes to go on living as a community." [3]

The concept of the refugees as a community, albeit a scattered one,[4] serves as a reminder that there were two rival nationalisms, Arab and Jewish, disputing the same geographical area. This type of dispute is bound to engender bitter hostility on the side that is displaced from the territory in dispute. Since the Palestine Arab community was left without a polity which might have cushioned some of that hostility through sublimation in tasks such as economic development or social welfare, the host states were made to serve as vehicles for expressing the hostility of the refugee community.

Israel's exclusion from political intercourse in the area further had the effect of blurring the distinction between primary and secondary interests for the states involved, so that disputes over secondary interests which ordinarily would be amenable to settlement by negotiation appeared to involve primary interests and engendered military conflict. For example, the differences with Syria over fishing rights on Lake Tiberias repeatedly led to violence; in a general atmosphere conducive to negotiation, such a dispute could be settled by give and take. But Israel's sensitivity was based not on concern for the fish, but for Syria's attitude to the permanency of the armistice line, which ran east of the lake, and to the status of the demilitarized zone further north. To Israel, demilitarization did not affect sovereignty. To Syria, it meant an impingement on Israel's sovereign rights.

In Israel, the absence of diplomatic contact strengthened the tendency to regard speeches by Arab figures and Arab press and radio comment as accurate indicators of policy. The most extreme statements of Arab leaders were viewed as reflecting policy aims which would be translated into action if the Arab states had the ability, or if Israel let down its defenses. Under such conditions, "the psychological element of the political relationship is lost." Military power is substituted for political power, "the essence of which is the psychological relation between two minds." [5]

This interpretation of Arab aspirations did not change even though official Arab policy eventually proclaimed that it sought an accommodation based on the 1947 Partition Resolution. In Israeli eyes, this ambition was tantamount to destruction. A return to partition was now unthinkable, since it would involve both major amputations of territory and return of large numbers of refugees.

Erosion of the Armistice System (I): "Belligerent Rights"

With the final breakdown of the P.C.C. talks, the avenue for an overall settlement which would ratify the *status quo* achieved through military action appeared foreclosed. The alternative was for Israel to seek to stabilize the *modus vivendi* embodied in the armistice agreements.

The principal defect of the armistice agreements lay in their indefinite character as to duration; they were meant to be transitory arrangements leading to treaties of peace; their time limit was not defined, nor was there any provision for unilateral abrogation.

By the time the P.C.C. made its final attempt at conciliation in Paris in the fall of 1951, Israel was fully conscious of this flaw in the agreements.[6] When the Arabs countered the Israel demand for a nonaggression pact by an offer to reaffirm their adherence to the armistice agreements themselves, the Commission went along, but the Israelis balked. The language of the armistice agreement with Egypt, they pointed out, was limited to prohibition of "hostile acts" by armed forces only; it made no reference to marauding by nonmilitary personnel, restrictions on shipping through the Suez Canal, or boycott and blacklisting. Israel was reinforced in its unwillingness to freeze the armistice agreements as the *status quo* by Egypt's insistence on "belligerent rights" under the armistice.

Only a few months before, in connection with Israel's complaint to the Security Council on the Suez Canal shipping ban, Egypt had claimed that "We are exercising a right of war. . . . We are still legally at war with Israel. An armistice does not put an end to a state of war. It does not prohibit a country from exercising certain rights of war."[7] In support of this position the Egyptian delegate later quoted from Lauterpacht's 1944 edition of Oppenheim's *International Law:*

Armistices or truces, in the wider sense of the term, are all agreements between belligerent forces for a temporary cessation of hostilities. They are in no wise to be compared with peace, and ought not to be called temporary peace, because the condition of war remains between the belligerents themselves, and between the belligerents and the neutrals, on all points beyond the mere cessation of hostilities.

100

In spite of such cessation the right to visit and search over neutral merchantmen therefore remains intact.[8]

The Security Council in its resolution of 1 September 1951 endorsed Israel's point of view that the exercise of belligerent rights was contrary to the Charter when it declared that "neither party can reasonably assert that it is actively belligerent," and called on Egypt to terminate restrictions on international shipping maintained on these grounds.[9] Egypt nevertheless continued to insist on its "belligerent rights" and to bar Israeli shipping from the Canal under that doctrine. It used the same argument when the subject came up again before the Council on a renewed Israeli complaint in 1954.[10] This time the Soviet Union vetoed the draft resolution reiterating the earlier stand. The Soviet delegate said, perhaps with tongue in cheek, that there was no point to adopting a new resolution as long as the earlier one had not been carried out.

In his authoritative treatise on the armistice agreements, Israel's Shabtai Rosenne concedes that under the traditional concept in international law, an armistice leaves the juridical state of war intact; it merely prohibits or limits the exercise of certain rights which flow from the state of war.[11] But he also points out that the exercise of belligerent rights is contrary to the Charter, and that therefore an armistice concluded in response to Security Council action cannot be considered an armistice in the traditional sense. A later Israeli study which confines itself to the legality of the Egyptian blockade of the Suez Canal also bases Israel's argument on the fact that "the scope of an armistice is dictated by the provisions of the agreement" and that each armistice is *sui generis*.[12]

An important contribution to this topic is a survey of relevant literature by Nathan Feinberg, in which he too concludes that Egypt's claim to belligerency is incompatible with the U.N. Charter. "The argument that, after the cessation of hostilities, a member state should be entitled to claim to be in a state of

101

war with a fellow member is patently untenable." Feinberg also shows that the termination of war without peace treaties has become the accepted procedure (Korea, Indochina) and that in the Suez invasion in 1956 peace was restored even without benefit of an armistice. Furthermore, the question whether a state of war existed between Egypt and Israel even during the hostilities remains controversial.[13]

The discussion on whether a state of war exists, or can exist, between the two states is made somewhat academic by the fact that the Egyptians themselves did not claim to be at war; their claim to "belligerent rights" clearly aimed at something less for which there was no international legal definition. The Egyptian representative told the Security Council at one time: "To those who wished to know what our attitude was, I said these few words, 'No war, no peace'." [14] Feinberg does note that there have been attempts in the past to "have one's cake and eat it too" in this regard [15] and that Philip Jessup in 1954 called for acknowledgment in law as well as in fact that there is an intermediate status between peace and war.[16] In the meantime, however, there is no such status in positive international law, and Cicero's maxim still holds: *Inter pacem et bellum nihil est media.*

The experience with the P.C.C. had a twofold significance for Israel's future policy. For one thing, it showed that the effect of the military successes of 1948–1949 had worn off and was not capable of inducing the Arab states to make peace in terms that were satisfactory to Israel. For another, it left Israeli policymakers with the impression that the U.N. machinery would be of little help in promoting a settlement. The P.C.C. had served as a channel for bringing pressure for concessions, and when Israel had made what it considered a substantial offer on the repatriation of refugees, the P.C.C. members considered it inadequate and the Arabs failed to respond. Henceforth Israel increasingly called for "direct negotiations" with the Arab states in official statements about peace.

Appeals for Peace

It was the short-term goal, however—that of ensuring compliance with the armistice agreements—which was pursued actively through concrete measures and initiative. This was the policy of security. Peace, on the other hand, was regarded more as a long-range goal and therefore primarily the subject of official statements and pronouncements rather than of unilateral initiative.[17] The existence of this dichotomy, however, was rarely acknowledged; indeed, Moshe Sharett said later, to proclaim that "the prospect of early peace does not exist serves as encouragement of the Arab refusal to make peace." Israel, he declared on the same occasion, had been blamed for wanting total peace or nothing. Yet Israel did explore partial approaches and Arab reaction had been negative. The Prime Minister reiterated Israel's readiness to enter into negotiations for a full or partial agreement. But it would have to be a settlement "with Israel as it is within the present boundaries and without the admission of refugees." [18]

How wide the gap was between this position and that of even the more moderate Arab statesmen becomes clear when a statement made in the Security Council earlier in the same year by Dr. Charles Malik of Lebanon is juxtaposed with Sharett's:

During the last few months, I have repeatedly stated what are some of the conditions on which the Arab world might accept a *modus vivendi* with Israel. I have not heard a single word in reply to any of the suggestions I put forward either from the representative of Israel, from you, the representative of New Zealand, or from any other representative. If you or others here representing their countries think that Israel can get away with what it has already got, completely unconditionally, and without making costly concessions to its own world with which it wants a permanent settlement, then let me tell

103

you in all frankness that you are all mistaken. This is never going to come about.[19]

In addition to general appeals and professions of Israel's readiness to make peace, usually made by the Prime Minister in parliament or in interviews with the foreign press, Israel also advanced detailed proposals of what it was prepared to offer as a basis for peace negotiations.

These proposals were generally based on the concessions which Israel had previously offered in secret negotiations to Jordan and/or Egypt, such as a free port for Jordan at Haifa with transit rights across Israel, free transit for other Arab traffic through Israeli territory, compensation for property left behind by Arab refugees, and minor frontier adjustments to adjacent villages. The basic such "blueprint for peace" was put forward by Israel at the Seventh General Assembly in 1952,[20] where it failed to evoke any positive response. Its provisions were summarized and reiterated from time to time, until the last comprehensive offer before the Sinai Campaign was made on 19 December 1955. Responding to strong State Department urging, Israel recapitulated the various previous offers in a "Seven-Point Proposal for Peace." [21] The list did not include any new concessions on the two main stumbling blocks of the P.C.C. talks— refugee repatriation and major border revisions. Nevertheless the Israel government exposed itself to much internal criticism each time a public announcement was made, and it became clear that the main impetus for these announcements was pressure from the Western powers for a more conciliatory attitude.

A third major point at issue, payment of compensation to Arab refugees accepting resettlement, while conceded by Israel, came to be hedged with various provisos at one time or another: that the property left behind by Jewish refugees in Arab states would have to be offset in eventual accounting; that the Arab states must first abandon their economic boycott of Israel, or that compensation should come only as part of a general peace settlement. However, when on at least one occasion an Israeli spokesman did not bring up the bill for Jewish property in offering payment or compensation there was no serious response on the part of the Arab states. Michael Comay told the U.N. General Assembly in 1954 that, if the Arabs stopped their boycott and Israel obtained international financing for the purpose, Israel was ready to approach the payment of compensation. He made no mention of an offsetting claim.[22]

Israel has been criticized on the score that its peace offers did not involve any unilateral or unconditional steps, and that the first move was always left to the other side.[23] With regard to two measures actually implemented by Israel, unfreezing of Arab bank accounts and the reunion of families separated at the time of the armistice, this criticism is unjustified. But from their experience with these measures, the Israelis concluded that talk of concessions on their side, or even concrete measures taken unilaterally, would not only evoke no response from the other side but might also be mistaken for weakness and lead to pressure for further unilateral moves.

Walter Eytan lists in the same category the offer for the return of a hundred thousand refugees, made through the P.C.C., and the undertaking to pay compensation for abandoned Arab lands. He notes that not a single conciliatory move came from the Arab side. Disillusion set in, he relates, and domestic critics began charging the government with appeasement. The more offers were made, the more the Arabs accepted, without showing the slightest sign of accepting Israel herself, the critics claimed.[24]

The fear that a conciliatory attitude on Israel's part might lead to a faulty appreciation of Israel's strength by the Arab leadership also played a part in the style of some of the calls for peace. Such declarations, after stressing Israel's willingness for peace, generally went on to emphasize that Israel was ready for war if the Arabs so wished.

105

Erosion of the Armistice System (II): The Use of Force

On the active level, Israel policy sought to accomplish two distinct aims: one positive, to obtain compliance with some as yet unimplemented parts of the armistice agreements; and one negative or preventive, to forestall infringement of the *status quo* or Arab gains in disputed areas such as the demilitarized zones.

To obtain compliance from the Arab states on specific matters, Israel—in the absence of direct diplomatic relations—had to rely on the machinery of the United Nations. Two types of situations were involved, one governed by an unequivocal provision of the armistice agreements, and the other where the agreement was not explicit and each side insisted on its own interpretation.

Relations between Israel and the Arab states were almost wholly of a negative nature; that is, they involved disputes over infractions of provisions of the agreements, or over interpretations of provisions which were ambiguous. Positive efforts, looking toward implementation of provisions which were not operative at the time, generally proved abortive. One provision included for future implementation was article 8 in the agreement with Jordan governing access to Mount Scopus and the Holy Places, and the opening of the main road to Jerusalem.

Such relations of a positive nature as were not strictly laid down in the armistice agreements were of minor significance and generally took place under the auspices of the U.N. Truce Supervision machinery: arrangements for crossings by Christians into Jordan during the holiday season; exchange of information on pest and epidemic control and joint implementation of health measures relative thereto; the return of individuals who had strayed across the demarcation lines; and certain arrangements requiring cooperation such as the reunion in Israel of refugees separated from their families or the unblocking and transfer of Arab bank accounts in Israel.[25]

Disputes over infractions were also in the province of the U.N. Truce Supervision Organization, which in turn dealt with the separate points at issue through its Mixed Armistice Commissions made up of a representative of each of the parties and an impartial chairman from the U.N.T.S.O. A main weakness of the M.A.C.'s was that they were largely reduced to assessing blame after the fact, with the chairman acting as referee over the conflicting claims. This put the chairman into a delicate and exposed position; any suspicion of partiality on his part by one of the parties might end his usefulness and paralyze the machinery, as illustrated by the case of Commander Hutchison. During the period when Israel boycotted the Israel-Jordan Mixed Armistice Commission, 1,500 complaints accumulated on which the Commission was unable to act because of Israel's absence.[26] The unpopularity of Commander Hutchison came to be matched by that of Major-General Vagn Bennike, the Danish officer who was Chief of Staff of the U.N.T.S.O. at the time of the Qibya raid and the dispute with Syria over the Jordan waters. The suspicion that a particular U.N. official who ruled against Israel was anti-Israel or anti-Semitic was always latent. Through the same alchemy which seems to have made British Mandate officials more sympathetic to the Arab than to the Jewish cause, some of the U.N.T.S.O. representatives did in fact come away with unfriendly feelings toward Israel, as shown in later statements or writings.[27] Major-General Burns, who was Chief of Staff from August 1954 to November 1956, felt impelled to begin his memoirs with an *a priori* denial that he is anti-Semitic.[28]

At the Israel-Lebanese border, where infractions were at a minimum, the M.A.C. functioned smoothly. The M.A.C. machinery was clearly intended to deal with an occasional infraction in a predominantly quiet situation; it was unable to cope effectively with continuously hostile action and counteraction such as characterized the Jordan-Israel frontier in 1953 and 1954 and the Egyptian demarcation line thereafter.

If the U.N. officials could not prevent infractions of such basic provisions of the armistice agreements as violation of the demarcation lines, they were even more powerless to impose their rulings in issues regarding which the agreements were ambiguous. Such disputes occurred over the status of the demilitarized zones both at the Syrian border and at al-Awja (Nitzana) in the south. Each side insisted on its own interpretation, with the U.N. officials unable to have their rulings accepted by both parties to the dispute.

The nub of the dispute with the Syrians concerned Israel's sovereignty over the demilitarized zone, and it was here that the language of the Israel-Syria General Armistice Agreement lacked clarity. Establishment of the demilitarized zone, as well as of the defensive zone along the upper reaches of the Jordan and the Sea of Galilee, was the result of Syrian military operations on Palestine territory on the western side of the Jordan between Lake Huleh and the Sea of Galilee in 1948, and Syrian occupation of certain positions on the western side of the Jordan at the time of the truce. Israel refused to sign an armistice agreement while Syrian troops were on its territory. The compromise worked out in the protracted negotiations leading to the signing of the agreement provided that the Syrian troops be withdrawn, but that the territory they had occupied be demilitarized. Israel was not to gain any military advantage through activity in the zone. When Israel began its drainage and reclamation project of the Huleh swamps in 1951, Syria promptly complained to the M.A.C. that the project would result in military advantage to Israel in the zone, thereby violating article II (1) of the armistice agreement.[29] The M.A.C. sought the opinion of the U.N.T.S.O. Chief of Staff, General William Riley, who ruled that the reclamation work in itself offered Syria no grounds for objection, being entirely civilian in nature, but that the construction of a projected dam would violate the agreement because the flooding of Arab-owned lands in the zone was an obstacle to the return to normal civilian life of its inhabitants. In his ruling, General Riley expressed the view that sovereign rights in the zone were in abeyance. He asked Israel to cease its operations within the zone until agreement with Syria, through the chairman, could be arranged. When Israel refused to accept the Chief of Staff's recommendation and continued the work, violence broke out, and both sides appealed to the Security Council. The Council in its resolution of 18 May sustained General Riley's ruling for a temporary suspension of the work, and Israel eventually complied. Shortly thereafter, on 11 June, the Chief of Staff authorized Israel to resume dredging on non–Arab-owned land—a decision which Syria protested to the Security Council. As for Israel, it stood fast in its refusal to acknowledge the United Nations' authority over civilian matters in the demilitarized zone and withdrew its delegation from all meetings of the M.A.C. which dealt with incidents occurring in the zone.[30]

Syria's complaint on the Jordan River diversion and hydro-electric project was also directed first to the M.A.C. and subsequently to the Security Council.[31] This time the issue of sovereignty and of military advantage was compounded by the claims over water rights, and General Riley's successor, General Vagn Bennike, in his report to the Security Council supported Syria's contention that Israel was violating several provisions of the armistice agreement.[32] Israel rejected these claims, citing the Huleh precedent, but eventually agreed to suspend the work under strong pressure from the United States.

The distribution of the waters of the Jordan was a point at dispute which was not covered at all by the armistice agreements. To avoid putting off the solution of this complex problem until the indefinite future when a peace treaty might be signed, President Eisenhower took the initiative and on 16 October 1953 appointed Eric Johnston as his special envoy, charged with finding a formula acceptable to all parties concerned.[33] Although Mr. Johnston's plan was finally shelved because of the Arabs'

109

fear of the political consequences of acceptance, his intensive diplomatic activity kept the issue from boiling over during that period.

The Rationale for Retaliation (I): Jordan

Characteristic of the security policy was the view that only through internal strength would peace eventually come about.[34] The Arabs, this view held, had no incentive to make peace with a weak Israel—only when they became convinced that Israel was too strong for them to defeat would they want to come to terms. But while internal strength was thus viewed as a means to a political end, it also had its counterpart in the concept of deterrent strength as military policy. The essence of the military doctrine of General Moshe Dayan, who took over as Chief of Staff from General Mordecai Makleff in 1953, was that the Arabs needed to understand that it would not pay them to attack Israel.[35] Indeed, military doctrine tended to overwhelm the political aspect of deterrence. It banked on armed superiority to deter the Arab states from attack rather than on the hope that a strong Israel might induce them to negotiate. "While others have networks of alliances," Ambassador Abba Eban told American Jews, "we only have our own unaided military strength as the shield of our independence and our very lives." [36]

The trouble with a deterrent policy in a situation where neither diplomatic nor other relations exist between states doing the deterring and those that are to be deterred, is that the message which the policy intends to express is difficult to get across, except through actual demonstration. The retaliation raids—in addition to their punitive aspect—constituted such a demonstration.

With regard to Jordan, Israeli officials felt that infiltration was more than the attempt of refugee desperadoes to stage raids into their former lands; they saw in it a deliberate policy—if not of open, then of tacit encouragement—on the part of the Jordan government to harass Israeli settlers, to destroy the morale of the immigrants in the border villages, and eventually to challenge the validity of the armistice lines as frontiers.[37]

Israel's military doctrine as far as Jordan was concerned was a simple one. As General Dayan put it: "There is no means to prevent the blowing up of water pipers or the killing of a family in its sleep, but we set a high price for our blood." The price must be so high that the Arab governments across the borders will feel obligated to take unpopular measures and punish the marauders.[38] In that sense the policy may be called successful. The raids declined in 1954. Relative quiet on the Jordan border was restored. There were indications that the Jordanian authorities had gotten the point and were doing their best to suppress infiltration. Brigadier Glubb, former commander of the Arab Legion, reports that at night "the whole border area was criss-crossed with police and army patrols." [39] From October 1954 to March 1955, 997 Jordanians were jailed for actual or attempted illegal border crossings.[40] General Burns saw the Israelis' contention that the Arab governments could put a stop to infiltration borne out by the absence of serious trouble between Israel and Jordan from the summer of 1954 until March 1956.[41] To repeat, in the sense that the retaliation policy was designed to demonstrate Israel's military superiority, there is no doubt about its success. But the means employed would seem to have exceeded the requirements. The Jordanian authorities were well aware of Israel's military superiority, and in fact carefully avoided military engagements.[42] Yet the knowledge of Israel's superiority was insufficient to prod Jordan toward peace.

As if to test out the effectiveness of this policy in making Jordan more amenable to negotiation, Israel shortly after the Security Council censure of the Qibya raid asked Secretary-General Dag Hammarskjold to call for a top-level meeting under article 12 of the Armistice Agreement. That article provided for an exchange of views between the parties in case of a break-

111

down in the implementation of the Agreement. Hammarskjold consequently invited the parties to meet with him in Jerusalem to discuss "concrete and limited issues arising out of the Armistice Agreement implementation." But Jordan declined, declaring that the M.A.C. was adequate for a discussion of outstanding problems. The Jordanians manifestly did not want to be first to initiate discussions on a higher level, being painfully aware of the stigma attached to King Abdallah's negotiations.

On 25 March 1954, the U.N. Secretary gave up his efforts at calling a meeting. Ambassador Eban called the refusal "the most serious breach of the armistice agreement since it was signed," and the diplomatic correspondent of the *Jerusalem Post* wrote that it crumbled the armistice pact itself.[43]

On the negative side, the retaliation policy against Jordan brought with it a serious public relations problem. Israel's efforts to explain the reprisals in terms of its own losses in lives and property were handicapped by the fact that infiltration was unspectacular, case by case. With at most two or three deaths at a time, no single incident attracted world-wide attention. The reprisals were massive in character, with the number of victims large enough to make the front pages. Therefore the argument that the number of Arabs killed in these raids was far smaller than the number of Israelis murdered over a period of time made little impact.

The storm of disapproval throughout the world which followed Qibya took Israelis by surprise. In the Knesset debate following the Security Council's resolution on Qibya, most of the speakers blamed the great powers for ganging up on Israel and favoring the Arabs.[44]

Subsequently the Foreign Minister warned that the censure would encourage the Arabs in their refusal to make peace. Those who had drafted the resolution, Sharett told the Knesset, had other interests in mind than peace in the Middle East: Britain was aiming at strengthening her uneasy position in Jordan; the

112

United States apparently hoped for improved relations with the Arab world; France adapted herself to the line taken by her two partners, although with little enthusiasm. At the same time, Sharett blamed the sponsors of the resolution for neglecting to urge the parties to make peace. Qibya, he said, was the result of Jordan's failure to honor her obligations under the armistice by permitting infiltration. In the larger sense, the Arab states had frustrated the organic passage of the armistice agreements to a final peace settlement.

But Sharett also gave a forthright account of the extraordinarily adverse reaction to the Qibya raid outside of Israel. It had aroused, he said, "feelings of antagonism and anger, mingled with astonishment and distress throughout the world." [45]

The Qibya raid had a sobering effect on sections of the population even before the Security Council deliberations. An editorial in the German-language weekly of the Progressive party made this plea for a return to a peace policy: "It is the task of our foreign policy to examine exactly at what price an agreement and peace with the Arab neighbor states is attainable. Today, and not tomorrow. It is the task of every political factor in the country to examine this question coolly." [46]

The Rationale for Retaliation (II): Egypt

The basic difference in the nature of the operations against Jordan and Egypt was that the raids against Jordan served immediate security needs, whereas those against Egypt were also related to longer-range considerations. At the time the weight of military activity shifted toward Egypt, the latter was about to reach agreement with Great Britain on the evacuation of the Suez base, and thereby attain a new dimension of military power. The treaty made no provision for the passage of Israel ships through the Canal and in general ignored the interests of Israel.[47]

113

Israel, according to Eban, had received assurance that, once the Canal question was settled, Egypt would be ready for an accommodation.[48] When nothing came of this promise, Israel tested Egypt's attitude by attempting to send a vessel under its own flag, the Bat Galim, through the Canal. But Egypt refused to budge from its determination to bar the Canal to Israeli traffic, continuing to assert that the armistice had not put an end to the state of war with Israel.[49] There was evidence of increasing American backing for Nasser and offers of arms; [50] and in January there took place the trial of the Israeli spy ring and the subsequent execution of two of the thirteen accused.[51] At the same time, there was a steep increase of infiltrations from the Gaza Strip, with twenty-seven forays counted in the first two months of 1955 in which seven Israelis were killed and twenty-four wounded.

Israel's raid against Gaza, although it came in immediate response to the last-named incursions, must be viewed in the light of all the foregoing developments. Its purpose was punitive and preventive, and it also fitted into an overall policy designed to demonstrate Israel's military superiority.

General Dayan later that year spoke in terms of the political rationale for retaliation which existed side by side with the military doctrine. Clashes with Israeli forces had important repercussions among the Arab states, the Chief of Staff believed, for the outcome of any battle was interpreted as a measure of strength of the parties involved. Therefore an act of retaliation by Israel could serve as an encouragement to an Arab government considering the possibility of accepting the existence of Israel, rather than to lose face by continuing to oppose it.[52]

To what extent there was a cause-and-effect relationship between Israel's retaliation policy and Egypt's decision to acquire massive armaments from Eastern European sources of supply will remain a moot question. Obviously, Egypt was interested in

114

stressing the causal relationship while Israel would have it otherwise.

Nasser said that it was the Gaza raid which made him negotiate for Soviet arms, and that it was the Khan Yunis attack which made him decide to accept the offer.[53] He had requested American arms under the Mutual Security program even before 28 February, and it was presumably only after he found the terms offered to him unsatisfactory that he turned to the Soviet Union.[54] Moreover, his quarrel with Iraq over the Baghdad Pact and, implicitly, over leadership of the Arab world, was in itself incentive enough for wanting to accumulate strength, and his resentment of the West enough motive for turning to the Eastern bloc for arms.

In an interview with a *New York Times* correspondent, Nasser complained that the United States and Britain had violated a "gentlemen's agreement" that Egypt should be permitted to take the lead in constructing a purely Arab defense alliance free from formal links with outside powers. The report continued:

Nothing in his conversations with Western statesmen, including Secretary of State Dulles, had prepared Egypt for abandonment of this policy or for the shock of the Turkish-Iraqi pact, the Premier said.

"No one told me of dissatisfaction with that policy or of the adoption of another one," Premier Nasser said. "I cannot base all my plans on one solution and see that cast aside for another on which I was given no information, that neglects Egypt's interests and would turn the Arab countries over to Turkey to shepherd." [55]

That the Egyptian premier had envisaged military cooperation with the West, including future arms shipments, as giving shape to the Arab League collective security pact under his leadership is strongly hinted at in his article in *Foreign Affairs* which appeared in January 1955.[56] But it was the Arab League's military organization rather than a Western-sponsored instrument which he expected to fill the military vacuum in the area. Iraq's par-

115

ticipation in the Western defense scheme thus not only crossed Nasser's striving for a strong Arab bloc under his leadership, but it also gave Great Britain—in Egyptian eyes—an opening for a comeback in the area. At the same time, the Baghdad Pact and the concept underlying it were regarded as a strong provocation by the Soviet rulers, who lost no time in exploiting the opportunity offered by the disgruntled Egyptian leader for leapfrogging the Western defense arrangement.

Perhaps the wisest interpretation is that the two events had a cumulative effect on the Egyptian Prime Minister, coming as they did within a few days of each other. The negotiations for a Middle East defense alliance reached a decisive phase on 12 January with the announcement that Iraq and Turkey were about to conclude a treaty of mutual defense, with other interested countries to join the pact later. Egypt, contending that the alliance would contravene the spirit of the collective security pact of the Arab League, summoned a special meeting of the League Council in Cairo on 22 January where it demanded nothing less than that all Arab countries should abstain from adhering to the pact. Prime Minister Nuri es-Said of Iraq was conspicuously absent, having been "forbidden by his doctors to attend." [57] The Iraqi-Turkish pact was signed on 24 February; the Gaza raid came on the twenty-eighth. The determination to obtain arms, it is clear, was present before the Gaza raid, but the raid strengthened it; the signing of the pact provided the rationale for accepting the Soviet offer which was quick in forthcoming. Put somewhat differently, the Gaza raid produced a military effect which resulted in the escalation of violence; the Baghdad Pact had political repercussions which included an "opening to the left" of which the arms purchase was a part.

A policy of reprisals, when applied to a state of potentially equal strength, is apt to lead to an escalation of violence as each side wants to prove to its foe, to itself, and to others that it cannot be defeated.

The Gaza raid, in demonstrating Israel's superiority and Egypt's weakness, had the effect of a "stinging slap in the face of the Egyptian army—still sore from its defeats in 1948," [58] and the prestige of the government and the emotions of the men comprising it were bound up with that of the army. Although the army was not ready to challenge the Israelis in open warfare, its leaders would not allow the insult to pass without counteraction. Their first reaction was to step up guerrilla activities and the mining of roads. Then "illegitimate force" was used to terrorize the civilian population through the *fidayun*.

Ambivalence and Illegitimate Force

Even while the policy of retaliation toward Egypt was in effect, various peace offers continued to be interspersed with the punitive raids.

With the Egyptian revolution which put General Muhammad Nagib into power, Israel had felt that the time might have arrived for turning over a new leaf in its relations with its strongest Arab foe. Prime Minister Ben-Gurion in effect welcomed the advent of Nagib and pointed out that there was no room for antagonism between the two neighbors. Israel, he declared, wished to see a free, independent and progressive Egypt.[59] He complimented Muhammad Nagib personally on his reported statement that he and most of his colleagues in the army had been opposed to the invasion of Palestine, for which former King Faruq bore the responsibilty. Ben-Gurion also emphasized that the strategic situation favored a rapprochement: "The two countries are separated by a broad and extensive desert, and therefore there is no room for border disputes." He added that Israel bore no grudge against Egypt "for what she did to our forefathers in the days of Pharaoh or even for what she did to us four years ago." Indeed, he pointed out graciously, the first en-

117

counter of the two nations in Joseph's days had resulted in mutual aid.

Expanding on this theme somewhat in his introductory article to the Government Year Book which appeared in October 1952, Ben-Gurion offered Israel's help in the political and social difficulties under which Egypt was laboring as an incentive for peace. "Peace with Israel would improve its (Egypt's) position. Its cultural and economic development and its international standing could only profit from such cooperation." [60]

But only a few months after President Nagib had shown himself in a conciliatory mood he decided to break the spell, attacking Israel as a "cancer in the body of the Arab nation." [61] The Egyptian press, taking its cue from the President, launched savage diatribes against Israel. It is difficult to judge whether there was ever any sincere desire on Egypt's part to come to terms, or whether the Egyptian leader simply wished to shelve the Palestine question over the short run while concentrating his attention on expelling the British.

The coming to power of Nasser had no immediate effect on Egyptian-Israeli relations. His first efforts were turned toward reaching agreement with Great Britain on the Suez Canal. In spite of Israel's apprehension over Egypt's enhanced status as the signing of the agreement approached, there was still hope that Nasser, in pursuing his announced program of social and agricultural reforms, would be willing to reach a *modus vivendi* with Israel. Accordingly, on 30 June 1954, Prime Minister Sharett made a conciliatory speech in connection with the Johnston plan, promising Egypt the right of passage through the Negev if desired. Two months later he told the Knesset that Israel did not begrudge Egypt its Suez victory but would like to see it linked to peace. [62] Mapam had insisted all along that Israel was on Egypt's side in demanding the removal of foreign troops from its territory. [63]

As for Nasser, his article in *Foreign Affairs* (prepared weeks

118

before the January 1955 publication date) contained an un-usually conciliatory statement. After describing in detail his plans for social reform, for bridging the gulf between economic and social classes, and for doubling the national income in ten years, he declared: "We do not want to start any conflict. War has no place in the reconstructive policy which we have designed to improve the lot of our people. . . . There is much to do in Egypt. . . . A war will cause us to lose much of what we seek to achieve."[64]

But the mood of moderation was soon dispelled by events. Shortly after the article appeared, two men convicted of carrying out acts of sabotage on behalf of Israel were hanged in Cairo (see below). The Israel government had tried feverishly to pre-vent their execution, and in fact was given to understand through an intermediary that the sentence would not be carried out. For Sharett, the fate of the condemned men became a gauge of Nasser's intentions, and when the news of the hangings came, he was convinced that the Egyptians had flung down the gauntlet.[65]

Ben-Gurion's return as Minister of Defense on 17 February 1955 heralded a tougher policy, which was reflected in his state-ments as well as in action. He told William Randolph Hearst, Jr., that peace with Egypt could be "negotiated in five minutes." Hearst reported that Nasser had assured him that Egypt also wanted peace with Israel, but Ben-Gurion replied, "I am afraid Nasser is not master in his own house. Until Egypt has a popular democratic government, I doubt whether its leadership will be capable of making peace with Israel." [66]

At the same time, the nature of Egypt's regime did not deter the Israeli leadership from seeking a basis for contact with Nasser when the opportunity offered itself. Some months before Sinai, a personal envoy of President Eisenhower made a secret trip to the Middle East in order to find common ground be-tween the two parties. Ben-Gurion later alluded to the pres-idential mission on at least two occasions [67] as proof that Israel

119

was willing to come to terms with Nasser but that the latter had refused the mediation. While the Prime Minister did not divulge the envoy's name, he has since been identified as Robert Anderson, Eisenhower's Secretary of the Treasury.

The episode of the saboteurs and its aftermath gave rise six years later to the protracted government crisis known as the "Lavon affair." In the course of that crisis there emerged a good deal of hitherto secret information which shed light on the differences prevailing at the time among the leadership concerning the assessment of Egypt's intentions and the means to be employed in checking that country's growing power.

The 1960–1961 crisis itself grew out of Pinhas Lavon's stubborn desire to be vindicated as to his role in what was euphemistically described as a "security mishap" during his incumbency as Minister of Defense. When he believed he had collected sufficient evidence to prove that witnesses testifying against him at a secret inquiry into the circumstances of the "mishap" had perjured themselves, Lavon requested that Ben-Gurion publicly clear his name or appoint a judicial committee to review the case. This Ben-Gurion refused to do, appointing instead a ministerial committee of inquiry whose conclusions he subsequently declined to accept. The ensuing clash of wills and personalities resulted in Lavon's removal from his post as Secretary-General of the Histadrut, and in his being stricken from the list of Mapai candidates for election to the Knesset after the Ben-Gurion government resigned in the wake of the "Affair."

But before this outcome was decided, the following circumstances had come to light:

(1) The security mishap for which Lavon disclaimed responsibility was the same operation for which the two Egyptian Jews had been convicted and executed. Although the exact nature of the operation was never revealed in Israel, it emerged from the confessions obtained in the Cairo trials that members of the ring had received orders to cause fires or explosions in the

U.S.I.S. libraries in Cairo and Alexandria at the time the negotiations on the evacuation of the Suez Canal base were at a critical stage. The aim of these acts appears to have been twofold: first, to cause confusion among the Egyptian public; and, second, to arouse American public opinion against Egypt at a time when the U.S. government seemed ready to follow Great Britain's evacuation of the Suez base with major deliveries of armaments, and efforts to include Egypt in a defense alliance.[68]

(2) Prime Minister and Foreign Minister Sharett was not informed of these orders either before or after they were handed down. He became aware that something was afoot only when he read of the Cairo trial in the papers. Even then he was merely told that a fatal error had occurred when an order to "plan" had been interpreted as an order to "execute." [69]

(3) There were serious conflicts between Lavon and senior members of the defense establishment—both civilian and military—responsible to him. Lavon resigned after Sharett refused to support him on his proposal to dismiss his main antagonists.

Two conclusions may be drawn from these revelations: the first is that the division of functions between the Prime Minister and the Ministry of Defense, by which the Defense Minister rather than the Prime Minister is in effect the commander-in-chief of the armed forces, is unsatisfactory at a time when the two ministerial offices are held by different persons.[70] This was the case, of course, during Ben-Gurion's retirement and until Sharett's resignation as Premier.

Second, one may conclude from these revelations that there was indeed a large measure of ambivalence surrounding the policy toward Egypt, which expressed itself in a rift between the foreign and defense policy of the government majority headed by Sharett, and that of the security establishment. The security heads, appointed by Ben-Gurion before his retirement, favored an emphatic security policy as the main instrument for Israel's survival. For them the Suez evacuation, the line of the

Republican administration in Washington, and the incapacity of the United Nations to guarantee Israel's security, strengthened the conviction that Israel must reply to any Arab use of force by strong counterforce.

Sharett—and with him, apparently, the majority of the government—did not share this assumption. For him there remained political possibilities in diplomacy, in ties with the United States, and in working with and through the United Nations. On at least one occasion, the Sharett government apparently took the initiative in establishing unofficial contact with Egyptian representatives on neutral ground, with a view to exploring the possibilities for a *modus vivendi* based on the *status quo*. On 4 August 1961, the two Tel Aviv afternoon papers simultaneously carried reports describing these contacts. According to *Yediot Ahronot,* Reuven Shiloah and Eliahu Sasson, both Middle East experts of the Israel Foreign Ministry, met with Arab representatives in Paris in 1954. *Ma'ariv*'s story added these details:

The representatives of Egypt's rulers revealed then, in undercover negotiations in Europe, a willingness to reach a secret agreement with Israel on the normalization of relations without a formal peace treaty. During the negotiations several proposals took shape which could serve as the basis for such an agreement. The main proposal was: to maintain a quiet border, to create and maintain contact in a European capital as a base for clearing up conflict situations. Egypt was to agree to the passage of Israeli cargo through the Suez Canal; though not under the Israeli flag. . . . The top Israeli Foreign Office people, headed by Mr. Sharett . . . regarded this as the beginning of a quiet normalization with other Arab countries, and a chance to break the ring of Arab hostility against Israel. But then something happened, initiated by another executive arm of the Israeli government. Immediately after this action, which caused a great stir at the time, all contact with the Egyptian representatives abruptly ceased.[71]

122

During the balance of Sharett's tenure, Israel's policy manifested the ambivalence prevailing among the leadership. It zigzagged between calls for peace and appeals to the United Nations, on the one hand, and retaliatory operations on the other. Each operation was preceded by debates between the civilian and military heads, and some operations had been planned for which no civilian approval was forthcoming. On the other hand, the scale of the operation carried out by the military sometimes exceeded that authorized by the civilian chiefs.[72]

While it was generally known that there were proponents of an activist policy and others who preferred to rely more on diplomacy—with the former represented by Ben-Gurion and the latter by Sharett—it was only through the Lavon affair that the extent of the division within the Sharett government itself, and the extent to which the defense establishment served as a pressure group for a more activist policy, became widely understood.

There had been one occasion in the last days of Lavon's incumbency when the rift showed up in open Knesset debate, but it was little noticed at the time. Sharett, replying to a nonconfidence motion by Herut at the close of the foreign policy debate in January 1955, pointed to the relative quiet on the frontiers and said he opposed the activist line advocated by Herut. He added that Israel had to make up its mind whether it wished to be a "state of law or of piracy." [73] Lavon, speaking from the same platform a few days later, said Israel had to be a state of "law and self-defense." In addition to international law, Israel also had to observe the "law of self-defense." How the two imperatives could be reconciled could not be discussed in the Knesset, he declared. It was his claim that the decline in infiltration which Sharett had cited was due to the Israel army's "preventive" operations on the borders.[74]

Lavon's resignation came because he himself had been shown not to have ultimate control over the activities of his establishment. There was perplexity among the members of the government when it came to finding a successor for Lavon. Ben-Gurion's name was suggested in an almost offhand fashion, and few really believed that he was ready to come out of retirement. But the ex-Premier accepted the call unhesitatingly.[75]

Ben-Gurion must have been disturbed by the evidence of dissension on the highest level of defense and foreign policy-making which he perceived from his desert vantage-point. The man he had hand-picked to succeed him as Minister of Defense did not get along with Moshe Dayan, the Chief of Staff whom Ben-Gurion had appointed the day before his retirement, nor with the young Director-General of the Defense Ministry, Shimon Peres, another Ben-Gurion appointee. And the defense establishment as a whole—Lavon included—differed sharply with Sharett, the Prime Minister and Minister of Foreign Affairs. Sharett's views were, of course, known to Ben-Gurion when the latter made his decision to withdraw from the scene. But he may have felt that Sharett deserved an opportunity to test them. Ben-Gurion's own role in maintaining contact with the defense establishment during his period of retirement remains nebulous. In any event, Ben-Gurion considered the time ripe, upon Lavon's resignation, for his return to the government to keep a firm rein on matters of security once again.

Sharett's conception of the international environment was colored by his experience in diplomacy before Israel had achieved statehood; as head of the Political Department of the Jewish Agency he had engaged in diplomatic and quasi-diplomatic negotiations with the mandatory power and also had contacts with other governmental bodies and the United Nations. This was necessarily a diplomacy without power, and its legacy, as it transmitted itself to Sharett, was a belief in the force of reason and the effectiveness of legal and logical argument. His eloquence was well suited to the idealistic fervor concerning Israel's spiritual mission which animated the older generation

of Zionist leaders. These qualities are reflected in this explanation to the Knesset of why Israel must pursue a global foreign
policy. Referring to Israel's isolation from land contact, he said:

This alone forces us to reinforce our ties with states further away
which can take us out of our isolation. The front of war or peace
between us and the Arab states extends over the whole world. We
must be in a constant struggle to explain our position and to prove
its justice and necessity. We must constantly recruit understanding
and support of our position.

But even with peace, we would have to maintain this network of
friendly relations and mutual understanding—not like every other
state, but in a special measure. . . . Our history is part of the
basic consciousness of the civilized world, in time and in space. We
do not see ourselves as just another state in the Middle East—although we are proud to belong, whether our neighbors wish it or not,
to the state system of this area.

We don't want to lose the world outlook we acquired in our wan-
dering and to isolate ourselves. And it is not just the heritage of our
wanderings, but also that of our ancient past which brings to the
fore that which is universal and worldly in our aspirations, our
morality, and our progress.

The miracle of the return to Zion is a central element of our times;
the interest, the intellectual tension, the moral expectations it caused,
are still there. Whoever visits abroad finds this special relationship to
Israel, the moral demands made on it, the ideological expectations.
Everyone wants to see and to learn how we will develop and solve
our problems, what contributions we will make to the weal of man-
kind as a whole.[76]

Sharett, in brief, was a small-state diplomat of the old school,
a man of intellect and a linguist, at home at international conferences, and conscious of the limitations of small-state diplomacy. But it was Ben-Gurion's characteristic pattern to establish
facts when the situation called for it, and to deal with facts
established by others as the need arose. For Ben-Gurion, its
architect, the establishment of the state itself was the ultimate

vindication of his approach and influenced his subsequent decisions. These decisions, however, were not so much in the realm of foreign policy as they were actions taken internally which affected Israel's relations with other states and thereby created issues of foreign policy. This was readily acknowledged by Sharett when he told the Knesset that many of Israel's foreign policy problems were the result of its own initiative.[77]

The fact that the Israel army staged a major retaliation raid against Gaza less than two weeks after Ben-Gurion's return as head of the defense establishment would indicate that his stewardship signaled an end to the experiment in moderation attempted by Sharett. Although the latter continued to head the government until November 1955 (general elections took place in July, but the negotiations for a new coalition dragged on until the fall), there was no mistaking Ben-Gurion's influence where defense and foreign policy were concerned. In the new government formed by Ben-Gurion after the elections, Sharett continued for some months as Foreign Minister but resigned his post in June 1956 with the announcement that he no longer found it possible to continue under Ben-Gurion's direction.[78]

As for Ben-Gurion himself, he said he had come to the conclusion that "complete harmony" between the Foreign and Defense ministries was now needed, as well as a different leadership in the Foreign Ministry.[79]

CHAPTER V

Policy Based on Influence:
Relations with the Great Powers

If Israel's relations with the states of the area were characterized by absence of diplomacy and resort to force, relations
with the great powers outside the area were based on a maximum
of diplomacy and the absence of force. To withstand great-
power policies which are detrimental to its own interests, the
small state relies on the protection of other great powers, through
alliances or the guarantee of its neutrality; failing that, it will
use the full extent of influence at its command in resisting the
great power's pressure, and only as a last resort will it muster
its physical force. In such recent instances where this occurred—
apart from the general wars in which small as well as great
powers were involved—only exceptional factors of geography
or of morale enabled the small state to offer successful resistance
to the great power for any length of time. In the case of Italy's
attack on Ethiopia, the Italians' extended supply line and the
difficulty of the Ethiopian terrain for a while inhibited Italy's
superior power; and in Soviet Russia's invasion of Finland in
1939 it was the fighting spirit of the Finns—added to the fact
that the Russians were able to commit only a small part of their
overwhelming power on this front—which permitted the former
to hold out considerably longer than had been predicted.

Israel was involved in no conflict situation with any great
power which would call for such desperate means. But the

127

pursuit of its goals in the area brought it into contact and at times also into controversy with outside powers with substantial interests in the area. These interests—related to economics, strategy, and prestige, and above all to the Cold War—were not immediately bound up with the Israel-Arab conflict. But eventually they could not be kept separate from the dispute and, to a greater or lesser extent, became interlaced with the powers' position in that dispute. Thus with the spread of the Cold War into the area the Arab-Israel dispute came to be played out against the backdrop of great-power rivalry.

Great-Power Policies as Threats to Israel's Interests

In each of the three developments which affected the distribution of power in the area to Israel's disadvantage—the Suez evacuation, the American arms supply to Iraq, and the Czech arms deal with Egypt—a hostile power in the area received an accretion of strength from a great power outside of it. Each development was instructive in its own way in that it showed one of the three great powers with interests in the area pursuing a policy which Israel felt called upon to oppose.

Britain's evacuation of the Suez base came after a period of withdrawal and lessening influence in the Middle East which began with the end of World War II and culminated in a "changing of the guard" as the area gradually moved into the strategic system of the United States. Because of the reduced scope of Britain's aspirations, the limited role of the Jewish community in British politics, and also because of the record of British-Jewish relations in Palestine, British policy was relatively impervious to Israeli influence. In the end, Israel realized the inevitability of the withdrawal decision (which was backed heavily by the United States), but it came as a disappointment when the final version of the Anglo-Egyptian treaty ignored Israel's interests entirely.

Although a remarkable improvement in relations had taken place since the British gave up the Palestine mandate in 1948, Israel was aware that Britain's major interest lay in the relationship with Egypt, and that the *rapprochement* with Israel was not allowed to interfere with this. Therefore Israel was apprehensive of Britain's influence on American policy and sought to minimize it. Since Britain was a signatory to the Tripartite Declaration, Israel attempted to convince it of the danger in continuing arms deliveries to the Arab states, but with indifferent success. A special source of friction was Britain's close treaty relationship with the Hashemite Kingdom of Jordan, and there was a lingering suspicion that British intrigue was still at work in fostering Jordanian enmity. On the whole, the relationship with Britain was marked by ambivalence. Because of Britain's commitments to the Arabs there was coolness and even hostility, especially in the press. But there also remained a genuine admiration for British political and social institutions which expressed itself in an oft-heard desire for better relations. During the Dulles visit to the Middle East, a curious temporary reversal of the traditional roles of the United States and the United Kingdom took place when Winston Churchill made a speech warmly praising Israel,[1] just six years after Ernest Bevin's Palestine policy had evoked severe criticism in the United States. But Israeli hopes that this might presage a new British policy which could serve as a counterweight to American leanings to the Arab side did not materialize; the Churchill statement had no further consequences. Britain intensively pursued its policy of securing an agreement with Egypt on evacuation of the Suez base. In the House of Commons debate of 29 July 1954, following the initialing of the agreement two days earlier, it was the Labor opposition which reminded the government that Britain had a duty to Israel; Clement Attlee even suggested that Haifa might serve as an alternative base. But Eden felt that Britain could help reduce tensions by entering on an era of good relations

129

with Egypt and saw no need for further assurances to Israel.[2]

While the Suez evacuation became an accomplished fact to which Israel had to accommodate itself, American arming of Iraq and the pursuit of the Northern Tier policy was a continuing process which was subject to modification and therefore to influence at its various stages. American policy throughout the period appeared tentative and uncertain, often on the verge of commitment but reluctant to take the plunge. Israel's influence base was broader in relation to the United States than to the other great powers, and the United States was now the most influential outside power in the area. Therefore it is Israel's relationship with the United States which will receive closer scrutiny in this chapter.

Israel was able to carry on a nearly continuous dialogue with the United States both in respect of *ad hoc* situations and of overall American policy. It was made easier by the fact that the United States had agreed and repeatedly proclaimed that the continued existence of Israel was in the interest of the United States, and had announced its opposition to arms deliveries which would upset the balance of strength in the area.[3] But this agreement on general principles did little to conciliate divergent views on what constituted a danger to Israel's existence, how that existence could best be secured, and what amount of arms would upset the balance of forces. However, the continuing nature of this dialogue kept the lines of communication open and the overall issue from being foreclosed.

No such dialogue could be conducted with the Soviet Union. Israel's influence base relative to that power was narrow. After Russia had broken off diplomatic relations in 1953, Israel's foreign policy was aimed at re-establishing those relations, and in this it succeeded, but it was powerless against the Soviet Union's determination to enlist the favor of the Arab states by siding with them in the United Nations and elsewhere.

Relations with the French Republic were affected by the fact that France was both a member of the Palestine Conciliation Commission and a partner to the Tripartite Declaration. It was understood that France still had some interests in the Levant and therefore was not overly friendly to Israel. In the early fifties France's U.N. votes and particularly its position on the internationalization of Jerusalem were of no great comfort to Israel. (However, with the outbreak of the rebellion in Algeria and Egypt's role in aiding the rebel leadership, a community of interests between France and Israel began to develop [see below, Chapter VIII].)

During this phase Israel began to extend the first feelers in the direction of Asia. Burma became the first country on the Asian continent to establish friendly relations with Israel. But there was scoffing in the opposition press about the new Asian policy,[4] and the pro-Arab resolutions adopted at the Bandung Conference in April 1955 seemed to justify this criticism. Israel's major diplomatic offensive in the direction of Asia and Africa did not get under way until after the Sinai Campaign.

The United Nations—Fulcrum of Great-Power Pressure

In addition to the four great powers, there was a fifth major power factor which Israel had to take into account, and that was the United Nations itself.

The United Nations, and for a time its subsidiary organ, the Palestine Conciliation Commission, became an arena for Israel's diplomatic struggle with forces outside the area. At each successive U.N. General Assembly session Israel was obliged to fend off attempts to revive and implement those parts of the 1947 Partition Resolution and subsequent resolutions which Israel felt itself no longer in a position to comply with. The existence of these resolutions, notably of Resolution 194 (III/1) of 11 December 1948 concerning the repatriation of the Arab refugees, constituted an instrument for pressure on Israel, most

131

menacing at those times when the United States lent them its backing. For while Israel had no great regard for the power of the United Nations as a whole, the attitude of the United States and its allies endowed the U.N. resolutions with added significance. It was evident that the effect of the resolutions which were still on the books was in direct relation to the determination of the great powers to enforce or support them. Thus the United Nations became a fulcrum of pressure not only for repatriation of the refugees but also for the internationalization of Jerusalem and, to a lesser extent, for territorial concessions. Israel was also called upon repeatedly to account for its use of force before the Security Council. The resulting censure resolutions had an adverse effect on relations with the powers that supported them, and they created resentment in Israel at what was regarded as one-sidedness in the U.N. consensus.[5]

Israel was in an isolated position in the United Nations: belonging to no regional grouping or bloc, it was disregarded when appointments and the rotation of offices were distributed in accordance with a regional key. Having no bloc of votes assured to it in any decisions affecting its interests, Israel often saw its case defeated by the sheer weight of the political line-up.[6]

This added to the attitude of skepticism and disillusionment toward the United Nations and to the tendency of public opinion to discount U.N. resolutions. This tendency became even more pronounced after the Soviet Union consistently sided with the Arab cause and thereby prevented the Security Council from taking action favorable to Israel in even as clear-cut a case as Israel's 1954 complaint against Egyptian interference with its shipping.[7] The earlier vote calling on Egypt to open the Canal remained a dead letter and no attempt was ever made to enforce it. Nor did the Council's action in disallowing Egypt's claim to belligerency bring about any perceptible change in that country's attitude.

The United Nations was not merely a composite of its members as far as Israel's foreign policy was concerned. It also confronted Israel in the shape of the truce supervision machinery on the spot. The operations of the U.N.T.S.O. were a source of potential and frequently open conflict between it and Israeli officials. The most obvious source of friction was Israel's retaliation policy, and the T.S.O.'s role in assessing blame for the incidents. The procedures of the truce supervision officers in investigating complaints often clashed with what Israel considered the prerogatives of its sovereignty. Israel's conception of the role of the truce teams was a limited one; nevertheless, there was a natural tendency to blame the M.A.C. system for its inability to prevent incursions and crime from the Arab side.

In its dealings with the United Nations on the spot, Israel had the advantage of its sovereignty, while the U.N.T.S.O. remained a somewhat amorphous body in international law and usage, representing considerably less than the authority enjoyed by the United Nations on its home grounds where, in matters relating to Palestine, it was backed almost automatically by a consensus of member states. In other words: while in the General Assembly, the Security Council, and the various committees Israel often found itself in an isolated position, on its own territory it confronted the U.N. officials as a sovereign state. Moreover, the Israelis dealing with the U.N. team were frequently military men, and these were not normally subject to the same inhibitions as the professional diplomat. They were members of an army which, in General Burns' words, had "unbounded confidence in its ability to defeat any and all the Arab armies," a confidence born of the successes in the 1948 war. "This feeling of preponderant military power not surprisingly resulted in arrogance toward the U.N. military personnel." [8]

General Burns candidly writes that "neither I nor the U.N. had a carrot or a stick." The principal source of the Chief of Staff's authority was that the General enjoyed the unqualified backing of the U.N. consensus and above all of the Secretary

General. His reports, like those of his predecessors, formed the basis of deliberations on Palestine matters by the Security Council.

The Secretary General himself occasionally intervened in disputes in the area and thereby became a focus for Israeli diplomatic activity. Relations between the Israel government and Dag Hammarskjold were of a checkered nature; he was the subject of frequent attacks in the press for alleged one-sidedness or indecisiveness, but his prestige nevertheless remained high. Withal, he managed throughout his tenure to preserve the confidence of both sides in the dispute.

Conditions Governing Great-Power Relations

Israel's relations with the great powers were conducted under one of three conditions:

(1) Israel's interests coincided with those of the great power. In that case the task of Israel's foreign policy was simple. But such situations were rare, since by cooperating with Israel in matters affecting the Arab states the great power would risk antagonizing the latter and thereby create negative factors likely to outweigh any gains to be achieved by cooperating with Israel.

(2) Israel's interests were a subject of indifference to the great power; that is, they did not affect the interests of the great power either way. Here too the range was necessarily narrow: because of the spread of the Cold War, great-power interests were easily affected by intra-area developments.

(3) The great power opposed Israel's interests because they clashed with its own. In such a case Israel had three choices open to it: first, to probe the extent of the opposition and to pursue its own policy up to the point where it clashed head on with that opposition; second, to modify or abandon its policy;

third, to attempt to overcome opposition through the influence at its disposal.

Since foreign policy is most active where it encounters opposition to the national interest, Israel's policy toward the United States was mainly concerned with achieving its goals in spite of the opposition of the superior power. This meant, in the first instance, persuading the United States that its interests were not in fact opposed to those of Israel but were identical to, or at least unaffected by, Israel's interests. If this effort were successful, the United States could ultimately be persuaded first to refrain from actions which Israel considered to be harmful to its own interests, and second to undertake actions which would benefit Israel, such as guaranteeing its security. If Israel failed in this, then its foreign policy had to seek means of withstanding or overcoming the United States' opposition in either its positive or negative manifestations. In its positive aspect, U.S. policy engaged in initiatives which Israel considered harmful to its own interest, such as supplying arms to an Arab state. In its negative aspect, U.S. policy was in opposition to a move by Israel, such as the transfer of the capital to Jerusalem. The price of failure here, of course, would be accommodation of Israel's policy to that of the United States, as when it stopped work on the Jordan River hydroelectric project.

Positive acts of policy which Israel sought to obtain from the United States at one time or another included the following: (1) inclusion in an alliance or regional defense organization which would automatically guarantee Israel's security; (2) a unilateral guarantee of territorial integrity and security; (3) economic aid to overcome foreign exchange and supply difficulties; (4) supply of armaments; (5) pressure on Egypt concerning interference with shipping in the Suez Canal and the Gulf of Aqaba and relaxation of the economic boycott; (6) pressure on Arab states to induce them to conduct peace talks with Israel.

Conversely, Israel attempted to influence American policy to

135

desist from certain courses of action, including the following: (1) pressure for concessions on territory and refugee repatriation; (2) pressure for internationalization of Jerusalem; (3) arms deliveries to Arab states; (4) establishment of a regional defense organization to the exclusion of Israel.

There was also concern lest certain policy pronouncements might be translated into concrete measures, and consequently influence was exerted to forestall this.

Arguments of Persuasion

To persuade the United States that there was indeed a mutuality of interest between the two states, Israel resorted to arguments both of a material and of a moral nature. The Cold War presented the most obvious opportunity for demonstrating reciprocity of interest on the material plane. If Israel could convince the United States that an accretion in its strength meant an accretion of strength to the West in a critical area, then the West was bound to help Israel attain that strength. This was the basis for the alliance policy.

Although the United States showed no willingness to see Israel included in its plans for a Middle East defense organization, the theory that Israel's military strength should figure as a trump card in its foreign policy remained a keystone in the philosophy of Herut, articulated by its spokesmen in the Knesset. In their view, the policy of the United States toward Israel was not the result of objective facts but of Israel's own actions, and in particular of Sharett's failure to develop mutual interests with the United States. "We must find sufficient strength to change that policy," they said—and toward that end the army should serve as the principal instrument of Israel's policy not only in the area but in the world.[9]

The General Zionist spokesman, on the other hand, perceived that emphasis on Israel's military strength would have the effect of undercutting the demand for the supply of arms. Since one cannot protest one's strength and one's weakness at the same time, the answer from the West was likely to be: you are already strong enough to take care of yourself.[10]

There were two other ways in which the marginal use of power might affect relations with the states outside the region which would normally be impervious to small-state arguments based on power. One was the "illegitimate" use of power already described in the previous chapter, where violence in the area was used to influence relations between the United States and Egypt at a critical juncture. The second might be called the powder keg argument: the Middle East is a powder keg, and unless something is done, the Arab-Israel conflict could be the fuse to ignite it.[11]

It is quite natural for a small state to take advantage of great-power rivalry by taking a neutralist stance and have both sides bid for its favor. Then, if need be, one side can be relied upon to counterbalance pressure by the other. This appeared feasible in Israel's case for as long as it enjoyed Soviet support. When the United States was advising Israel to yield a portion of the Negev as a price for peace, Ambassador McDonald cabled the State Department that Israel would not do so unless forced by military pressure or such a degree of economic pressure as would be tantamount to war. Israel's opposition, he added significantly, would have the full moral support of the Soviet Union.[12] Whether or not this was a realistic estimate, the American diplomat's assessment was in itself a factor in the power position at the time. In order to preserve this balancing ability, Israel evolved the policy of "non-identification." But in the Tripartite Declaration of 25 May 1950 the Western powers stated their conviction that the Arab states and Israel all needed to "maintain a certain level of armed forces for the purpose of assuring their internal security and their legitimate self-defense, and to permit them to play their part in the defense of the area as a

137

whole." The latter phrase could only mean defense against Soviet attack.

When Israel subsequently voted with the West on the question of Korea in the United Nations, the end of the non-identification policy was clearly at hand.

But while the Korean War brought Israel closer to the position of the West, that conflict also enhanced American awareness of the importance of the Middle East to Western security. After Turkey joined the North Atlantic Treaty Organization in February 1952, the United States continued in its effort to set up a form of Middle Eastern Defense Organization which would to some extent fill the power vacuum being created by Great Britain's gradual withdrawal. For its part, the Soviet Union, which since Stalin's abortive attempt to break into the Middle East in 1945–1947 had been relatively inactive in the area, now began to view it in a different light and sought to extend its influence to counter the Western thrust.

Great-Power Inertia and Small-State Sovereignty

In view of the difficulty in establishing a clear-cut case of identity of interest, a more effective basis on which to deal with great-power opposition was to count on the great power's inertia; the reluctance, particularly on the part of the United States, to take significant action unless its primary interest was affected. If the small state so conducts its affairs as to avoid overt conflict with the great power's primary interest, opposition may remain limited to verbal expression of disapproval. For what to the small state may be of vital interest is likely to be of secondary or tertiary interest to the great power, and therefore not worth the disturbance of conflict even with a small state.

An effective source of influence for small states in their relations with the great powers is the nature of sovereignty itself. At a time when the sovereign equality of states is inscribed on the banner of the United Nations, this can be a potent argument, at least for as long as the vital interests of the great power are not directly affected.

David Ben-Gurion has said:

There is no identity of interest between any two states and certainly none between a rich and universal power of the world and a small embryo state in a distant corner of the Middle East. America has not undertaken nor will it undertake to back Israel in all it asks. America has its own considerations, and they differ from Israel's or even run counter to them. Israel too has its own considerations, and while they do not run counter to America's, they also need not be identical with them. . . . No external force, be it the strongest, most vehement and wealthiest imaginable, is going to decide Israel's needs and values. The foreign policy of Israel is going to be decided according to the fundamental values and needs of the Jewish nation and by no other determination.[13]

Shortly after the Czech-Egyptian arms deal, Moshe Sharett echoed these sentiments in this fashion:

Regardless of the motives and considerations of national or of world import which shape the policies of each of the world powers, for us the decisive point and the one which determines our attitude toward each power is the extent to which its policies or actions ensure or imperil, reinforce or undermine, the existence and security of Israel.[14]

The Appeal to Public Opinion:
The Role of American Jewry

Israel possessed a unique asset in the United States in the presence of a large and influential Jewish community deeply sympathetic to Israel's aspirations. Coupled with the structure of American political life and its system of checks and balances among the executive, legislative, and judicial branches of the government, and its susceptibility to pressure groups as well as to sentimental appeal, this circumstance facilitated Israel's efforts to present its goals effectively. The capacity to persuade important segments of the public of the identity of these goals with American interests, and at times to affect government policy, was thus a major element in Israel's influence base.

It is true that there was a large Jewish population in the Soviet Union as well. But in the absence of the features characteristic of the "open society," the existence of that population, far from being an asset in the conduct of foreign policy, was a potential liability in relations with the Soviet Union. Israel's periodic demands for special rights for that body of Jews, such as the right to emigration, served to antagonize the Soviet rulers and to make Israel's aspirations suspect in their eyes.

Ben-Gurion has astutely defined the conditions which made the United States a fertile field for influencing public opinion— conditions which did not obtain on the far side of the Iron Curtain:

If a totalitarian state adopts an unfavorable attitude towards one of Israel's vital interests, we cannot attempt to change its attitude by explaining our point of view to its public opinion. No letter opposing the Government's decision can be published in that country's press; no debate can be held in parliament; it is impossible to appeal to influential individuals; everyone is subordinate to the ruler, and his decision is final. In a country where there is freedom of speech, debate and criticism, it is possible to appeal to public opinion by means of all the channels through which it finds expression.[15]

While a democratic form of government is a *sine qua non* for access to public opinion, it is no guarantee of success. In Great Britain, the experience of Israel and of the Palestine *Yishuv* before it showed that it is possible to enlist sympathy and support among members of the party in opposition, only to have it pursue the same policy as the previous government, once in power.

In the United States, the sympathy of American Jews for the state of Israel, as Jewish spokesmen stressed on many occasions, derived not from any political loyalty or feeling of identification with the state as such, but with the idea of Jewish national and cultural renascence which it embodied, and from physical and emotional kinship to its population. The idea of the return to Zion after two millennia not only appealed strongly to the religious sentiments of many Jews, but it also seemed to offer an opportunity for testing the Jewish genius in a setting of territorial concentration and cultural homogeneity, which challenged the imagination of Jews in the dispersion. To this end, national sovereignty did not at first appear a prerequisite. But once the leadership of the World Zionist Organization had resolved to make sovereignty a basic part of the Zionist program, American Jews by and large went along, although there remained a vocal dissenting group, centered around a section of the Reform rabbinate.[16] After the war, the *Yishuv* of Palestine became the main instrument for receiving and rehabilitating the survivors of the Nazi crimes against Europe's Jews. When the state was established, therefore, defense of its interests became identified with the imperative to safeguard the physical existence of a precious remnant of Jewry, and to keep open a haven for others to enter.

Already in the struggle to create the state, American Jewry had proved an invaluable asset. Its influence on American public opinion through the media of communication, and on American policy mainly through supporters in the legislative branch, was reflected in the United States' role at the final countdown at the United Nations, the abandonment of the Trusteeship scheme and President Truman's quick *de facto* recognition of the new state.[17] It is easy to understand that Israel's policy-makers wished to preserve this asset to the fullest extent and for as long as possible. But with the attainment of sovereignty, the quality of the relationship was bound to change: an outside group can hardly lend its backing to a sovereign government as unqualifiedly as it did to a movement for national liberation. To most

141

American Jews, this was self-evident. The loss of interest in political activity on behalf of Israel on the part of individuals was reflected in the drop in membership of the Zionist Organization of America, for example, from 250,000 in 1948 to 87,000 a decade and a half later.[18]

The tacit assumption underlying much of this activity was that the concentration of Jewish voters in major centers of population would help create attitudes favorable to Israel among representatives to Congress from these key areas, which in turn would have its effect on administration policies. Also, the electoral system for the presidency gives ethnic groups in a few of the large cities a weight out of proportion to their numerical importance in the nation as a whole. The extent to which Zionist activities, public opinion, concern with the Jewish vote and similar considerations actually influenced American policy at various stages in the period under review cannot be empirically determined, in view of the many variables.[19] But it is probable that the effectiveness of these factors was sometimes overrated in Israel. There were occasional expressions of disappointment in the absence of results, especially on the right wing. Menahen Begin scored the Jews of America "for not rallying and demonstrating in the main cities" after the signing of the Suez agreement and American arms deliveries to Iraq, and even the moderate Meir Argov of Mapai was heard speculating in the same debate that "something must have happened in the United States if the Jews don't go out and protest the injustice their government was doing to Israel." [20]

After the striking successes leading to the U.N. Partition Resolution and the swift recognition of the new state by President Truman, it would appear that the effect of the presence of American Jewry was more easily measurable in the economic than in the political sphere. It is doubtful whether the generous economic aid which the United States accorded to Israel in its first difficult years would have been forthcoming to the same degree had not American Jewry effectively pleaded the cause of the new state and focused the attention of the American people and its policy-makers on its needs and progress.

In the political sphere, the fact of American Jewry's existence certainly constituted a reservoir of strength, but it also had its drawbacks. For American Jewry had interests which did not always coincide with those of Israel, and as a result the latter's interests were not always fairly presented on the American scene by the former. When the Cold War was at its height, American Jews, intent on demonstrating that Israel was on the same side as the United States, emphasized Israel's differences with the Soviet Union, whereas Israel desired to retain the good will of both powers. This tended to exaggerate Israel's hostility to the Soviet Union. After the partial *rapprochement* with the Soviet Union in the summer of 1953, American Jewry was slow in de-emphasizing the hostility.

Similarly, the American Zionists' campaign against Egypt brought added virulence to the Israel-Egyptian relationship.[21] The propaganda material disseminated by the Zionist groups was by definition one-sided, and therefore hardly conducive to an understanding of complex issues by the constituencies. For example, it tended to emphasize Israel's role as a "bulwark of democracy" in contrast to the Arab states' political backwardness, without taking into consideration the circumstances that made for the differences. Once launched on a campaign, the organizational machinery was too cumbersome for easy control and for subtle response to changes in the diplomatic setting of the conflict.

An American observer, in reporting on the state of the American-Israeli dialogue circa 1954, distinguished between two categories of disagreements which formed the substance of that dialogue. One he called a "classic," or general disagreement, not over a particular issue or of limited duration, but long-time and springing from fundamental causes. These causes were the emergence of Israel itself, the Arab refusal to accept it, and the American need to fit the Arabs into a global strategy. The second type arose from the first, but they were tactical and specific, concerned with day-to-day issues.

The basic disagreements were over two questions: Were the Arabs capable of regional cooperation? If so, how should their cooperation be enlisted? The United States not only believed the Arabs capable of it, but also indispensable to it. Israel strongly doubted that the Arabs could be effectively organized in a regional system of defense, and certainly not through the "application of sweet reasonableness." From this long-term Israeli view stemmed the argument urging the United States to dispel the Arabs' notion that the West feared them, and to make it clear to them that the West would go on with Israel alone. If the Arabs have no alternative and enough pressure is put on them, Israel reasoned, they may acquiesce and make peace, as they did once before when they signed the armistice agreements.

To this the United States replied with its own long-term view. While conceding a certain logic to the argument, it found a basic flaw in Israel's perspective: Israel saw clearly its own interests and grievances, but not the immensely larger frame in which the Arab-Israeli conflict was set.

Israel is a pinpoint of territory with a population of less than two millions; the Arab world is almost a continent with more than 40 millions. Even if this mass were totally apathetic, it could not be ignored, nor could so huge a territory be treated as wasteland, the Americans point out. The people and the land are anything but apathetic. To test the soundness of Israeli assurances that firmness would bring tranquility, one would have to risk the alternative possibility of conflagration. Such a risk is unthinkable.[22]

Part Three

THE ROAD TO SINAI

CHAPTER VI ≺≺≺≺

The Balance Disturbed

The Soviet Involvement: Israel's Changed Position

That the Czech-Egyptian arms deal brought an entirely new element into the relationship with Egypt was immediately apparent in Israel, and under its impact the previous threats to the power relationship were acknowledged to have been relatively insignificant. It was the Czech arms deliveries which Moshe Sharett now characterized as an "unprecedented danger" apt to bring about ominous and revolutionary changes in Israel's security position.[1] Two weeks later, he declared that the arms deal had already resulted in a "decisive shift in the balance of military strength" which would put an end to Israel's qualitative superiority over Egypt. He explained that the new imbalance was much more serious than the condition caused by arms supplied by the West to Iraq, since Iraq was not on the borders of Israel.[2] Still later, he told the Knesset that the Soviet deal now conferred on Egypt "an overwhelming military superiority" and confronted Israel "with a danger such as has not threatened it since the War of Liberation."[3]

David Ben-Gurion, who became Premier in November, shared his colleague's judgment of the revolutionary nature of the event. Until recently, he told the Knesset, "our arms (apart from naval armaments) were not inferior in quality, and we were able to rely on the moral and spiritual superiority of the Israel fighting

147

man. But the Czech arms deal transformed the situation in the gravest and most dangerous manner." [4] In his retrospective article on the Sinai Campaign, Ben-Gurion avers that the "balance of forces between Israel and her neighbors was grievously undermined to Israel's detriment" by the Czech deal, because through it "quantitative inferiority became qualitative as well." [5]

While the precise extent of the arms deliveries scheduled under the agreement was shrouded in secrecy, there was no doubt that this time the threat to the power balance was taken seriously not only by the politicians but also by the military.[6] Nevertheless, the danger could hardly be considered immediate. General Burns estimated that it would take the Egyptian army two years to master its new weapons and to be ready for offensive action. And apart from the weapons it was to receive, the army needed better morale, training, and discipline before it could be a match for the Israelis.[7] Thus the new Egyptian edge in the quantity and even in the quality of armaments by no means wiped out Israel's advantage in training, organization, and morale.

The question which now faced the Israeli leadership was how to react to the new situation. Given a period of grace—be it two years or less—before Egypt fully realized the new dimension of power afforded it by the supply of arms, how best to utilize that span of time? What choices were open?

The response had to take account of the fact that the Czech-Egyptian agreement brought a new element not only to the confrontation between Israel and the Arab states through the accretion of power it vouchsafed to Egypt, but also to the position of the Middle East as a whole in the Cold War. In that sense as well Israel correctly perceived the event to be of "revolutionary importance," symptomizing, for the first time, "a purposeful attempt by the Soviet Union to establish its direct influence in the Middle East." [8] By fulfilling the Egyptian request for arms, through its Czechoslovak Satellite, the Soviet Union formally abandoned its neutrality in the Palestine conflict and entered the charged arena of Middle Eastern politics with both feet.

The effect on the Arab-Israel power relationship can be described in simple terms. At the beginning of 1955 both Egypt and Israel were without true allies among the great powers; at the end of the year, Egypt could count on the Soviet Union as its ally. Israel had suffered a telling setback in one of the major tenets of its foreign policy: to prevent accretion of power to the Arab side through foreign assistance. This was dictated by the knowledge that Israel's own power was sufficient only for facing the Arabs alone, but not for a combination of Arab and outside powers. Now the entrance of the Soviet Union onto the scene presented an ominous challenge to Israel's military superiority: the equilibrium of armed peace which had obtained since the armistice was likely to be upset, but not in the direction of co-operation. A new approach was required.

Egypt's Intentions

An uncertain factor in the Egypt-Israel equation remained the precise intentions of the Egyptian leader. If the Czech arms deal was indeed a turning point in the relationship, then it was essential for Israel to arrive at an assessment of Egypt's intentions in the new situation. It has been shown that, in the past, there had been considerable ambivalence among the Israelis as to the nature of Egypt's ambitions. The absence of conflicting interests between Egypt and Israel had been stressed, until disillusionment had set in early in 1955 among those who believed that, given time, Egypt would be amenable to a settlement. Abdel Nasser continued to disclaim any outright intention to make war on Israel; he spoke about helping the Arab refugees regain their rights:

No Arab state intends to destroy Israel. The Arabs only want the refugees to obtain their natural rights to life and to their lost properties, promised to them by the United Nations resolutions seven years ago. We are not aggressors. The threat is from the other side. I have stated many times that I am interested in the reconstruction of my

149

country. Now, I am forced to grant defense priority over development. The situation was otherwise before Ben Gurion's attack on Gaza. . . . I haven't ceased to expect an Israeli attack, but this danger will decrease to the degree that the Arab-Israeli arms balance is restored.[9]

Israelis, however, preferred to lend credence to the more violent Egyptian press and radio propaganda which constantly threatened them with destruction. Ben-Gurion quoted Egyptian newspaper opinion to the effect that it was "inconceivable" that Egypt would recognize or make peace with Israel.[10] But the Egyptian Premier's frequent mention of compliance with the U.N. resolutions and "justice" for the refugees as his price of peace, while not new, caused uneasiness. It was feared that Egypt's strengthened position and the West's sensitivity to Russian penetration of the area might bring active Western support of the idea of resuscitating the partition plan—a fear promptly borne out by the Eden Guildhall speech on 9 November (see below, p. 169).

Ambassador Eban said that Israel had been deceived again and again by assurances that with Egypt moderation was just around the corner:

We were told at the time (of the Suez Canal agreement) in the most authoritative way, chiefly by American sources, that if only we would look with complacency, or even with support, upon the spectacle of Egypt's achieving its national aspirations, all would be well for Israel. . . . Shortly after the evacuation of British troops, we were told, Nasser would first relax and then abolish the blockade. He would enter into conversations and into contact leading to a settlement with Israel. . . . Instead, he has progressively intensified the blockade, extended it to other waters, namely the Gulf of Aqaba. . . . He hasn't made a single move at any time towards a stabilization of his relations with Israel.[11]

Eban said he was trying to convey a clear impression of Israel's conviction that an assurance by Egypt was not worth the paper on which it was written. He said he was doing this not merely for the historical record, but because Israel feared there might be a tendency to be lulled into false optimism by other assessments. Eban also saw an ominous sign in the fact that the Egyptian President had refused the arms proffered by the United States because he was asked to make the commitment required by the Mutual Security Act to abstain from aggression.

Nasser explained in an interview that he had refused the offer because it would have meant stationing an American mission in Egypt, "and an American mission means American influence." He said he told the British and American ambassadors after the Gaza raid that he was negotiating with the Soviet Union. While Great Britain threatened him, the United States offered him $27 million worth of arms in June, but on conditions that he pay cash on delivery. He could not do it, he said. His request for credit was not answered: "The U.S. thought we were bluffing on Russia." Moreover, he added, he understood that Iraq never received the type of arms from the United States which it wanted; the supplies consisted mostly of ambulances.[12]

Nor was Israel impressed by the argument that for Nasser the problem of Israel was secondary in importance to his rivalry with Iraq and opposition to the Baghdad Pact, as foreign observers were wont to report before the Gaza raid. From Israel's point of view, while it was apparent that the Northern Tier concept developed by Dulles and the nurturing of the Baghdad Pact under Western sponsorship intensified the bitter feeling between Egypt and Iraq, it seemed more important that the two protagonists of this inter-Arab rivalry were competing also on the plane of anti-Zionism.

Nor did it particularly matter to Israel whether Nasser had a precise timetable for his next move. It seemed inherent in the dynamics of his policy that he would be led toward an adventure—it was inconceivable, Ben-Gurion warned the Knesset on 2 November, that he should have sought the Soviet arms with

151

any other purpose in mind but to destroy Israel. The Arabs had been the allies of Hitler, and with him had wanted to annihilate the Jews. These pronouncements came as part of the program for the new government being formed by Ben-Gurion, which put its greatest emphasis on a strengthening of the army.[13]

An analysis of the foreign policy of the revolutionary regime in Egypt presented to the 1956 symposium cited earlier saw the anti-Israel plank at the core of Egyptian foreign policy.[14] After initially concentrating its energy on the Suez problem, the symposium was told, Egyptian policy now was directed at the Arab area, and at the center of Arab policy was the anti-Israel campaign. Eventually, it was reasoned, military action against Israel must appear to Egypt to be the logical outcome of that policy. The military strength derived from the Soviet Union now made Egypt appear capable of standing up against Israel, and as a result enabled it to take the lead in the anti-Israel campaign. It was recalled that the advent of the officers' regime was greeted with high hopes in Israel as well as in the West. But, the speaker admitted somewhat ruefully, its character was not at first understood; and besides, about halfway along its course, the regime underwent a change of direction as far as its foreign policy was concerned. That turning point came with the conclusion of the Suez treaty in October 1954.

A significant pointer to Egyptian intentions was seen in the reorganization of the Egyptian General Staff, which was being implemented together with the receipt of the Czech arms. According to the reorganization plan, the land forces were to be increased to four motorized infantry divisions, an armored division, and a combat group of heavy tanks. An air force of 240 jet fighters and 60 bombers was to be built up, with all of the weapons assured by the agreement. The creation of an alliance system encircling Israel furnished additional evidence, in Israeli eyes, of the strategic intention. In October 1955, a military pact between Egypt and Syria provided for a joint supreme command

and general staff, standardization of weapons, and training and operational plans. This meant that Syria's six infantry brigades, one armored brigade, and 120 jets would also come under Egyptian command. A week later, an alliance was signed with Saudi Arabia, putting at Egypt's disposal not only the Saudi bases in the Gulf of Aqaba but also the financial means for political action to further an Arab unity movement under Egyptian hegemony in Jordan and elsewhere.[15]

Ben-Gurion later wrote that he had read Nasser's *Philosophy of the Revolution,* and found the Egyptian's ambitions too dangerous for Israel to tolerate passively, even apart from any designs on Israel's integrity. These aims, as Ben-Gurion paraphrased them, were "to gain power over all the Arab countries, to become the head of all Muslim peoples and the leader of Africa." [16] Thus by the time the Prime Minister made his policy statement to the Knesset, Egypt's intentions had already been assessed as being both imperialist in general and aimed at the destruction of Israel in particular.

According to that assessment, Israel was now faced with the kind of situation "where the mere possibility of overwhelming power constitutes a potential supreme threat. Under these circumstances the other party is left no choice whatever, assuming it is to survive and maintain its identity; it has to acquire the same power in order to compensate, and it has to do this in the shortest possible time interval, lest the first party interfere in the process of equalization or neutralization. It can do so by preventive war." [17]

CHAPTER VII

Last Chance for Diplomacy

The Debate on Preventive War

The change in the government in November 1955 could hardly be attributed to the new security situation which confronted Israel after the Soviet-Egyptian arms deal, since it grew out of the elections to the Third Knesset which took place in July. But a significant aspect of the election results was the startling gain in the strength of Herut, the rightist party which stood for an activist policy. The party nearly doubled its representation in the Knesset, increasing its percentage of the popular vote from 6.7 to 12.5 per cent. Ahdut ha-Avodah, the labor party which also advocated an activist line, equally enhanced its position. On the other hand, Mapai lost 4.2 per cent of the vote. These results were interpreted as popular support for a more aggressive foreign policy than had been conducted by Moshe Sharett. Mapai itself, it will be recalled, was divided between a moderate and an activist wing, the former represented by Sharett and the latter by Ben-Gurion. Before the Ben-Gurion wing formally won out, the fight between moderates and activists was waged in the Mapai Center, the elected party forum, and was decided by majority vote.[1] It cannot, however, be assumed that the moderate wing favored a peace policy over a security policy. Both the "activists" and the antiactivists gave priority to defense over other policy considerations; where they differed was in the extent that demon-

154

strations of power were required to carry out that policy. Perhaps it is fair to say that there was less ambivalence among the activists than among the moderates. The activists wished to respond doubly to every military threat, and they felt that a political benefit would flow from a demonstration of power itself.[2] General Burns speaks of a "negotiation" party as opposed to a "retaliation" party and also relates that Sharett at one time spoke to him of the two trends in Israel's defense and foreign policy. "Many others . . . mainly people in the Foreign Affairs Ministry, propounded the same thesis." [3] Herut's success in the elections lent new weight to the party's foreign policy arguments. As early as 30 August 1954, Menahem Begin had advocated in the Knesset that Israel destroy the enemy bases of aggression by a deliberate strategy at the appropriate time. Israel was not faced with a choice between peace or war, he declared, but the question was "how to stop the war." What he was advocating was not a preventive war, but a way to stop the war already being waged. "No one in Israel hates war more than we do." The chances for an Arab counterattack would be weak, Begin thought. "Why did the Arabs not attack us after Qibya or Nahalin? Because they knew we were strong. But tomorrow they will be stronger than ourselves, or at least they will be convinced of it, and they will attack us. Even without a Qibya, without retaliation." He accused the Sharett government of telling the people to resign itself to a war of annihilation.[4]

Sharett, at the next opportunity, had dismissed Begin's suggestions as "fantastic and irresponsible." While granting that the armistice agreements were deteriorating, he asked whether Israel for its part should not be interested in the maintenance of these agreements in order to continue its work and build up its strength, rather than to let them disintegrate into bloody strife and international complications, the end of which no one could predict.[5]

Fourteen months later, in the debate on the program of the

155

new government and after the Soviet-Egyptian arms agreement, Begin again came forward with the same arguments. But this time he spoke as the head of the leading opposition party, second in strength only to Mapai. Preventive war, he proclaimed, was a negative idea. The Arabs have been waging war on us, and if we react, it will be a "defensive war," designed to put an end to their warlike acts. At the same time, he stressed the significance of language: one can undertake "operations," without declaring "war." This need not cost much blood: Caesar changed the course of history at Pharsalus in a battle that cost two hundred legionnaires and thirty officers. Begin again berated the government for not knowing what to do in the preceding seven years. "This government cannot solve our most important problem," he charged. "It flounders between restraint and reacting. Between extremist talk and inactivity." [6] Once again Begin was answered in the debate by a leader of Mapai. Meir Argov said Begin's program sounded as though Israel had not signed the armistice agreements. Even in Korea, he pointed out, there was as yet no peace—only an armistice. The same was true in Indochina. Furthermore, Begin took no account of the great powers, their ability to exert pressure, and he spoke as though permanent peace depended only on Israel's own policy. The fact is, he declared, that the Arab peoples, and not only their rulers, have not resigned themselves to Israel's existence. [7]

While the Mapai leadership thus objected to Herut's line on the basis of Israel's international obligations, another voice spoke up in opposition on grounds of the same kind of *Realpolitik* which motivated Herut. Gershom Schocken, Progressive party deputy and publisher of the influential *Ha-Arez,* pointed out that only Begin had spoken with assurance in the debate: he wanted to use military initiative to break out of the political and security *cul de sac* in which Israel found itself. But no one could know the end of such a course, Schocken warned: Begin, of all people, should know the force that was in the fanaticism of nations awakening to national consciousness. Even victory was not the end. Israel had won over Egypt seven years ago—today Egypt was stronger than ever in the world arena since Arabi Pasha. There was something to the saying, "Defeat makes stronger." Possibly an additional defeat would awaken the Egyptians and the other Arab peoples to double and triple their national efforts. "It is not our job to be midwives to a strong Egypt." Schocken then conceded that the recent developments had strengthened Begin's argument: "Not that we should take his advice—but that he has more cause for questioning our past policies." [8]

Schocken then spoke about the role of the powers with a bitterness that was unusual in one known to be staunchly pro-Western in his views: Israel's foreign policy, he declared, had been based on the principle of international cooperation. No state today could do what it wanted; states were interdependent, especially a small state like Israel. That is why Israel put so much emphasis on the United Nations and on the great powers. But it seemed now that Israel's hopes were disappointed. Since 1949 the United Nations had not succeeded in anything in the Middle East. The great powers, instead of playing a stabilizing role, were playing the role of disturbers of the peace. What was called in Washington the "arms race" was competition between Moscow and Washington for various stakes in the Middle East. Israel and the Arabs were horses; the riders sat in the two world capitals. Israel had a special complaint to America, Schocken said, as the power on which it had based its main hopes. Dulles in his 26 August speech complained about Israel's borders. But the State Department was partly responsible for an explosive border: the Gaza Strip, from which spies and saboteurs were sent into Israel. Otherwise, Israel's natural and historic frontier with Egypt would have been the Sinai desert. "Our heavy sacrifice seven years ago of giving in to American demands has not brought us peace." [9]

Of the two left-wing labor parties that were included in the new government, Ahdut ha-Avodah took an activist attitude while the Mapam deputies came out unequivocally against "all sorts of preventive war." Said Mapam's Ya'qov Hazan: "Preventive war does not prevent war—it is war itself. It makes the real attacked the attacker. We had enough of destruction and blood. We came to build and to rescue, not to be killed and to kill." [10]

The Ahdut ha-Avodah line was somewhat ambiguous. The party's leader, Israel Galili, cautioned that "we must not initiate war" but also warned against "letting Egypt choose the time and place . . . at its convenience." [11] Later the same party's General Yigal Allon called the preventive war argument harmful to Israel in terms reminiscent of Herut: "Israel is already at war—the only question is, when will the decisive battle be fought?" [12] Hazan disagreed with this theme and called it a dangerous play on words. In an eloquent speech he chided those who claimed the war was already on. He said, "We still live at peace. True, it is a dangerous peace, but it is still peace. Unlike those who ask themselves, 'how can we finish the war victoriously?' those who believe we are still at peace ask, 'how can we save the peace?' " [13]

A fresh note was brought to the debate by a young Mapai deputy, Shlomo Hillel, who thus defined the various possibilities facing Israel:

(1) *The Arabs concede and resign themselves to Israel's existence in its present form.* Hillel thought there had been a possibility of attaining this goal with one or the other of the Arab states at various times if it had been pursued vigorously. But the opportunities were missed; there was no chance for this now. Recognition of Israel's existence could no longer be attained without serious concessions on Israel's part, he concluded.

(2) *Israel makes concessions to ensure peace.* All the proposals made by the Western powers for concessions were intended to satisfy the appetite and the prestige of the Arab rulers.

But no party—except the Communists—would get a mandate from the voters for such a course.

(3) *A realistic alternative is an extensive war in the future.* This was even a certainty under present conditions, according to Hillel. There was no possibility of avoiding war, even if the balance of power were restored. If a country like Egypt invested all its economic potential in armament, the arms would be ruling the government and not vice versa. Israel's attempt to solve the problem by retaliation raids would be met by more determined resistance which could only lead to total war.

Hillel thought the only point worth discussing was whether an Arab attack was a possibility or a certainty. He agreed that whoever saw war as inevitable must come to the conclusion that Israel should not permit the enemy to choose his time. As for the great powers, he doubted whether they would do more to prevent an Arab attack than they had done in 1948. In that year both the Soviet Union and the United States had been interested in preventing it, but had failed. Israel should, however, enlist their help through influencing its leaders and public opinion.[14]

David Hacohen, another outspoken Mapai politician, also felt sure that war would break out once Egypt had the arms. "She will feel strong, and then she will attack as she has long openly announced. The possibility is not to be excluded that, out of fear of such an attack, we shall attack first. I am not afraid to say this, but the world understands this—the world knows that we want to live." [15]

A deputy of Ha-Po'el ha-Mizrahi, Ya'qov Greenberg, contributed this thought to the debate: "There are two opinions among the public—(1) that war is inevitable, or that it is already here, and that we must not lose the initiative; (2) that war is not inevitable, and that we must strive for peace."

As to the first, we have not heard from its spokesmen what will happen once we win. Will peace come then, and will the tension subside;

159

or will we prepare for a third or a fourth round? We cannot occupy all the Arab states. . . . We cannot force tens of millions of Arabs to make peace with us. If we conquer a few strategic points, such as Gaza, the Triangle, etc., it is obvious that the war will not end thereby. But we will bring economic and spiritual disaster upon ourselves. We cannot digest that many inhabitants. We will endanger our special culture and quality. We will bring in a foreign body with a foreign culture.

Furthermore, what are we to expect from a leader whom we have frustrated and humiliated, and who rules over a defeated people? What desperate steps will he be capable of? The West is not always wrong: Nasser stuck a knife in their backs—yet they do not denounce, they appease him. Why? Because they are afraid of what a frustrated dictator is capable of. We must also remember the price in victims which a war will cost us. We will also estrange world public opinion, which will brand us as the aggressor. Yet we will have to depend to a large extent on public opinion for victory, to buy arms, and so forth. To begin a dubious war will bring us only temporary victory, and almost certain damage. The idea of peace suits our hearts better. It is better suited to our mentality and to our psychology. There is no objective reason why there should not be peace between us and the Arab states. The gulf is not so wide that it cannot be bridged. It is not a question of borders, only a matter of prestige. . . . Objective conditions do not prevent a peace settlement.

The failure of our propaganda is the failure to penetrate to the Arab masses. . . . It is not enough for Ben-Gurion to say that peace takes goodwill on both sides. Sometimes planned, intelligent, intensive action is required. Declarations and even proposals will not bring peace. I am sure that, from the time of the armistice until today, we had opportunities to make peace. We lost many opportunities, for we remained passive and satisfied with good will and half-hearted action.

It is true, the situation has changed for the worse. But it may not be too late. 'Make peace!' it is written. Peace must be made by energetic action. The Talmud says, 'Do not be ashamed before those who ridicule!' In fulfilling the commandment one mustn't think of prestige and false pride and not be afraid lest others say we want peace out of

160

weakness. We have two ways open to us: A war offensive or a peace offensive. Let us choose peace.[16]

But the main thrust of the argument continued inconclusively between the spokesmen of Herut and Ben-Gurion, after the latter had returned as Prime Minister. Said he:

We cannot obtain security through military victory—not even the most complete. We do not want, we are not permitted, and we cannot annihilate tens of millions of Arabs in the Middle East, and no war-like rhetoric can change this. Our defense lies in constant readiness and increasing our strength in every field and front.[17]

To which Herut's Ben Eliezer replied that his party never claimed it was necessary to kill 40 million Arabs: "No one plans to kill even one Arab." Retaliation raids did not solve the problem, he declared. Nasser was still in 1933 from the viewpoint of his power to attack Israel. "We can still keep him from carrying out the program, make the Egyptians return to Egypt and put a desert barrier between us. This will create conditions which may give us an opportunity for real peace with the Egyptian people, with whom we have no quarrel once its armies are in Egypt. We want to prevent a horrible war when conditions will be against us." [18] Thus the Herut line seemed to be that Israel should push Egypt out of Gaza and/or Sinai in a limited military operation.[19]

In the next debate on foreign policy Ben-Gurion sought to put an end to the argument by telling the Knesset that, while Israel would protect its borders against attack, it was firmly decided against the initiation of war because it considered that "the maintenance of peace is preferable even to victory in war." No lasting solution could be derived from war, he declared. Nor was war inevitable. As for retaliation, Israel was retaliating only after giving the United Nations a chance to set things aright.[20]

But Herut came back to the attack. In the debate on the defense levy on 22 April 1956, the party's Ya'qov Meridor said the

161

danger on the borders was rooted in the armistice lines, and in the war that was not finished in 1948.

If we had extended the borders to Jordan and Gaza in 1948, we would not need tens of thousands of soldiers to guard them all these years and suffer heavy losses. We have 960 kilometers of land borders which cannot be defended. We should have seized the opportunity—and there were opportunities—when public opinion was with us. . . . The danger grows because each day Nasser gets more pilots, tanks, drivers and heavy ammunition. To be strong is not the solution. Nasser will be stronger. If Israel had taken Gaza, Nasser would have fallen within a week. No one would have interfered. Russia would not have interfered, for fear of a new World War.

We have freedom of action as long as we still hold the advantage, especially on land, with our faithful army and the spirit of our forces. But what happens? We hold maneuvers, dress them for battle, open the supply depots, give them orders, but after a day we close them down again. Can one keep an army, and especially its officers, in perpetual suspense of that kind? The question must be solved once and for all.

After the liberation of Gaza, the conquest of Israel from the South will be impossible with the forces over which Egypt disposes today. Egypt would have to prepare another 50 years for such an attack, and we would have quiet. There would be incidents, yes, but no danger of annihilation. And if Jordan intervenes, we will have to solve that problem too.

Meridor said it was tragic for the national home that the government was divided on this question of all things, that there were such profound differences of opinion between the Prime Minister and the Foreign Minister. Let the majority of the Knesset decide in secret session for or against a liberation campaign, he said. "I maintain there is a majority here in favor of it—there is no other solution!" [21]

Two months later, on 18 June 1956, the differences between the Prime Minister and his Foreign Minister were resolved by Sharett's resignation.

Area Policy: The Sword and the Olive Branch

Until that day in June when Sharett resigned, the outward aspect of Israel's foreign policy after the Soviet arms deal was little different from what had gone before, except perhaps in its heightened intensity. In the area, there was still the ambivalence toward Egypt: the threat of retaliation, coupled with invitations to peaceful cooperation. Toward the powers, Israel renewed the plea for armaments to compensate for Egypt's superiority, and for an effective guarantee of its territorial integrity. To attain those aims, Israel's policy employed the gamut of means available to the small state. It sought to influence and mobilize friendly public opinion; turned to the world organization on the basis of the Charter and international law; drew attention to its nuisance value as a factor in the area, and appealed to the great powers' sense of fairness and justice. It was as though Israel, aware that a new situation confronted it, yet decided to give all the familiar means of policy another try, to test the efficacy of small-state diplomacy once more before embarking on a radically different course.

On 3 October 1955, only a few days after the announcement of the Soviet-Egyptian arms agreement, Ambassador Eban told the U.N. General Assembly that there were no problems outstanding between Israel and the Arab states which would by so much as a few weeks survive a mutual decision to solve them by negotiation.[22] Ben-Gurion, in his 2 November speech introducing the new government to the Knesset, made a new plea for peace with Egypt, professing his own readiness to meet with Nasser to prevent the dangers awaiting the two countries in the current situation and to negotiate a mutual agreement without any preconditions. This could be either a permanent peace with cooperation in the political, economic, and social spheres; or, if the other side was not ready for this, Israel would agree to a

163

limited arrangement based on full compliance with the armistice agreement, cessation of hostilities, including freedom of navigation, and the like. Egypt and the other Arab states, Ben-Gurion said, now had the opportunity to show whether they wanted war or peace.[23]

But there was an anticlimax the following day when an Israel force of battalion strength attacked Egyptian troops which had occupied positions in the al-Awja demilitarized zone within Israel and in a few hours' dogged fighting inflicted over one hundred casualties, among them about fifty dead.[24] The Egyptian force had entered Israeli territory on 26 October, and Israel at first appealed to the U.N. Truce Supervision Organization for its withdrawal. Egypt refused to withdraw and instead, according to the Israel report, increased its troops in the al-Awja area. In a statement after the attack, the Foreign Ministry spokesman reiterated Ben-Gurion's pledge to the Knesset that "Israel had never initiated a war and never will." But, said the spokesman, if Israel territory is invaded, the invader will be thrown out.

The al-Awja battle was the culmination of a protracted dispute over the demilitarized zone in which both sides were at one time in partial violation of the armistice agreement (see p. 108), but the Egyptian action in occupying positions on the Israel side of the international frontier was the most flagrant breach until the attack. Israel therefore had some justification for its drastic riposte on the basis of Begin's dictum that "in sovereignty, one kilometer is like a hundred."[25] Nevertheless, the timing of the attack was bound to deflate the Prime Minister's appeal to peace.

In a speech to the Knesset the day after the battle, Ben-Gurion was unambiguous about his attitude to the Egyptian leader: "I regret, too, the fact that 50 Egyptian soldiers were killed, for they were sacrificed not because of their evil intent and will, but because of the aggression of an ambitious dictator who plays with the lives of his countrymen."[26] A few days later, when General Burns paid his first call on the new Premier, Ben-Gurion told him that Israel wanted peace with Egypt but that, if Egypt would not make peace, Israel expected, as a minimum, strict adherence to the General Armistice Agreement. He reiterated that he would meet Nasser at any time to discuss peace or an improvement in relations. Burns remarked that it seemed to him that what stood between Israel and the Arab states was the refugees who had been displaced from Arab Palestine in 1948. To this Ben-Gurion replied by "giving the stereotyped Israeli answer"—that the refugees had left Palestine of their own accord, or rather on the orders of the Arab Higher Committee, and in accordance with its war plan against the newborn state. Nasser, too, reiterated that Egypt wanted peace when General Burns saw him a few days later. Orders to the forward troops not to fire were in effect; and there would be no retaliation by Egypt for the recent events in the demilitarized zone. But to Ben-Gurion's offer to meet him, Nasser made no comment. Burns reports that, to his knowledge, there were about four or five people who saw both Nasser and Ben-Gurion during the period from about midsummer 1955 to midsummer 1956, and who endeavored to discover common ground for the beginning of peace negotiations. "Both leaders were apparently very ready to give audiences and even encouragements to these amateur heralds of peace, whose well-intentioned efforts were unfortunately uniformly and completely unproductive." [27]

During the winter of 1955 there also took place a major Israel military operation on the Syrian border. In an attack on Syrian positions near the northern shore of Lake Tiberias on 11 December, 56 Syrians were killed, including 41 military personnel, 7 policemen and 8 civilians. A statement issued by the Foreign Ministry the same night said the attack was made because Syrian positions had opened fire on an Israeli police boat protecting fishermen on the east side of the lake. But even in the light of repeated earlier interference by Syrian fire with Israeli fishing in the lake, the retaliation seemed disproportionate to the

165

provocation. General Burns believes that the underlying reason for the attack was that Syria and Egypt had earlier concluded a mutual defense pact which provided for placing the forces of the two nations under a single command. He quotes an editorial in the *Jerusalem Post* of 14 December 1955 which strongly hints at a relationship between the raid and the military pact, asserting that "Egypt must now be considered as operating out of Syria, as well as through the Gaza Strip and Sinai." Burns reasoned that part of the motive for the Lake Tiberias action was to convey to the Syrians that they would do well not to link themselves too closely to Egypt, which did not have the power to defend Syrian territory.[28] Burns's report to the Security Council also pointed to embittered feelings in Israel because of the failure to agree on an exchange of prisoners with Syria; public opinion in Israel was "extremely agitated" about the fate of the Israeli captives who had been taken prisoner during an earlier foray into Syrian territory.

Before the next major punitive operation took place, now again directed against Egypt, Foreign Minister Sharett informed the Knesset on 2 January 1956 of the "peace plan" which Israel had communicated to the U.S. government as a basis for negotiation. He made it evident that the plan had been put forward in response to Washington's pressure for an indication of the price Israel was prepared to pay for peace, and also to counter the Western tendency to make proposals "which menace our vital interests." The plan itself, he wanted it known, merely subsumed under a single heading ideas which had been advanced at various stages in the past "concerning the forms of cooperation with neighboring countries and the facilities we should be ready to offer them in the spheres of commerce, communication and development on a reciprocal basis within the framework of peaceful relations." Sharett added that most of the suggestions were based on practices and customs which, in the civilized world, would normally govern the relationships of peoples living side

166

by side in peace and friendship. Only one of the proposals, "concerning the payment of compensation for abandoned Arab landed property, derived from the special circumstance of relations between Israel and her neighbors." Sharett made it clear that he himself was "extremely doubtful" whether all the talk about negotiations and settlement had any basis in the reality of the relationship between Israel and Egypt or the other Arab states. Nevertheless, he warned, "despite all our skepticism and caution, we are duty bound to seize every opportunity to explore the possibility of a settlement. . . . In one hand we will hold a weapon, and the other will be stretched out for peace." [29]

The Test of Diplomacy (I)—Security through a Guarantee

The "peace plan" was but the latest phase in what was to be Sharett's final effort at solving Israel's major problem through diplomacy. During the fall and winter he had been diligently pursuing a twofold aim: to obtain for Israel a firm guarantee of territorial integrity in the face of the new Egyptian-Soviet threat, and to obtain a supply of arms to match the Czech deliveries.

Neither of these objectives was new, of course: Israel had pleaded for both arms and a guarantee in the past. But now Sharett sounded the plea with a new, special urgency.

The result of Israel's earliest demand for a guarantee, it will be recalled, had been the Tripartite Declaration of 25 May 1950, which Israel had considered inadequate. The Declaration, in the words of Sharett, "undertook to preserve, as between Israel and the Arab states, the present territorial *status quo,* based on the armistice lines, as well as the existing balance of armed strength." While the government of Israel had heartily endorsed these two principles, it had failed to perceive, in the Declaration *per se* or in its actual text, any effective guarantee of their implementation. Now the advocates of a security treaty between Israel and the United States were simply "pursuing to its logical conclusion the

167

obligation enshrined in the three-power declaration, to prevent any attempt to alter by force the existing borders between Israel and her neighbors." [30]

Israel, in other words, wanted an automatic enforcement provision for the Tripartite Declaration. But up to now none of the Western powers had given any indication that they were serious about the Declaration as it stood. Not long before the Soviet-Egyptian arms agreement both the United Kingdom and the United States, in separate policy statements, had explicitly rejected the kind of guarantee Israel now asked for. Foreign Minister Eden told the House of Commons on 4 April 1955 that the final borders between Israel and its neighbors would be guaranteed provided the parties agreed on them.[31] And Secretary of State Dulles, in a major speech on the problems of the Middle East which he delivered on 26 August, also tied the signing of a future treaty and border guarantee to agreement by the Arab states.[32] President Eisenhower himself reiterated some months later that the United States would be willing to join in a formal treaty to guarantee the integrity of the Egypt-Israel border "if the two countries would settle their problems." [33] Naturally, all this was unacceptable to the Israelis, the more so since Dulles again spoke about "territory now occupied by Israel," a phrase which had proved to be unpopular once before. Said Begin:

There are no territories occupied by Israel. There is a legal state, and there are territories belonging to it, which are occupied by the enemy and the foreigner. . . . Dulles says that both sides have justified territorial demands. Yet Israel didn't demand parts outside its present territory—only the Arabs do. Israel's demand is to hold on to what she has. They are both justified—so let's compromise. Israel has to give up.[34]

Sharett, though welcoming the Dulles speech as giving signs, "in spite of certain prejudices on the part of the U.S. government, of recognizing the special problems of Israel," criticized its references to the borders as a tendency to "curtail the territory of Israel and to satisfy the Arab desire for aggrandizement, especially with regard to the Negev and Eilat." [35]

Sharett carried his case for a treaty of guarantee to Geneva, where the Big Four Foreign Ministers were meeting at the end of October, but President Eisenhower's message to the Madison Square Garden rally called to protest the arms shipments to Egypt showed no sign that Sharett's arguments had made any impact on U.S. policy. As for Eden's Guildhall speech, it represented a step backward as far as Israel was concerned. Quite apart from the suggestion that Israel agree to a compromise on its territory as between the present position and the 1947 partition borders, the speech did not so much as mention the Tripartite Declaration. In its editorial comment on the speech, the *Times* said the signatories of the Declaration had never regarded Israel's present boundaries as permanent, or the present guarantee against their violent infringement as more than a temporary stabilizing expedient. [36]

Among the political parties, the desire for a security treaty with the United States and a guarantee of the border was by no means unanimous. Begin and his group were, as usual, in the opposition. The quest for a guarantee was an illusion, Begin said. Israel had one guarantee only: its fighting youth. "To ask for a guarantee was a mistake, to receive it would be a disaster. Our fate would be like that of the Czechoslovakia of Benes." [37] Begin was caustic about the "mutuality" of a security treaty with the United States. "If the Mexican army will invade the United States, we will help," he mocked. "In this generation he [Sharett] wants a guarantee from a great power to a small state surrounded by enemies—when all the guarantees go up in smoke. This is an illusion."

Meir Argov of Mapai disagreed. He recalled how the powers honored their guarantee of Belgium's neutrality in World War I. He did not believe that a guarantee was an anachronism—every state belonged to some security framework. A fervent supporter of the idea of guarantees, Argov said that "whoever negates this demand refuses to face reality, and relies on the doubtful anchor which is called neutrality. Even mighty Russia has allies for her defense . . . even the U.S. and Britain do not rely on their own power alone." If a guarantee is not given to Israel, he warned, "a situation may be created which will force on Israel a defensive war." [38]

Mapam called for a change toward neutrality—the kind of guarantee that was needed was a four-power gaurantee. The party spokesman said he was not afraid of Communist penetration of the Middle East.[39]

The communique issued at the conclusion of the talks between President Eisenhower and Prime Minister Eden in Washington on 1 February 1956 was particularly inconclusive when it came to the two powers' position on the application of the Tripartite Declaration. "We made arrangements for joint discussions as to the nature of action to be taken if the contingency arises," it said.[40] Thus the original language and intent of the Declaration were diluted. It was apparent that the two powers' differences in interpreting the Declaration, already revealed in 1955, had not been overcome. A month later, Anthony Nutting made his government's attitude unmistakable in a House of Commons debate. He said he was against a territorial guarantee committing the United Kingdom to a permanent recognition of a frontier which was not agreed upon—which resulted from an armistice and not from a peace treaty; which was bitterly opposed by all the Arab states. Such a guarantee, he said, would be the biggest step away from a peace settlement.[41]

The Tripartite Declaration was a declaration of intention by the signatory powers in two separate areas: one concerned the prevention of an imbalance in armaments as between the Arab states and Israel; the second the alteration of the armistice lines by force. There was a basic difference in the mode of enforcement required for each area. The first required observance on a continuing basis, but there was room for differing opinions as to whether it was being observed properly. Israel frequently complained that it was not; the Western powers asserted that the arms they were supplying to some of the Arab states were not creating the imbalance of which the Declaration spoke. This part of the Declaration lost its significance in September 1955, when the great power which was not a signatory began to ship arms to one side in large quantities.

The second part required a binding commitment of enforcement to give it meaning. Israel's quest for a separate security guarantee showed that it had no faith in the Declaration without such a commitment, and the powers' refusal to grant such a guarantee pointed up the flaw in the Declaration. But its *de facto* demise came in April 1956, when Washington announced that, in the event of aggression, it would place primary emphasis on action through the United Nations, which in effect meant subjecting enforcement measures to a Soviet veto in the Security Council. Moreover, President Eisenhower stressed his intention to act only "within constitutional means," indicating that no forces would be sent to the area without approval of Congress.

The Test of Diplomacy (II)—The Quest for Armaments

Simultaneously with the demand for a guarantee, Israel asked the West for arms. Like the request for a guarantee, the call for weapons had been sounded before without substantial success.[42] The new U.S. Assistant Secretary of State for Near East Affairs, John D. Jernegan, had explained before the Czech arms deal why the United States had turned a deaf ear to Israel's request:

In my opinion, Israel as a nation is not in danger, except to the extent that all other states in the Near East are in danger from common threats of outside aggression. . . . Relative to others in the region, the Israeli military establishment is highly developed, and enjoys the advantage of holding interior lines. What is even more important,

I do not see evidence on the part of any of her neighbors to attack Israel.[43]

Would the impact of the arms transaction be sufficient to cause the State Department to change its mind?

Israel's request now was for quantities large enough to redress the balance which the Czech arms deal had upset. Ambassador Eban launched the campaign for arms in the United States when he declared that "the dynamic efforts of Egypt must be met by equally dynamic efforts . . . to create a counter-balance by specific acts, by those who want stability in the Middle East." The framework, he said, was the agreement signed in 1954 under the Mutual Security Act in which the United States offered Israel, in principle, an opportunity to purchase arms under a reimbursement arrangement. Israel was not asking for a new policy, only an application of the old.[44]

Sharett set the keynote for his own campaign of personal diplomacy when by telling the Knesset on 18 October: "Because the obtaining of arms is for us an imperative military and defensive necessity—that is to say, a first essential for existence—we will not hesitate to obtain them from every possible source." [45] But at the Big Four Foreign Ministers' Meeting in Geneva Sharett was told by the U.S. Secretary of State that any military aid which the United States would give would be primarily in the form of defensive weapons; the United States had no intention of matching the Czech supplies to Egypt. Britain's Macmillan stuck by the terms of the Tripartite Declaration, seeing no need to go beyond it. The two Western powers, above all, disliked the idea of a four-power approach, because it interfered with their carefully nurtured Northern Tier concept. This did not keep Sharett from seeing Soviet Foreign Minister Molotov and warning him that the Soviet arms supplies to Egypt were threatening to set the Middle East in flames which might spread beyond control. The Soviet action, he told the Russian, was contrary to the Geneva Spirit of settling international disputes by peaceful means.[46]

Sharett's arguments seem to have impressed both the French Foreign Minister, Antoine Pinay, and Premier Edgar Faure (whom he saw in Paris). For a number of months previously, top officials of Israel's defense establishment had been making friends for Israel's cause among their counterparts in France, but the resistance of the Quai d'Orsay had prevented a consummation of these secret negotiations. On 12 November, however, an agreement was signed at last whereby Israel was to receive twelve of France's latest jet fighter planes, the Mystère IV, as well as an equal number of the earlier Ouragan model. Although delivery of these coveted weapons was still a good many months away, the ice had been broken.[47]

Sharett also drew some encouragement from the fact that Washington at least had agreed to "consider sympathetically" Israel's request for defensive arms. Consequently, a detailed list of requirements was submitted to the U.S. government in the middle of November. At the beginning of January Sharett was still not able to give the Knesset any positive word on the status of the request, except to report that the list had been the subject of detailed negotiations, with the Defense Department giving it "swift and active consideration." But the decision in principle—presumably by the Department of State—had been delayed and "we still have not received the promised reply." However, he assured the House, the government would renew its effort in the new year to bring negotiations to a quick conclusion.[48]

There had been persistent reports in Israel that Washington was using the 11 December raid against Syria as grounds for shelving Israel's request, and that the raid had pulled the rug out from under Sharett while he was abroad on his mission. Sharett made no reference to this in his statement to the Knesset.

At the same Knesset session, Ben-Gurion joined his Foreign Minister in the plea for arms. He said it was his duty to draw the attention of the Knesset and the people of Israel, and of decent public opinion in the world, to the terrible danger and pernicious objective of this flow of Soviet arms to Egypt, which was being augmented by a flow of British arms, also being sent to the military junta in Cairo. These arms, Soviet and British, were intended exclusively for an attack against Israel. "We demand, and we have the right to obtain, defensive arms not inferior in quality to the aggressive arms streaming into Egypt." If Israel receives the arms to redress the balance of power, he added significantly, it is almost certain that there will be no war.[49]

The arguments Israel used to back up its demands were mainly of two kinds: (1) Israel addressed itself to the international community at large, calling on it to forestall a local conflict which might result in a much wider conflagration, and which would become well-nigh inevitable if the balance of armaments were not redressed; and (2) at the same time Israel also addressed the West, and in particular the United States, on a twofold basis—the Western powers had an obligation to implement the Tripartite Declaration which called for maintenance of a balance of armaments, and since Egypt had now aligned itself with the Soviet bloc, it was logical that Israel should receive support from the West.[50]

It was to be expected that the theme of Egypt's alignment with the East as against Israel's loyalty to the West should be taken up with fervor by American Jewish organizations and their public relations arms. The call for a stepped-up information campaign to bring Israel's case to the U.S. public once again went forth in the Knesset,[51] and indeed Sharett's American tour in December 1955 had been devoted to a large extent to bringing Israel's case before the mass media.

Although there was no official rejection from the State Department for some months to come, there were intermittent hints that nothing would come of Israel's request for arms. Notwithstanding the Soviet arms deliveries to Egypt, the Department professed to see no immediate danger to Israel.[52] On 7 February 1956, Dulles wrote to a group of forty members of the House of Representatives solicitous of Israel's welfare that Israel could never win an arms race against the Arabs, who had access to Soviet-controlled supplies. While reiterating that U.S. foreign policy embraced the preservation of Israel, he said that the disparity in arms could not be offset by additional purchases on Israel's part. After all, he commented, Israel's population was only two million, and its security would be better assured by means other than an arms race. Equal or superior arms in Israel's hands were not the only deterrent to aggression, he wrote to the Congressmen. Israel was the creation of the United Nations, by whose charter all states were bound. He also made reference to the Tripartite Declaration, even though it was only two days since the inconclusive Anglo-American communique had been released.[53]

The Test of Diplomacy (III)—Pressure for Concessions

Under these circumstances, the United States–Israel dialogue had once again taken on the form of pressure on the part of the United States and determination on Israel's part to resist it. Sharett said as much when he told the Knesset in November that "the powers are now more interested in the possibility of a solution, perhaps in the belief that our difficulties make us more amenable to concessions. This is an illusion we must constantly dispel." [54] With all the increase in its military preparedness, he said, Israel would continue to work for peace, but would not buy peace at the price of concessions that sapped its ability to live, and encourage further encroachments and destructive schemes against it.

What were these concessions which were now being urged upon Israel as the price of possible peace? Both Britain and the United States had suggestions to make, the former in more general terms but from the public platform, the latter making more detailed proposals in diplomatic conversations. There are indications that the thinking of the two governments had been coordinated, and that some plan for a settlement based on substantial concessions on the part of Israel had been worked out before the Soviet arms deal was consummated. After that, as Sharett emphasized, Israel's worsened diplomatic position made the time seem propitious for a concerted approach. Eden writes that after the signing of the Suez treaty, the United States and the United Kingdom for a whole year "plodded steadily after schemes" to improve relations between Israel and the Arabs." [55] This is corroborated by a former State Department official who relates that the United States and Britain in October of 1954 "made a thorough study of all the possibilities" and even worked out draft peace treaties which they planned to discuss separately with Egypt and Israel. In his view, it was the Gaza raid, revealing as it did the utter weakness of Egypt's defenses, which made the project come to naught.[56]

Secretary Dulles' speech of 26 August 1955 before the Council on Foreign Relations [57] brought in its wake protracted discussions in the course of which Washington suggested that Israel cede a part of the Southern Negev as a land bridge to Egypt. Sharett told the Knesset that Israel was determined to reject these demands—it was inconceivable that Eilat should be given up.[58]

In his Guildhall speech, Sir Anthony Eden called for a settlement based on a compromise between the area allotted to Israel in the Partition Resolution, and its present territory. The reaction in Israel was far more violent than it had been to the State Department's suggestions. Sharett gave two reasons for the difference in Israel's attitude: "The United States did not make its proposals public, and it does not support the 1947 settlement, as far as we know." [59] The 1947 resolution, he explained, was a mere recommendation, applicable under the prevailing circumstances and then only as an integral whole. Eden's proposal, while it has the "semblance of impartiality and equal justice, is in effect logically fallacious, legally incongruous and morally untenable," Sharett contended.[60]

176

Ben-Gurion had said much the same thing—though with not quite the same flourish—in an explosive reaction shortly after the Eden speech: The invasion of Israel by the Arab states had made all the U.N. resolutions null and void; Sir Anthony Eden's proposals amounted to dismemberment of Israel and a reward to the Arab aggressors of 1948. They were likely to encourage and intensify Arab aggressiveness. Israel, the Premier vowed, would not conduct negotiations on such a basis.[61]

The fact that Nasser seemed not displeased with the Guildhall speech, discerning in it a "constructive attitude," no doubt increased the Israelis' resentment.[62] Israel had discarded the 1947 resolution as a basis for peace negotiations five years earlier in the talks with the P.C.C.; the Arabs were quite content to revert to it now that Israel was under pressure. In October, Victor Khoury of Lebanon had told the U.N. General Assembly that a solution to the Palestine problem might be found if "a real, sincere effort was made to exert pressure on Israel to abide by the resolutions of the General Assembly and to respond to the requirements of justice and fairness." [63] The fact that Nuri es-Said was willing to see a settlement of the Palestine question based on "U.N. resolutions" and was urging Foreign Secretary Eden to press Israel for concessions also could not have escaped Jerusalem's attention.[64] Indeed, there were reports from Cairo that British Ambassador Humphrey Trevelyan was talking "almost daily" with the Prime Minister and with Foreign Minister Mahmud Fawzi and that "major developments toward a solution" might be expected in the immediate future. According to these reports, the British were not discouraged by the Israeli outburst against the Eden proposals, hoping that, if territorial concessions in the Negev should prove to be the price of peace, "Israel will regard the immediate economic gains of peace as decisively outweighing the loss of still largely barren territory." [65]

The reports were given added substance when Foreign Minister Macmillan told Commons in opening a foreign policy debate on 12 December that he had "heard for the first time from many leading Arab figures who take the view that a final settlement must now be worked for." He, too, admonished the Israelis that "any compromise must involve some sacrifice from them also," while holding out the prospect of the material and moral gains to be won through peace.[66] Yet in his memoirs, Sir Anthony thought the Guildhall speech was a mistake. "Once Russian arms had begun to flow into Egypt, it was unwise to raise the issue of frontiers," he reflected.[67]

It became clear to Israel's policy-makers, during this period of pressure for concessions, that Egypt's price for peace had not become cheaper as a result of its newly acquired strength. Nasser said so bluntly to Richard Crossman, who later told it to General Yigal Allon: no peace was possible unless Israel surrendered the Southern Negev and Eilat. Once there was peace, his reasoning went, Israel would not need an outlet on the Red Sea, as it could then use the Suez Canal.[68]

With the price for peace spelled out, it was also obvious that the *status quo* represented the optimum Israel could expect, and that there was nothing to gain from negotiation. Negotiations are entered into under one of two conditions: expectation of gain, or duress. While the attainment of peaceful relations with the Arab states would have been a gain, it was feared that the concessions would outweigh the gain, so that the outcome would be a net loss. As long as this was believed to be the case, pressure for negotiation and offers of mediation would continue to be resisted. The pressure did not assume proportions of duress. Begin's question—"the decisive question of our day," as he told the Knesset—was whether a small state could resist the pressure of great powers. In the thirties, he said, the impression was that it could not. In the fifties, it was proved possible, provided the powers found they had something hard in their grip. He cited as examples Yugoslavia and Formosa. The small state, he warned, must not be ready to make concessions, for once it offers concessions at a time of pressure it only invites more pressure upon itself.[69]

Israel offered no new concessions, and found it possible to resist great-power pressure. The day after Sharett's resignation as Foreign Minister, Ben-Gurion told the Knesset that "we must strengthen ourselves in order to be able to say 'no' to the greatest powers in the world and to stick to it." [70]

A New Cycle of Violence

In March of 1956 another cycle of infiltration and retaliation began on the Gaza demarcation line. On 22 March, eleven Israeli settlers were wounded near Gvulot, opposite the Strip, when a tractor-drawn cart was blown up by a land mine. A week later, Israel asked the United Nations to investigate three Egyptian attacks on the border; one Egyptian infiltrator was killed, one captured, and five others wounded in the engagements. On 30 March, Egypt accused an Israeli patrol of killing two Arab farmers in a burst of fire across the line. The following day, Egyptian infiltrators attempting to harvest Israeli grain were fired upon. The Israelis charged that the Egyptians had opened machine-gun fire to protect the illicit harvesters. On 3 April, an Israeli soldier was killed and three wounded in a clash in the Nirim area, just two days after the Egyptian command in Gaza had announced new measures to stop infiltration. The Israeli army charged that one of their patrols had been ambushed, and that a relief unit approaching the scene was also attacked. On 4 April, three Israeli soldiers were killed in an exchange of fire near Qisufim. Not since September 1955 had the Gaza line seen such heavy firing. On 5 April the Israelis retaliated, this time by shelling Gaza with 120-mm. mortar fire which killed 56 of the town's inhabitants and wounded 103 more.

According to General Burns, the shelling was ordered by a local Israeli commander following a day in which machine-gun, mortar, and artillery fire had been exchanged almost incessantly, notwithstanding the appeals of the chairman of the Egyptian-Israeli M.A.C. for a cease-fire. Israel contended that the shelling had been aimed at a military headquarters in Gaza; but the United Nations "found no evidence that there was such a headquarters in the vicinity of the impact area." [71] The argument on this point soon subsided, however, for within a few days a series of Egyptian *fidayun* raids took up the limelight. General Burns recalls: "By about 10 o'clock on the night of April 7th messages began to come in reporting attacks during the day on vehicles on the Beersheba–Tel Aviv road. By 1 A.M., seven attacks had been reported, including grenade throwings and demolitions. It was clear that the *fidayun* operations had begun on a large scale." [72]

By the time the attacks ceased on 11 April, nearly a dozen Israelis had been killed and more injured. Among the victims of the attacks were five children in a religious boarding school near Ramleh who had been killed while reciting their prayers. All the other victims were also civilians. The Egyptian press hailed the *fidayun* in extravagant terms, acclaiming them as "heroes back from the battlefield . . . who taught Israel a lesson she will never forget." [73]

The end of the raids coincided with the arrival of Secretary General Hammarskjold in the Middle East on a mission on behalf of the Security Council. The Council's resolution called upon him to prepare a survey of the various aspects of enforcement of, and compliance with, the four General Armistice Agreements between Israel and its Arab neighbors, as well as compliance with the Security Council resolutions passed during the previous year. [74] Thus the United Nations once more stepped into the breach in an effort to prop up the *status quo*.

In contrast to the Western powers' efforts, Hammarskjold's attempts at mediation took place, as it were, on a tactical level. By obtaining assurances on observation of the armistice from

Egypt and Israel, as well as from Syria, Lebanon, and Jordan, Hammarskjold temporarily prevented escalation of the guerrilla warfare into a more serious explosion. But he did not bring the parties any closer to a permanent settlement. He was not able to obtain from Egypt the assurances which Israel sought concerning freedom of navigation in the Suez Canal and the Gulf of Aqaba. Hammarskjold himself was content with a narrow interpretation of his mandate from the Security Council, which asked him to negotiate about the demarcation line, the demilitarized zone and defensive areas. Questions outside that mandate, he pointed out in his report, depended on the "governments' willingness to discuss them." [75] General Burns writes that, had the engagements obtained by the Secretary General been kept, they would have ensured stability under the general framework of the armistice agreements. At the same time, he concedes that, looking back, "one can see that by the spring of 1956, the currents which were bearing the antagonists in the Middle East toward the whirlpool of war, were too strong to be stemmed just by diplomatic intervention, or changed by simple mediation by third parties, including the United Nations, and its agent, the Secretary General." [76]

CHAPTER VIII ≺≺≺≺
The Final Phase

Any nation which faces war as a possibility is necessarily engaged in the formulation of strategic plans, and it is clear from General Dayan's diary that Israel had evolved a strategic plan having as its objective the penetration of the Sinai Peninsula and the Gaza Strip some considerable time before the start of the campaign. The crucial element, however, is the plan's execution, and here speculation was rife following the campaign as to when Israel made the decision to intervene at its southern border. One observer saw in the al-Awja battle the key to the campaign, since it secured Israel's access to the vital road junction which was the gateway to the peninsula. In support of his hypothesis he noted that Dag Hammarskjold had been fully aware of the demilitarized area's strategic importance and had asked Israel to evacuate it. He saw another piece of circumstantial evidence pointing in the same direction in the fact that, in the agreement to station U.N. observers on the Gaza border which Hammarskjold worked out during his mission in the spring, Israel put a six-month time limit on the arrangement which expired on 31 October, two days after D-day.[1] Dayan puts such speculation to rest. He reveals that, on 23 October 1955, Ben-Gurion, while still only Minister of Defense, instructed him to be prepared to capture the Egyptian positions controlling the Straits of Tiran in order to open the waterway to Israel shipping—an operation which obviously required invasion of the Sinai peninsula. Ten days later, Ben-

182

Gurion assumed the premiership in place of Moshe Sharett, and promptly thereafter he sought the approval of the Cabinet for his plan. The Cabinet turned him down, deciding that the moment was not propitious. But Ben-Gurion's colleagues did not rule out the idea categorically. Israel should act, they decided, "in the place and at the time she deems appropriate." [2] When General Dayan was informed of this, he protested that time would weaken Israel's position relative to the Egyptian armed forces, especially in the air. Failure to act immediately, he contended in a letter to Ben-Gurion, would be a *de facto* surrender of freedom of shipping and of overflight in the Straits. (Since 1953, Egypt had blocked passage of Israel ships through the Straits of Tiran; in September of 1955 it also interdicted flights of the El Al Airline over the narrow waterway—the shortest route from Israel to South Africa without flying over Arab territory). General Dayan advocated capture of the Straits positions "within one month," but the Prime Minister let himself be governed by the Cabinet's negative attitude.[3]

Less than a year later, shortly before launching the Sinai Campaign, Ben-Gurion again went before the Cabinet to request its approval.[4] This time consent was forthcoming. What were the new circumstances that now made "time and place" seem appropriate?

The Friendship with France

In the spring and summer, Israel's position vis-à-vis Egypt was affected by two new elements which had the effect of bringing preventive war within the realm of feasibility.

By April, it was "clear beyond doubt that the U.S. will not give us any arms." [5] And yet arms were received—from a different source. If neither the United States nor Britain found it compatible with their interests to supply Israel with its defensive requirements, the position of the third Western ally, France, was

183

entirely different. Here a genuine community of interest between the two countries had developed, unrelated to the Cold War: namely common opposition to Abdel Nasser and his policies. It happened that his accession to power coincided with France's military involvement in Algeria, and his policy of granting aid and comfort to the rebellion manifested itself at about the same time that military clashes along the Israeli demarcation line occurred with increasing frequency.

Agents of Israel's Ministry of Defense had been active in France ever since 1954 attempting to persuade military and government circles that the sale of arms to Israel would be in France's interest. But, much as in Israel at that time, the Defense and Foreign ministries were pursuing divergent and often uncoordinated policies, and the Israelis' efforts were repeatedly frustrated by the Quai d'Orsay just when they seemed on the verge of success. It was only with the advent of the Guy Mollet government in January 1956 that a more consistent policy began to evolve. This policy became clearly pro-Israel later in the spring, after the new government's steps in the direction of an understanding with both the Algerian rebels and President Nasser ended in failure.[6] Despite Nasser's assurance to Foreign Minister Pineau during the latter's visit to Cairo on 14 March that Egypt wished to help in a peaceful settlement of the North African problem, the Arab League Council two weeks later resolved to "support the sons of Arabia in Algeria." At about the same time the United States, never unsympathetic to Israel's request but apprehensive about its effect on the Arab states if American arms were to go to Israel in quantity, referred the Israeli list to France, indicating that there would be no objection if certain types of French arms were delivered to Israel. On 15 April France announced the sale to Israel of the twelve Mystère jet fighters on which agreement had been reached earlier; shortly thereafter it became known that the United States had given its blessing to the transaction as fitting in with the concept of balanced arms de-

altered Israel's position in relation to the West. For the first time, it ranged the United States and Britain squarely in opposition to Nasser and therefore temporarily removed the danger of appeasement of Egypt at Israel's expense. Secretary Dulles' intent to reduce the Egyptian leader's prestige, if successful, could only redound to Israel's advantage. The immediate official motive cited by Dulles for his decision, that the Egyptian economy would be unable to meet its share of the construction cost of the dam,[13] was also of direct interest to Israel: the pressure on the economy resulted primarily from the Czech arms deal by which Egypt was said to have mortgaged $200 million worth of as yet unplanted cotton. Israel now had the satisfaction of knowing that the American Secretary of State shared its assessment of the Egyptian leader and his intentions. As for Britain, a basic change in policy toward Egypt had already been under way as a result of the frustrated Templer mission to Jordan in December 1955 and the subsequent dismissal of Brigadier Glubb, both of which were strongly associated in British minds with Egyptian machinations.

There was also a moral in the substantive act of withdrawing the offer, which had been made quite unabashedly in an effort to outbid the Soviets in the economic sphere.[14] Now Dulles' move, made on the assumption that the Russians were unwilling at this point to finance the project, came to show Nasser that he could not indefinitely play off the East against the West. But while the blow to his prestige came from the direction of the United States, Egypt's coup was directed primarily at the British and the French. While the United States saw the area not in terms of its own vital interest, but as one sector in a far-flung front in which the foe was not the Egyptian ruler but the Soviet Union, the stakes for Britain and France were much higher: the nationalization posed a threat to their economic life and that of Western Europe as a whole. Not surprisingly, the British thought in terms of force at once and made no secret of it. "Failure to keep the canal international would inevitably lead to the loss, one by one, of all of our interests and assets in the Middle East, and even if Her Majesty's Government had to act alone, they could not stop short of using force to protect their position." [15] This was the recorded opinion of the British government the day after the nationalization was announced. France, too, while not as immediately affected as Britain by the seizure, was in no mood to let Nasser have his way. The French were concerned, above all, that Egypt's success would give heart to the Algerian nationalists and further undermine the French position in North Africa. Although at this point Dulles still assured his partners that the United States would not object to the use of force if all other measures should fail,[16] it was apparent that the U.S. interests were not engaged to a comparable extent, and that it would therefore be far more reluctant to precipitate an armed conflict than its European allies.[17]

For Israel, July 26 brought another turning point. Nasser countered the American attempt to reduce his influence and prestige and "converted what had looked like a major fiasco into a popular triumph which resounded throughout the Arab world." [18] Now all depended on the manner in which the West would answer the Egyptian's challenge. If the West succeeded in making him "disgorge," [19] then the Egyptian danger to Israel too might recede. If, on the other hand, he could get away with the nationalization without having significant restraints put upon him, then the outlook for Israel would be bleak.

The Israelis therefore viewed with mounting apprehension the evidence that the American government was prepared to accept Egyptian control of the Canal, with only "such concessions to appearances as could be wheedled out of Col. Nasser." [20]

Dulles' alternative to force at first was the proposal to reroute shipping around the Cape so as to bypass the Canal. But he did not make any concrete offer to have the United States pay the extra cost. By this omission the chance to counter the nationalization by leaving Egypt the Canal without the revenue was dissipated. There began a series of negotiations culminating in Dulles' second major alternative to force, namely the establishment of an international board to supervise the operation of the Canal, of which Egypt would be one member, with an arbitral commission to settle disputes. The proposal also provided for maintenance of the Canal as a "free, open and secure international waterway"; "insulation of the Canal from the influence of the politics of any nation"; and "due regard to the sovereign rights of Egypt." [21] Of the twenty-two user nations convened in London between 16 and 23 August, four—Ceylon, India, Indonesia, and the Soviet Union—refused to approve the proposal. The other eighteen set up a committee headed by Australian Prime Minister Robert Menzies to present the proposal to Egypt.

The Menzies mission, which was in Cairo from 3 to 7 September, met with a point-blank refusal by Nasser to accept the eighteen-nation proposal.

Dulles' next suggestion was for the creation of a Suez Canal Users Association which would employ pilots, be responsible for coordination of traffic through the Canal, and collect dues. Egypt was to receive appropriate payment for facilities provided by it. Egypt's President denounced the idea vehemently, but the S.C.U.A. was nevertheless brought into being on 21 September at a third meeting in London by the eighteen states that had previously backed the Menzies assignment. The Association was apparently written off as still-born by Britain and France, who viewed it as another effort by Dulles to press them to postpone their operational plans and tie their hands militarily.[22] In the meantime, the initial resolution on the part of the Conservative cabinet to resort to force was blunted when the Labor party decided to oppose a policy of resolute action, and their decision found a wide echo in the country at large, causing misgivings even in the cabinet itself. Then, in addition to pressure from the United States against the use of force, India ranged itself on the side of those opposing action and assumed its customary role as a mediator. The Soviet Union, although it had attended the twenty-two-nation conference of principal Suez users, was determined to obstruct rather than support effective Western action.

On 23 September the British and French governments, discouraged by the failure of direct negotiations, took their case to the Security Council over the opposition of Dulles,[23] who correctly foresaw that the Soviets would veto any meaningful resolution and thereby score a point in the Cold War. After strenuous efforts by Mr. Hammarskjold had resulted in agreement among Britain, France, and Egypt on "six principles" to be applied to the operation of the Canal, the Soviets vetoed the implementing section of the resolution which called on Egypt to cooperate with the S.C.U.A.[24]

With that Soviet veto, the U.N. chapter of the Suez episode came to an inconclusive end. The Users' Association continued in existence, on paper at least, but a difference developed among the members as to whether tolls should be withheld from the newly constituted Egyptian Canal Authority. France and Great Britain once again felt they did not have the backing of the United States in this crucial question and were being pressed to negotiate further from a position of weakness, while Egypt consolidated its unilateral control of the Canal.

For Israel, the outcome of the Security Council deliberations confirmed the worst apprehensions. The course of events had shown that the United States not only was unwilling to make Egypt "disgorge," but also was determined to keep Britain and France from using force. Moreover, Israel's own interests had been ignored in all the diplomatic activity leading up to the submission of the dispute to the United Nations, the question of freedom of shipping for Israel having been studiously avoided by all the powers concerned. While the 13 October draft resolution proclaimed the principle of freedom of navigation in the Canal, Israel's experience with the 1951 and 1954 resolutions had been that none of the powers would stand up for Israel's rights. And with the section on implementation proposed by Britain and France cut from the resolution by the Russian veto, all that remained was a set of principles with no provision for enforcement. There was no doubt in the minds of the Israelis that, if the U.N. decision was to be the last word in the Suez dispute, Egypt would emerge stronger from the affair than she had been before.

Although freedom for its shipping in the Canal was the test for any international arrangement for settlement of the dispute as far as Israel was concerned,[25] its policy had been one of restraint. This brought a grudging compliment from Cairo radio, which congratulated Israel for "not siding with the imperialists." [26] Moreover, Egypt again allowed some ships under Israel orders—but not under the Israel flag—to transit the Canal in August.[27]

While Herut's Menahem Begin continued to call for preventive war, Ben-Gurion told a Mapai congress late in August that Israel would not start such a war, because there was no certainty it would end in victory. Great forces outside the Arab world would deploy their power against Israel, he predicted, yet Israel's army was not designed to measure its strength against forces outside the region.

All of the advice to start a preventive war, even if its source is not in fascistic demagoguery, is false and misleading. A war which is not forced upon us by others will not solve any of our problems, even if it ends in a victory, and there is no assurance that a war initiated by us will end in a victory. Because great powers outside the Arab realm may in such an event intervene against us with their military might, both in the East and the West, and the Defense Army of Israel is not designed to stand up against such world powers. And so the first principle of our policy is to maintain the peace— even a bad peace, to the extent that this depends upon us.[28]

In an interview on the occasion of his seventieth birthday, he told a reporter for the *Jerusalem Post* on 21 September: "A war? There is no need for a war. They can see our strength with-

191

out that. As long as it is for me to decide, we shall make no war. . . . I will never make war. Never. You can tell anybody that." But he added: "Of course, if anybody attacks us, that is another matter." [29]

The Strategic Position

It has been shown, nevertheless, that the thought of preventive war had been very much in the minds of the Israelis since the Czech arms deal.

Access to French armament, especially aircraft, armor, and antitank weapons of a type designed to match the Egyptian acquisitions, could only temporarily offset the Egyptian advantage. The French weapons deliveries, in spite of the political affinity which made them possible, were being paid for at commercial rates; Egypt's relationship with the Soviet Union was such that it assured Egypt almost unlimited access to the weapons production and technology of a great power, on terms far more advantageous than anything Israel had been able to obtain. Granted that both powers were incapable of engaging in all-out warfare on the basis of their own means, Egypt had proved to be in a better position to exploit its influence base for weapons procurement.

From the Israel army's viewpoint, a ratio of three to one in equipment (when applied to all the Arab armies combined, or 2.5 to one when applied to Egypt alone) was considered acceptable, in that Arab superiority on that scale could be countered by superior morale and technical and combat skills. But the Soviet arms deal threatened to bring Arab superiority to as high as six to one, and this the army chiefs found alarming.[30]

Even if the three powers had been sincere in enforcing the arms ban provision of the Tripartite Declaration and Israel had exaggerated the effect of the Western supplies to Egypt and Iraq on the military balance, the Russian involvement had made their influence in this sphere meaningless.

The prospect of decisive Egyptian superiority also called into question the Israeli strategy of being ready to defend against attack, to halt a possible Egyptian offensive before it could penetrate deeply, and to hit back with a counteroffensive. Egyptian superiority in armor and aircraft would make the lack of depth of Israel's defensive position more of a liability than before. At the same time, Egypt had shown that it had developed in the *fidayun* an effective weapon of guerrilla warfare as an answer to Israel's policy of retaliation and demonstration of force. It was reasonable to expect that the prestige success in the contest with the West over Suez would give the Egyptian leader a new impetus for planning a second round against Israel, and it became increasingly doubtful whether the concept of strategic defense which had hitherto prevailed among Israel's planners would stand up against an attack under these circumstances.

But in October of 1956 the Soviet deliveries had, according to all estimates, not yet resulted in Egyptian tactical superiority. The equipment was there, to be sure, but not the ability to use it. The officer material was as yet the Egyptian army's weakest link, and the fighting personnel as a whole had not had time to become sufficiently acquainted with the Soviet weapons, on the ground and in the air. Whatever reforms Nasser had succeeded in bringing about had scarcely made a dent as yet in Egypt's traditionally low standards of living and education, militating against startling changes.[31] As against this, the prestige and morale of the Israeli army was high. In a Knesset speech on 30 October 1960, Ben-Gurion recalled that in July 1953 he had asked for an extended leave which he utilized to make a basic examination of the security situation. On 18 October of that year, shortly before his retirement, he gave the government a detailed report of his study and recommended a three-year plan to strengthen the country's defenses. After the Cabinet approved this plan, he announced his wish to resign. The three-year plan, Ben-Gurion revealed, was carried out almost in its entirety and proved its efficiency in the supreme test, the Sinai Compaign.[32] Ben-Gurion's study may have been prompted by the fact that the large numbers of new immigrants who had come into the army after the War of Independence had perceptibly lowered its efficiency from the peak combat effectiveness attained in the fighting. As part of the reforms recommended by Ben-Gurion, the newly appointed Chief of Staff, General Moshe Dayan, sent the best and most intelligent cadres into the fighting units instead of assigning them to staff jobs as before. He instituted a toughening up program, especially among officers, and insisted that they take the lead in battle as had been the tradition during the 1948–1949 fighting. As a result of these and similar measures, the Israel Defense Army was by 1956 once again a hard-hitting, aggressive force.[33]

While Nasser was busy at the Suez Canal, offensive preparations in the Sinai Peninsula area bordering Israel had consisted mainly in setting up supply dumps of Russian materiel; the positions established earlier under German advisers continued to be of an essentially defensive nature. Moreover, under the threat of armed intervention in the Canal dispute by Britain and France, Egypt had withdrawn a large part of its Sinai garrison to the area of the Canal.

But while the tactical advantage thus continued to be with Israel, its strategic position was further eroded by the latest and apparently effective attempt at establishing a unified Arab command. Such endeavors, under Egyptian initiative, had been made previously; but no effective joint command which could have been a threat to Israel's security had resulted from any of the paper pacts. Now, however, there arose a distinct possibility that the three states whose strategic position in relation to Israel complemented one another might bring their armies under a common direction. Following the return of the pro-Nasser government in Jordan's elections of 21 October, an agreement among Egypt,

194

Jordan, and Syria was announced on the twenty-fourth, its main provision being a joint command of the three armies under the overall orders of General Abd al-Hakim Amir of Egypt.

The Crisis Over Jordan

Throughout September and the first half of October, renewed reprisals against Jordan drew attention away from any planning in the direction of Egypt. The number of incidents along the Jordan border had registered a steady increase ever since the dismissal of General Glubb in the spring, culminating in what may be loosely described as *fidayun* activity from Jordan in early September. In the two months from 29 July to 25 September, Israel lodged fifty-nine complaints with the M.A.C., concerning crossings of the demarcation line by military or civilians, or firing across it. Nineteen Israelis has been killed and 28 wounded in these incidents.[34] During the same period, Jordan lodged fifty-three complaints and counted 72 killed and 24 wounded.

On 11 September an Israel army unit, retaliating for a frontier incident at Dawiyima in which six Israelis had been killed, struck out at the Jordan post of Rahwa, on the Hebron-Beersheba road several kilometers inside Jordan, killing five Jordanian police and ten soldiers. The next evening, in what General Burns describes as an unconnected incident, three Druze guards at an oil rig in the Negev were murdered by marauders whose tracks led to Jordan. The following day an Israeli force destroyed a Jordanian police post at Gharandal, killing nine policemen and two civilians. A few days later, a Jordanian legionnaire opened fire on a party of Israeli amateur archaeologists at Ramat Rahel, on the southern outskirts of Jerusalem, killing four and wounding sixteen members of the group. The Israelis rejected the Jordanian plea that the incident was an unpremeditated act by a soldier seized with a sudden fit of insanity. On the night of 25 September, after two more Israelis, including a young girl, had been killed

195

by infiltrators on the twenty-fourth, a punitive raid was carried out. The Sharafa police post near Husan was blown up, and thirty-nine Jordanians lost their lives.[35] At the M.A.C. meeting on the Ramat Rahel incident on 3 October, the chairman accepted the Jordanian proposal to examine the mental state of the soldier who had done the firing. But the Israelis objected strenuously and announced that they would no longer participate in the proceedings of the M.A.C., since they were "useless." Nor would Israel agree to the investigation by U.N. observers of incidents that occurred inside Israeli territory.[36]

The next retaliation raid—as it turned out, the last in the series—was the bloodiest in the entire record of punitive operations. Its target was the police station at Qalqilya, the date the night of 10 October, and the provocation the murder of two Israeli workers in an orange grove at Even Yehuda, about ten kilometers away. The count: 83 dead and 15 wounded, mostly police and military personnel. This time the Arab Legion gave battle, which resulted in 18 Israelis being killed and 68 wounded.[37]

From General Dayan's diary it is evident that by this time the die had been cast in favor of a major strike against Egypt. Although Dayan describes the Qalqilya raid in considerable detail, he provides no satisfactory explanation as to why an operation of such severity and consequence, involving an Israeli paratroop brigade as well as armor and artillery, was launched on another front at this particular time. Part of the answer, it would appear, was to mislead Egypt and the powers as to Israel's true intentions —a tactic pursued assiduously and successfully until the very eve of the campaign. Nearly a decade later, a political commentator, writing in *Ha-Arez*, speculated on some additional considerations which may have influenced the decision:

(1) Qalqilya may have been intended as a warning to Jordan not to intervene on Egypt's side later on.

(2) The army may have used the losses suffered in the Qal-

196

qilya operation as an argument in persuading the government to approve the Sinai plans, on the grounds that—in Dayan's words —"we have reached the end of the chapter of night reprisal actions" and that more drastic action was called for. (At a public appearance in connection with the publication of his book in Israel, Dayan denied that this was a factor in planning the Qalqilya operation. Asked why the same paratroop brigade which was to be assigned a key job in the Sinai Campaign was used at Qalqilya, Dayan replied that this was the only unit ready for action at a few hours' notice.)

(3) It is possible, too, that Qalqilya was simply the final manifestation of the dynamics of the retaliation policy which, since 1953, had developed from a tactical response to infiltration into a major strategy of foreign policy in Israel's relations with the neighboring states, producing an almost automatic response to the kind of incursion which preceded Qalqilya.[38]

After the Husan raid on 25 September, Jordan turned to Iraq with a view to forming a joint Iraq-Jordan army and thereby strengthening Jordan's position vis-à-vis both Israel and Egypt. Subsequently, two Iraqi divisions moved into position near the Jordan frontier. They did not actually enter Jordan, as the talks for a joint command broke down about 4 October. But the negotiations were reopened after the Qalqilya battle, and by this time Israel made it known that the move of Iraqi troops into Jordan would be a direct threat to the security of Israel and the validity of the Jordan-Israel General Armistice Agreement. The implication was that Israel would take action in such a case. At this point Britain intervened and issued a strongly worded warning to Israel against any attack upon Jordan. In the case of such an attack, the British government pointed out through its chargé d'affaires in Tel Aviv, it would come to Jordan's assistance under the Anglo-Jordanian Treaty of 1948.[39]

In Israel, amid mounting tension and a sense of fateful decision in the making, there appeared to be official anger over the Brit-

197

ish warning. Every indication was that military action, if it were to come, would be directed against Jordan. Ben-Gurion's Knesset speech opening foreign policy debate on 15 October was distinctly unfriendly to Britain. The Prime Minister also alluded cryptically to "momentous decisions and events" which were "perhaps" being faced. But two days later, there was a shift in direction, as though a sudden gust of wind had made him change his tack. Twice in his brief speech to the Knesset on 17 October he described "the Egyptian dictator" as the "bitterest and most dangerous enemy." [40] His stated reason for saying this was that, a few days earlier, Egypt had broken the *détente* which had marked its relations with Israel during the Suez crisis and had resumed its raids into Israel territory.

The speech contains another passage which emerges as significant on post-factum analysis, though in its context it was scarcely sufficient to arouse attention at the time. Ben-Gurion referred to the argument of Peretz Bernstein, the General Zionist leader, in the debate, asking why the government had pleaded for "defensive arms," thereby limiting the types of weapons with which the army was to be equipped. Ben-Gurion explained that this was not so; all weapons had but one purpose—to destroy and to kill. There were no offensive and defensive arms, except in the mind of the beholder, he said. If a country needed weapons in order to defend itself, then they were defensive arms. He went on to say that even in a defensive operation one must take offensive action. "Most of the time, the most effective way to defend oneself is by offensive actions. And if we are compelled to defend ourselves, we are not going to sit in our homes and defend ourselves. We are going to carry the war to the other side and defend ourselves through offensive shock tactics, for defense requires offensive means." [41]

At the same time, Ben-Gurion once more and in strong language reiterated his distaste for the solution advocated by Herut.

The Meshing of the Plans

A precondition for successful military action by a small state is the open or tacit support of one or more great powers with interests in the area, and the noninvolvement of others. The failure of Western strategy in the Suez affair meant also the end of Israel's policy of letting the West European powers try their hand at "cutting Nasser down to size"; it meant that Nasser had emerged as the "bitterest and most dangerous enemy." But the interests of Israel now continued to coincide with those of Britain and France as they sought "to pursue policy by other means." In relation to Jordan, Great Britain had made it clear that it would not sit back passively if Israel were to cross the border. Under these circumstances, Israeli action against Jordan would not make sense, in spite of the fact that the major irritation at the moment came from that direction. But action against Egypt would. Ben-Gurion's 17 October speech prepared Israel public opinion, brought to a pitch of animosity toward the Jordanians, for the shift in direction.

A crucial juncture had been reached on the previous day when the Prime Ministers and Foreign Ministers of France and Britain had met in secret at Paris without any of their aides being present. No official account of what went on at that meeting has been released, but there is every indication that it was then that the final decision was made to seize the Canal by force and to coordinate this operation with Israel. Only after Ben-Gurion was so informed did he begin to prepare public opinion in Israel for the forthcoming encounter with Egypt.

For while discussions with France regarding an attack on the common adversary had by this time reached an advanced stage, the attitude of Britain toward Israel continued equivocal, especially so after the latest flare-up over Jordan. France, it has been said, was anti-Egypt and pro-Israel, whereas Britain was pro-Arab and anti-Israel.

Until a week before D-day, therefore, Israel conducted military discussions exclusively with France. Contacts were initiated, it will be recalled, already much earlier when Israeli Defense Ministry officials had talks with their French counterparts regarding purchase of armaments. In August 1956, shortly after the Suez nationalization, top-secret meetings between Israeli emissaries and high officials of the French Defense Ministry took place in Paris, resulting in a new major arms purchase agreement the extent of which was kept secret from France's partners in the Tripartite Declaration. At this point the French apparently were not yet ready to reveal their intentions in detail —but on 1 September Israel's military attaché in Paris signaled Tel Aviv of the existence of an Anglo-French plan to seize the Canal.[42] This threw the Israeli planning machinery into high gear: "the propitious moment" was within sight. The branches of the General Staff were ordered to examine the various operational plans on the Egyptian front, from the capture of the whole of the Sinai Peninsula to securing control of the Straits of Tiran or of the Gaza Strip.[43] At a meeting of the Operations Branch on 17 September, Dayan explained (in accordance with Ben-Gurion's guidance) that, while the operation which was likely to be launched by Britain and France will have been prompted by the abrogation of the international status of the Suez Canal, this was not a specific Israeli problem. Israel had no aspirations to reach Suez and to become an involved party in this dispute. The Straits of Tiran and the Gaza Strip, on the other hand, were "problems specific to us," the one being used by Egypt to blockade shipping to Eilat, the other as a base for Egyptian terrorist raids on Israel. Military action against these targets might be taken by Israel at its own initiative, "either in association with the forces operating against Egypt or without any contact with them, whenever the Government of Israel decides that the situation warrants it." [44]

General Dayan later put it more graphically: "When I explained our relationship to the Anglo-French forces, I said that if our assessment is confirmed and they do indeed attack Egypt, we should behave like the cyclist who is riding uphill when a truck chances by and he grabs hold. We should get what help we can, hanging on to their vehicle and exploiting its movement as much as possible, and only when our routes fork should we break off and proceed along our separate way with our own force alone." [45]

In the second half of September, two representatives of the French Defense Ministry had come to Israel to propose that France should aid an Israel attack upon Egypt, and that the French air force should give active support to such an operation. By then the French had concluded that "diplomatic pretexts" for an attack on Egypt had been exhausted, and that the best remaining hope for toppling Nasser was a clash between Egypt and Israel.

On 1 October Dayan and his assistants met in Paris with the French Chief of Staff, General Ely, and various staff officers to submit a shopping list of equipment, including one hundred tanks, three hundred half-tracks and a squadron of transport planes. The French promised to do their best to comply, but still proved reluctant to talk about their own timetable and plans. Upon returning to Israel the next day, Dayan issued an early warning order to his General Staff, telling them of the likelihood of a campaign against Egypt, even though no decision had as yet been taken. The estimated date of the opening of hostilities was 20 October and the campaign might last three weeks, the order stipulated. The plan was to capture the Sinai Peninsula in order to break the Egyptian blockade of the straits. Preparations would be explained in terms of the possible entry of Iraqi troops into Jordan.[46] Three days later, on 5 October, the first planning order for Kadesh, the code name given to the campaign, was issued. To avoid political complications, the campaign was to last no longer than two weeks; its tasks were to bring about the collapse of enemy forces and achieve control of Sinai.[47]

On 10 October, specific agreement was reached in Paris between France and Israel about the French naval, air, and supply drop aid that was to start immediately with the Israel attack. On that same day, Israel carried out the Qalqilya reprisal raid, and two days later was told by the British that future operations against Jordan would cause the Anglo-Jordanian security treaty to be invoked. By that time the British did not yet know the details of the Israeli plan: it was only on 15 October that France's General Challe flew to London to inform Sir Anthony that Israel had a plan for marching into Sinai. By then the Soviet veto had disposed of the U.N. option; it had become clear that nothing was to be expected from the Suez Canal Users' Association and that the United States would be opposed to the use of force. The Israeli plan, the French now felt, would provide the opportunity for two-power intervention, and they set out to sell the idea to the British. General Challe's visit was followed by the secret Paris meeting on the next day, at which Sir Anthony agreed to go along provided Great Britain was not to be allied with Israel. In sum, to quote Barraclough, "circumstantial evidence provides a strong presumption that decisions were taken (at the 16 October meeting) which led to the Israel attack on Egypt on October 29 and the subsequent Anglo-French intervention at Port Said." [48] After 16 October a communications blackout descended on relations between the Western allies and the United States; contact with American diplomats in the European capitals was avoided, and exchanges of messages held to a minimum.

Ben-Gurion made a flying visit to France during the week before mobilization where he met with Premier Guy Mollet and, according to some reports, also briefly with British Foreign Minister Selwyn Lloyd, and their top aides. The Israeli Premier had two purposes in mind: (1) to obtain a promise of air support, as the Israel air force felt inadequate to the twin tasks of protecting population centers against bomber attacks and providing air cover for land operations; and (2) since he was still suspicious of British intentions, he wanted to take back a "piece of paper" in which the conditions of Anglo-French interventions were spelled out. He was granted both, and in turn appears to have been persuaded to play along with Britain's desire not to become openly identified with Israel's plans.[49] General Dayan, who had accompanied the Prime Minister to Paris, issued a revised order of operations after their return on 25 October which differed in some significant respects from the earlier planning order. The changes, it is now apparent, were made to bring the Israeli operation more closely into line with the plans of the allies. Thus stress was now placed on creating a threat to the Suez Canal, and only after that came the basic purpose of the campaign for Israel—capture of the Straits of Tiran and defeat of the Egyptian forces.[50] The intention obviously was to provide the context for the Anglo-French ultimatum on 30 October. The new order provided for the campaign to start with a paratroop drop at the Mitla Pass, near the southern end of the Canal, presenting the impression that here was a rather large-scale reprisal raid and thereby minimizing the risk of Egyptian air attack on Israeli cities until the Anglo-French bombing of Egyptian air fields would take effect.

War Aims and Mobilization

It is significant that in his reply to President Eisenhower's warning against offensive action, which was received on 27 October, Ben-Gurion gave first precedence to the establishment of the joint command among the reasons he cited for Israel's mobilization:

In view of the establishment of the Joint Command of Egypt, Syria and Jordan, the decisive influence of Egypt in Jordan, and the renewed penetration by Egyptian bands into Israel, my government would be betraying its principal responsibility if it did not take all possible measures to ensure the frustration of the declared policy of the Arab rulers—the liquidation of Israel.[51]

The recrudescence of infiltration is mentioned in third place only—a sign that, at the time the signal for the campaign was given, renewed Egyptian activity across the borders had not yet assumed dimensions that would in themselves justify so drastic a riposte. By 30 October, however, when Eban addressed the Security Council, the record of Arab raids became the core of Israel's argument. In his initial announcement at the Council's morning session, Eban announced that the Israel move across the border came after three *fidayun* units from Egypt had invaded Israel territory on 28 October. This, he said had followed the Amman conference of chiefs of staff of the armies of Egypt, Syria, and Jordan, at which decisions were reached for the immediate and drastic intensification of aggression against Israel. Later that day, Eban presented "a diary of attacks by *fidayun*" since April 1956, which included seven instances of penetration from Egypt between 12 and 28 October including one, on 20 October, in which three Israeli soldiers were killed when an army command car hit a mine in the Nitzana-Rafah area.

Israel's Sinai Campaign was in the nature of a limited war, it being understood by all concerned that total destruction of the enemy was neither within Israel's means nor essential to its interest. It will be recalled that even the constant prodding of Herut for military action was for a strictly circumscribed military operation. In limited war it is not only necessary that the aims pursued be limited, but also that this limitation be announced without delay. Israel, in its announcements accompanying the move across the frontier, at first understated the purpose of the operation and created the impression of an extensive retaliation raid the aim of which was the cleaning out of the nests of *fidayun*.[52] Only gradually, as the scope of the campaign became apparent, did Israel reveal its aims as being more inclusive, but still well within the confines of limited war. Ben-Gurion thus made it known that there was no intention of crossing the Canal into Egypt proper, but that operations were to be limited to the Sinai Peninsula and the Gaza Strip. As subsequently ranked by Ben-Gurion, the goals of the campaign were, first, to "strengthen the security of Israel and to break the military power of Nasser," then to "lower the stature of the Egyptian dictator," and third, "to open the waterway from Eilat to the Red Sea." [53] This last aim had actually been the principal rationale for the operation first projected by Ben-Gurion and Dayan in November 1955. Its significance—granting Israel access to the eastern seas and lines of commerce to the Afro-Asian world—was underscored when it became clear that Nasser stuck to his determination to block passage of Israeli ships through the Canal, even though the Security Council resolution of 13 October included freedom of navigation among the six principles to which Egypt was ready to subscribe.

An Israeli staff officer familiar with the circumstances surrounding the campaign asserts that peace with Egypt was not a result Israel expected to achieve through its operation, although it was hoped that Nasser might abdicate and a pro-Western government succeed him. The minimum goal, according to this officer, was to make Nasser realize that he could not win in an engagement with Israel, and perhaps to bring peace nearer by neutralizing his capacity to attack.[54] For a short time, Ben-Gurion seems to have felt it might be possible for Israel to retain the Sinai Peninsula and thereby turn the Suez Canal into a true international waterway.[55] But this thought was quickly abandoned. In his reply to President Eisenhower's letter of 7 November, which he read over the air, the Premier said: "Neither I nor any authorized spokesman of the Israel government has said that we intend to annex the Sinai desert to the State of Israel. In view of the resolution of the U.N. with regard to the withdrawal of foreign forces from Egypt and the establishment of an international force, we shall willingly withdraw our forces as soon as suitable arrangements have been made by the U.N. for the entry of an international force into the Suez Canal Zone." [56]

Nor was any decision reached to retain the Gaza Strip, because of the difficult refugee problem this would entail. On the other hand, both Sinai and the Gaza Strip were considered as bargaining counters in later dealings with Egypt:

Israel had not the strength to hold large areas of enemy territory permanently, nor did she want to do so, but she envisaged and hoped for some form of demilitarized zone under U.N. supervision. Israel did attempt to hold the Gaza Strip, Rafa, Abu Agueila, a narrow strip of territory stretching from Eilat to Sharm-el Sheikh and the island of Tiran, until she had concluded a satisfactory agreement with Egypt.[57]

On the evening of 25 October, Israel secretly mobilized. "So well briefed and so well organized was the citizen army of Israel, that the mobilization by secret code words on the radio was achieved with no dislocation of daily life . . . and in such secrecy that only the most alert foreign diplomats could gauge its scale." [58]

Even so experienced an observer as General Burns confesses that, "prior to October 28, the reports of the mobilization did not excite me greatly," and this in spite of the fact that he had virtually predicted the attack on Sinai in a memorandum submitted to the Secretary General on 14 September, and that a number of observers had reported troop movements in a southward direction on 27 and 28 October. The crisis over Jordan earlier in the month had concentrated attention on that section of the front, where tension had subsequently lessened after the sharp British warning. To account for his lack of acumen, Burns explains that he underestimated the Israeli determination to break the ring of hostility that surrounded the country "and perhaps over-estimated the sincerity of Ben-Gurion's public announcements that Israel would never engage in a preventive war." [59]

The Israel Foreign Ministry, in publishing a statement on the mobilization on 28 October, explained that reserves had been called up because of *fidayun* attacks, and because of the new military alliance between Egypt, Jordan, and Syria. The third reason given was the presence of Iraqi troops close to the Jordanian border,[60] a claim to which General Eisenhower responded by assuring Ben-Gurion that no troops had crossed. In a second cable to Ben-Gurion, the President assured the Prime Minister that he would discuss the problem of Israel's security with Britain and France on the basis of the Tripartite Declaration—a promise which led General Dayan to exclaim in his diary, "How uninformed he is of the situation!" Ben-Gurion kept his intentions even from his Cabinet until the day before the attack when he sought—and received—its approval. Small wonder that Nasser himself was caught by surprise, and when the attack came at first was convinced that he was faced merely with a reprisal raid on a larger scale. On 29 October, at last, General Burns reported on the Israeli mobilization to the Secretary General, including an appreciation that there was imminent danger of war.

In the afternoon and evening of that same day, units of the Israeli Defense Forces crossed the border into Egypt on land and in the air. The Sinai Campaign had begun.

CONCLUSION ≺≺≺≺

After Sinai

Military analysts have classed the Sinai Campaign as a text-book example of soundly planned, skillfully executed modern desert warfare. But as in any military operation conducted for political ends, the ultimate measure of success is the attainment of those ends. And on that score there is room for doubt.

The political results of Sinai may be divided into two categories: short-term and long-term. On a short-term basis, the campaign achieved its aim of advancing Israel's security. In effect, it epitomized the security policy by preserving the *status quo* and projecting the short-term into the indefinite future, minus some of the irritations which had been a part of the *status quo ante* Sinai.

The campaign achieved this aim primarily by proving that Israel continued to be the dominant military factor in the area. It thereby dashed any hopes of conquest which Egypt might have entertained for the short-term future on the basis of its newly acquired Soviet arms.

Apart from this demonstration effect, the operation upset any preparations for possible offensive action on Egypt's part through Israel's capture of the stores of Soviet supplies in the peninsula.

Furthermore, the military success of the campaign had an important psychological effect on the Israelis themselves. It confirmed conclusively that Israel could overcome its shortcomings in physical resources, population, and territory through such intangible assets as high morale, organization, and technical and combat skills; and that it could muster an effective fighting machine capable of dealing with the challenge posed by Egyptian superiority in numbers and equipment. That this could be accomplished in spite of the handicaps placed upon Israel's development through Arab hostility greatly boosted the population's self-confidence. The campaign also reassured the Israelis on another crucial point: in spite of military pacts and declarations of solidarity, the Arab states were still far from acting in unison in time of crisis.

Irritation in the form of *fidayun* activity and other kinds of illegal border crossings was greatly reduced as a result of Israel's initiative, and by the subsequent stationing of the United Nations Emergency Force on the Egyptian side of the Gaza demarcation line. Relief of another kind was obtained by the opening of the Gulf of Aqaba to Israeli shipping, after Israel's forces had flushed the Egyptian garrisons out of the forts governing access to the Gulf. Here extension of the military success into a long-range gain was assured when the U.N. force took over occupation of the strategic coastal points after the Israelis evacuated the Sinai Peninsula.*

The prolongation of the *status quo* also comprised the fending off of efforts on the part of the powers to impose a political settlement detrimental to Israel's interests. The reaction to Western attempts at peacemaking and conciliation in the period before Sinai indicates that Israel regarded the possibility of a concerted political drive on its territorial integrity with utmost suspicion. In their statements from time to time, Arab spokesmen had scaled down their objective from absolute annihilation of the State of Israel to something considerably short of it, such as return to the 1947 partition frontiers, but still unacceptable

---

* As this book went to press, the hasty withdrawal of the United Nations Emergency Force from these positions at President Nasser's behest and Egypt's renewed blockade of the Gulf entirely erased Israel's advantage.

to the Israelis. There were signs that Western statesmen of high rank tended to favor a settlement on such terms. The Sinai Campaign (and the general upheavel in the area as a result of the Suez crisis) postponed similar attempts for several years. It was only with the advent of the Kennedy administration that substantial pressure for concessions (on the refugee question) was again being applied to Israel by a great power.

As for long-range results, freedom for its shipping through the Gulf of Aqaba was the only strategic gain Israel was able to retain. The territory occupied by the Israel army had to be evacuated under U.S. and U.N. pressure. Neither the underlying causes nor the symptoms of Arab hostility were removed by the campaign. The refugee situation was brought no nearer a solution. Egypt's military capacity, while temporarily impaired, was not decisively affected over the long term. Its ability to obtain aid from both the Soviet Union and the United States remained intact.

In the Arab world, Nasser's prestige remained unaffected by his military reverses in Sinai, and from the contest with the Western powers he emerged with added stature. No firm guarantees were exacted from him after control of the Suez Canal was restored to Egypt, so that he was in a position to turn his military defeat into a diplomatic triumph.

Ben-Gurion later revealed that he took the Sinai risk in the face of his Cabinet colleagues' fears that the campaign would arouse antagonism on the part of the Asian and African peoples and also spoil relations with diaspora Jewry. But three years after the campaign he felt that these fears had shown themselves to have been groundless.[1] Nevertheless Israel sustained a setback in the intangible realm of its reputation as a law-abiding member of the community of nations. As had happened in connection with the retaliation policy, the provocation was not of sufficient magnitude to keep the label of aggressor from being hung upon Israel. Israel had not been able to convince world opinion that an Egyptian attempt upon its integrity was imminent. After Great Britain and France issued their ultimatum and jumped off on their own ill-starred attack, the charge of collusion was added to this. It is true that Israel's image did not suffer any long-term damage among the Jews of the diaspora; and the initial disapproval among the nations of Asia and Africa with whom Israel maintained relations was mingled with respect for Israel's military prowess. But in the Arab states, the image of Israel as an aggressor and tool of imperialism was reinforced. It is hard to say whether this had the effect of postponing a possible readiness of the Arab states to come to terms, since there had been so little evidence of such readiness prior to Sinai.

In Egypt, the military experience of Sinai strengthened the determination to match Israel's power, rather than to accept Israel's superiority as ineluctable. In the subsequent years, Egypt built up its navy, air force, and armor far beyond their pre-Sinai state, thereby leading Israel to equip its own deterrent force with newer and more powerful types of weapons.

The Lessons of Sinai

The experience in Sinai demonstrated a series of "facts of life" to Israel's policy makers. Some of these were axioms of small-state behavior; others were peculiar to Israel's circumstances.

The first lesson concerned the limits of small-state liberty of action and of great-power inertia. Israel's assumption that the two superpowers would be either too preoccupied with their own affairs or would not consider their interests sufficiently affected to intervene proved unfounded. Both the United States and the Soviet Union viewed the Sinai-Suez operation as affecting their interests and decided to take an active role toward bringing it to an end. The United States went so far as to take up a position opposing its traditional allies and siding with its Cold War adversary. The Soviet Union, direct and brutal in its approach, warned

Israel of dire consequences unless it complied with the U.N. resolution calling on it to withdraw its troops behind the armistice lines. The United States was more temperate but hinted that it would support sanctions in the United Nations if Israel failed to comply.[2] Twenty-four hours after announcing in the Knesset that the armistice with Egypt was null and void and that the armistice lines had ceased to exist, Ben-Gurion assured President Eisenhower that "we shall willingly withdraw our forces as soon as suitable arrangements have been made by the U.N. for the entry of an international force into the Suez Canal." There was more defiance in the simultaneous reply to Bulganin, who was told that "our foreign policy is dictated by our vital needs and our desire for peace, and no foreign factor determines, or will determine, our policy. As a sovereign State, we ourselves determine our course." But the Prime Minister learned the limits of a small nation's liberty of action, and ordered the withdrawal.

Thus the scope of Israel's military success was determined not by the power Israel possessed in relation to its immediate adversaries, but by the degree of great-power toleration of the employment of that power. The success of the campaign showed that Israel had sufficient power for its strategic needs in the area. But the political setbacks it suffered after the cease-fire indicated that its influence was not sufficient to consolidate the military gains on the political level. Israel had overextended its political lines, as it were, because it did not correctly anticipate the attitude and actions of the great powers nor the failure of the Anglo-French expedition. The lesson to be learned from this was that, while it is possible for a small state to predicate *military* success on the power relationship with the enemy at a given time, it is far more difficult to plan and execute on the *political* level where great-power interests are affected.

A corollary lesson was this: a preventive attack carries the risk that the political goals for which it is intended cannot be attained, in spite of military success, because of the stigma of

213

aggression that becomes attached to it. Had the Arabs indeed attacked first, and Israel marched into Sinai under more un-ambiguous conditions of self-defense, the political outcome might have been different.

The meager results of Israel's efforts to salvage its objectives in the face of overwhelming pressure showed that the power inventory of a small state, no matter how effective in relation to the forces within its own orbit, remains ineffectual against con-certed great-power pressure. That it was possible to extract even limited enduring gains was due mainly to Israel's strategy of giving in to pressure only step by step rather than capitulating all at once. It must be added that the limited strategic gains re-tained were in areas where Israel had legitimate grievances recog-nized by the international community, namely the guerrilla raids from the Gaza Strip and the interference with its navigation in the Gulf of Aqaba.

The aid which Israel was able to obtain from France, both military in the preparation and execution of the campaign, and political in the struggle at the United Nations, showed that there is no substitute for a community of interests. Notwithstand-ing the dialogue which Israel had carried on with the United States, and the manifest sympathy of American public opinion for Israel's aims, it was the United States which opposed Israel's aims while France supported them. But the limitations of France's influence and the extent of its own commitments rendered French political aid ineffective. Moreover, it was shown that Israel's interests, although they converged with those of France and Great Britain at a certain juncture, were by no means identical with those of the two powers. Yet Israel's ob-jectives became caught up with the aims of those two countries: Israel was the cyclist who had grabbed hold of the truck but, as one of General Dayan's aides had anticipated, it was dragged along to where it did not wish to go. It became clear that there was such a thing as too much outside support for the aims of the small state; that a point can be reached where the small state loses control over its policies as they are swept along in the wake of the great power's actions.

An important lesson for Israel concerned the limits of the utility of Jewish support, particularly in the United States. Jewish opinion in America was at first no less disconcerted by Israel's action than public opinion in general, and only gradually came around to the Israeli point of view. Later on, the attempts on the part of Jewish leadership to soften the American stand in the United Nations (when Israel was compelled to give up one position after another) had little effect. The results of the presidential election showed, furthermore, that in a critical situation the "Jewish vote" can fail to affect either American policy or the outcome of the balloting.

If there was a lesson to be learned by the world community at large, it lay in the motive for Israel's attack, as distinguished from that of the two Western powers. At the time Britain and France went into Suez, the crisis precipitated by the nationalization of the Canal was no longer acute; the threat to the West European lifeline which had appeared so imminent a few months earlier, had turned out to be a highly contingent one; Egypt had shown itself capable of operating the Canal, and the quarrel was now over the terms and conditions by which it should be permitted to do so. This was no longer a matter of vital interest to the West but one of prestige.

From Israel's subjective point of view, its own vital interests *were* still at stake; with Egypt's success in the Canal zone the danger Israel saw itself in had not abated but grown. But it would be difficult to maintain that the use of force to safeguard its vital interests remained as the sole option open to Israel at this particular juncture. This is one criterion for the validity of the plea of self-defense under Article 51 of the U.N. Charter.

The Sequel: 1967

If the Arab states found out at Sinai that Israel could not be defeated in war, Israel learned that even a victorious campaign could not force the peace. The combination of circumstances which made Sinai possible, moreover, is not likely to recur. The major problem of Israel's foreign policy, therefore—that of making the Arab world accept the *status quo*—remains to be resolved by diplomacy.

Preceded by some pages of cautious prediction and speculation about the future, the above stood as the concluding paragraph of the book as it was composed months before 15 May 1967. But on that day, which was also the nineteenth anniversary of the birth of the State of Israel, there was set into motion a sequence of events which made past speculation idle and predictions miss their mark. Even the lines above, so incontrovertible only a few days earlier in the light of ten post-Sinai years, became subject to re-examination. Only the initial clause, it would seem, has weathered the test of the Six-Day War, for the Arabs again learned that Israel could not be defeated on the battlefield. Israel, on the other hand, was once more trying to convert a victorious campaign into peace. As for making the Arab world accept the *status quo,* this had ceased to be the same proposition it had been since 1949: the territorial *status quo* for which Israel now sought acceptance was no longer that laid down in the armistice agreements. At the same time, the Arabs' stunning defeat, while augmenting their interest in coming to terms, also added to their ideological resistance to

217

sitting down at the peace table. Whether interest would now overcome ideology thus remained the crucial issue.

This leaves the central statement of that final paragraph. It is still true that the combination of circumstances which made Sinai possible did not recur—but the stark fact remains that Sinai itself did recur, ten years, seven months, and nine days later, its reenactment more swift, more startling, and more deadly than the original.

Why?

If the Sinai Campaign gave rise to an avalanche of books the end of which is not yet in sight, the Six-Day War has already forced the publishing pace in about the same ratio the battle itself stood to the—in retrospect—more leisurely Sinai Campaign.[1] It would serve little purpose, therefore, to recount here the course of the war itself, or to reconstruct the chronology of the crisis which preceded it. Instead, these rewritten concluding pages will attempt to relate the most recent events to the Sinai Campaign, its antecedents and its outcome.

When Egypt moved its troops into the Sinai Peninsula on 15 May 1967, the short-term era in Israel's foreign policy came to an end, and what had once appeared as the indefinite future suddenly became finite. The gains of the Sinai Campaign were about to be wiped out, and Israel once more found itself challenged to a fight for survival.

The most important political gain Israel carried away from Sinai, it will be recalled, was the opening of the Straits of Tiran; corollary results were the elimination of *fidayun* activity from the Gaza Strip and the removal of the military threat from the Sinai frontier. Yet the securing of these goals was based not on Israel's military victory alone but also on political commitments by others. Israel withdrew from the Sinai Peninsula under great-power pressure after the decision was taken to station a United Nations Emergency Force there at sensitive points; its ostensible purpose was to interpose a neutral body between the belligerents, but for Israel its main function was to safeguard the newly achieved *status quo*. Freedom of shipping was, of course, the keystone of this arrangement. The withdrawal from Sharm es-Sheikh, the point controlling passage through the Straits of Tiran, came about only when months of intricate negotiations brought forth, on 2 March 1957, a letter from President Eisenhower in which he expressed his "belief" that it was "reasonable" to entertain such "hopes and expectations" (regarding the right of innocent passage for Israel's ships) as were contained in the speech by Israel's Foreign Minister at the U.N. General Assembly the previous day. Mrs. Meir had in fact spoken about Israel's "assumptions" on these matters, but Israel nevertheless chose to regard the letter as sufficient to permit it to withdraw its troops. Actually, it was so tenuous a commitment that Foreign Minister Abba Eban found it necessary to produce the document when he met with President Johnson in Washington on 26 May 1967 to refresh his hosts' memories as to its terms and the circumstances in which it had been drafted.

While the American assurances were not in the end put to the test, the hollowness of the U.N. Emergency Force safeguard became manifest as soon as the Egyptian president asked for its evacuation. Although this was his prerogative under the arrangements worked out by Dag Hammarskjold, Secretary General U Thant was not required to respond to the request with such speed as to add momentum to the crisis.

The U.N. Emergency Force agreement was probably the best even a man of Hammarskjold's astuteness could have obtained, but now it stood exposed very much like the emperor without his clothes: a U.N. Emergency Force that took its effective orders from the suzerain of the territory on which it was stationed, that proved itself unequal to a genuine emergency, and that was enjoined from using force when the chips were down.

Egypt and Syria

In probing for the origin of the crisis which burst upon the world with such suddenness, one must go back in time beyond the Egyptian declarations and movements of troops of mid-May and take account of the relationship between Egypt and Syria.

These two countries had arrived at disparate attitudes toward the problem posed by Israel's existence. Egypt, while in agreement that the *status quo* was unacceptable, advocated postponement of the ultimate confrontation until such time as the Arab world was politically and militarily ready. Syria, by contrast, was clamoring for a showdown and, unlike Egypt, gave shelter and encouragement to the new *fidayun,* the members of the *El Fatah* terrorist group.

In the tension created by these two approaches, the more dynamic policy of Syria won out. The relationship between the two states was further complicated by the attitude of Jordan, whose pro-Western leanings and commitments made it the butt of the anger of both Egypt and Syria. An additional complicating element was the existence of the Palestine Liberation Organization created and headed by Ahmad Shuqairy, and its offshoot, the Egyptian-trained Palestine Liberation Army. The point has been made in the body of the book that the presence of the refugee population in the Arab states constituted a political factor extraneous to the state system and therefore impeding its functioning. Neither the Arab states nor Israel had taken any significant measures since 1950 to eliminate this focus of disturbance—the Arabs because its continued existence served their political purposes; Israel because it did not consider solution of the problem its primary responsibility.

At the time the bulk of this book was written, one was still justified to note that attempts to give political shape to the accumulated frustration of the refugee population had failed. Since then Shuqairy, dismissed from his post as Saudi Arabia's representative at the United Nations, came upon the scene as an effective catalyst who succeeded in using the presence of the refugees for the creation of a political body that was granted recognition of sorts by the Arab states and some powers friendly to them. The army, placed under Egyptian command and thence political control, had not yet become a disturbing factor in the area's relationships. But the affiliated terrorist group, operating out of Syria apparently without restraint, caused damage within Israel and wrought havoc with the delicate political balance in the area. Just as in 1956 the *fidayun* attacks had been a contributory reason for Israel's march into Sinai, so in 1967 the *El Fatah* raids, while not the immediate cause of the war, nevertheless helped produce in Israel a nearly irresistible determination to react. While in 1955 and 1956 the Egyptian government assumed responsibility for the *fidayun* activity as a reply to Israel's retaliation raids, the terrorists of the mid-1960's functioned extragovernmentally, and the regimes on whose territory the raids originated officially disclaimed responsibility. They could thus boast to have developed a doctrine permitting them to carry on the fight against Israel without laying themselves open to retaliatory attacks. These sporadic and frequently unsuccessful attempts at sabotage or murder presented Israel with less of a genuine security threat than with a policy dilemma. The border with Syria—and even more so that with Jordan—could not be effectively guarded by conventional means. But a U.S. offer to supply electronic detection equipment for use in conjunction with a barbed wire fence was not received with enthusiasm. Israel feared not only the cost, but also the prospect of seeing its territory fenced in, concentration camp style.

The dilemma was graphically illustrated by Israel's reaction to an incursion from Jordan in November 1966 in which three soldiers were killed near Arad. The reprisal raid on the Jordanian village of Samoa which claimed seventeen victims from among an Arab Legion detachment brought a world-wide outcry reminiscent of Qibya in 1953, censure by the Security Council, and a threat to internal stability in Jordan, in which Israel had an interest. But, with the infiltrators' tracks definitely leading to Jordan,

221

it would have made even less sense to strike at Syria. There was also a feeling that Syria enjoyed a measure of immunity because of the Soviet Union's aggressive backing.

Syria and Israel

Relations between Israel and Syria, already dangerously strained by the terrorist raids, were further exacerbated by the renewal of the periodic dispute over the cultivation of certain plots of land in the demilitarized zones east of Lake Tiberias. In the winter of 1966–1967 the U.N. Truce Supervision Organization succeeded in reviving the Israel-Syrian Mixed Armistice Commission to deal with the dispute. But the hopes which arose when both sides reiterated their commitment not to use force in their relationship were short-lived: after two sessions devoted mainly to procedural wrangling, the M.A.C. adjourned sine die. The next time the representatives of the opposing sides met again was in battle. Israel insisted that the M.A.C. agenda deal only with the problem of cultivation; Syria wished to extend the discussion to the question of sovereignty over the zones, and this Israel resisted. After the negotiations—or the attempt to open them— broke down, attitudes on both sides hardened again. Israel resumed its plowing, after halting it for several months to give U.N.T.S.O. Chief of Staff, General Odd Bull, an opportunity to arrange the talks, and the Syrians went back to firing at the tractorists. In a climactic incident on 7 April 1967 they opened up with artillery from fortified hill positions, and the Israelis used air power to silence the guns. When Syrian fighter planes took to the sky, the Israelis chased them as far as Damascus in hot pursuit and downed six of the MIGs.

It is generally acknowledged that this air engagement, with its disastrous results for Syria (over which the Jordanians were scarcely able to keep from gloating) marked a turning point in intra-Arab relationships even more than in the Israel-Arab confrontation. The loss of prestige was not only Syria's but Egypt's as well, and ultimately the Soviet Union's. Syria, as has been noted, had been most vocal about its eagerness to liberate Palestine immediately, and the poor showing of its air arm made those proclamations sound ludicrous. Egypt was tied to Syria in a military assistance pact and, while under no binding obligation to come to Syria's aid in the circumstances, its inaction nevertheless caused a loss of faith in its reliability as an ally. The Soviet Union found its advanced type of aircraft ineffective in Syrian hands, and its political backing incapable of preventing Syria's humiliation.

Escalation

Thus the stage was set for the next step up the ladder, with Israel perplexed as to how to meet the dual threat from Syrian guns and *fidayun;* Egypt anxious to recoup some of its damaged prestige in the Arab world; and Soviet Russia eager to reassure Syria that it could be counted on in time of need.

The defeat in the air did not deter the *El Fatah* terrorists from continuing their exploits on the ground: during April and May mines were again laid on roads in Northern Israel, causing damage but, by sheer coincidence, no loss of life. Israel did not retaliate, yet in a speech on 10 May Chief of Staff Yitzhak Rabin and Premier Levi Eshkol warned that further incursions would not go unpunished. Prime Minister Eshkol himself used the occasion of his traditional Independence Day radio address to drive home the same point.

Arab statesmen apparently took these warnings with the seriousness with which they were uttered, the more so since they came hard on the heels of reports, vigorously denied by Jerusalem, of large-scale concentrations of Israeli troops near the Syrian border. Russia now played a rather murky role by passing these reports on to Egypt, after having declined Eshkol's offer to the Soviet

Ambassador to check on them at first hand. Against the back-drop of these reports the Rabin-Eshkol speeches, though creating hardly a ripple at home, must have sounded alarming enough for Damascus to appeal to Cairo for assistance. The next step was Nasser's declaration, on 15 May, that he was moving troops across the Canal into the peninsula.

While this background is essential for an understanding of the events that followed, the claim cannot be sustained that the subsequent events stemmed solely from these antecedents. In Israel, someone ascribed the next sequence of developments to the "Minister of History." Certainly, predictability in international politics must be based on rationality on the part of the principal actors. The point was made earlier in the book that there is a negative correlation between the newness of states and the rationality of their leadership. But a striking thing about President Nasser was that his rationality—in spite of his periodic outbursts of rhetoric —was basically acknowledged even in Israel (*vide* the wish expressed repeatedly by both Ben-Gurion and Eshkol to meet with him "anytime, any place"). Nasser's declaration of 15 May was publicly interpreted by Israel within the framework of rational action: he was simply demonstrating to his ally Syria that he meant business—for if he was engaged in anything more than a "show," why would he move troops through the streets of Cairo in broad daylight and tell the world about it?

This was Israel's official line for an entire week—the country appeared to wake up to the danger only when it was face to face with Egyptian and Palestinian troops across the Sinai frontier. But Foreign Minister Eban still conceded that Egypt was within its rights in moving troops wherever it pleased on its own territory; even Nasser's demand to the United Nations to recall its "force" was accepted in the same spirit (though U Thant's overly prompt compliance was not). Thus the loss of two of the three long-term gains of Sinai was taken with equanimity (the first *fidayun* attack in ten years across the Gaza frontier was not long in coming); and the faith in Nasser's rationality was so strong that his determination to wipe out the third, crucial gain by closing the Straits caused shock and surprise.

That war was far from the Israelis' minds on their Independence Day was obvious to anyone who observed the elaborate preparations for the parade in Jerusalem, which then appeared to be the defense establishment's most pressing business. The parade itself was kept almost pathetically modest to comply with the terms of the Israel-Jordan Armistice Agreement limiting the amount and type of forces permitted in the Jerusalem area. There were no tanks and no planes—light antiaircraft cannon mounted on jeeps was the heaviest equipment on display. The decision to confine the parade to these limits had caused enough adverse comment among the more excitable politicians and press; but the government was determined not to give its external foes cause for complaint. (Another indication that the crisis caught Israel unaware was the departure of President Shazar on his long-scheduled state visit to Canada on 19 May. Partial mobilization orders were issued in the night of May 19–20.)

One of the characteristics of the Eshkol succession government which took office upon Ben-Gurion's resignation in 1963 was the adoption of a more conciliatory tone toward the Arab states. Shortly after taking over the Defense Ministry from his predecessor, Levi Eshkol removed Shimon Peres, architect of French-Israeli military cooperation, as deputy minister and replaced him with a financial expert. Nor was Eshkol himself known for his ambitions as a strategist. In the Foreign Ministry too, the change-over from Golda Meir to Abba Eban pointed in the direction of new initiatives toward peace. But the forces with which the Eshkol government was confronted proved stronger than its intentions. There is more than a little irony in this: Eshkol, planner of Israel's economic prosperity while Minister of Finance, as Premier was forced to cope with Israel's worst recession; as the arch-advocate of better relations with the Soviet Union, he had to see them deteriorate to the breaking point; and as a sincere moderate in his Arab policy it fell to his lot to give the signal for a third round of fighting.

Nasser's Motives

If Israel was so evidently interested in preserving the peace and also had the deterrent strength to ensure its security, why did Nasser, in closing the Straits, take the one additional step which Israel had repeatedly defined as a *casus belli?*

One answer given frequently is that Nasser was not looking for war but hoped to achieve his aims through bold action short of fighting. Whether his ultimate goal was Israel's total destruction or merely its reduction in territory and viability, he now embarked on an exercise in brinkmanship destined to bring him a step nearer to his goal and at the same time enhance his standing in the Arab world.

Whereas Israel had incorporated freedom of shipping through the Straits in the *status quo* it was determined to defend, Nasser made it clear that he did not consider the changes brought about by Sinai as irrevocable. Having smarted under the 1956 defeat and its consequences for a decade, he was now resolved to seize the opportunity for redress which presented itself when Israel accepted the withdrawal of the U.N. force without belligerency. On 23 May, while U Thant was on his way to Cairo to stave off that very move, Nasser declared the Straits closed to Israeli flag vessels and to ships of other flags carrying "strategic goods" to Eilat. This formula left a small loophole for negotiation, but Israel was convinced that Nasser meant to cut off its trade with the East and also prevent oil supplies from reaching it. Some highly placed Israelis continued to maintain that Nasser was only intent on proving to the Arab world that he was not standing idly by while Israel prepared to attack Syria, nor hiding behind the

U.N. Emergency Force. Therefore he asked the latter to evacuate its forward positions so it would not be in the way if he had to intervene. Having proved his readiness to act, and claimed to have drawn off Israeli forces from the north, he would have withdrawn, according to this view. But now a series of tragic misunderstandings and wrong moves took place, and Nasser showed himself quickly capable of exploiting these. India's General Rikye, the U.N. Emergency Force commander, transmitted Nasser's request to U Thant; the latter, instead of playing for time, complied immediately. Riding on the wave of enthusiasm in the Arab world, facing the taunts of Jordan to close the Straits, and in the absence of any vigorous reaction from Israel, poker player Nasser staked his all on one card and closed the Straits.[2]

But engaging in brinkmanship also means to be ready for war. Nasser apparently felt he was ready—at least he said so: *"Ahlan wa-sahlan!"* ("You are welcome to try!") Some months earlier he had declared that he was not planning to launch an attack on Israel until certain conditions were fulfilled: (1) There must be unity among the Arabs; (2) International circumstances must be favorable; (3) Egypt must be armed to the point where it has decisive superiority over Israel.

Of these three conditions the first two were now being met. With his bold moves culminating in the closing of the Straits, Nasser had banished, on the surface at least, most of the rivalries and contradictions which had plagued the Arab camp. When King Hussein flew to his Canossa on 30 May, Nasser became the undisputed leader of the Arab world, and it appeared to be merely a matter of time before the other Western-oriented monarch, Feisal of Saudi Arabia, would fall into line.

"International circumstances" were favorable because Egypt enjoyed the strong support of one of the superpowers and could draw freely on its arsenals, while American support of Israel was far more qualified and arms supplies limited. Of the Western European "semipowers," neither had any appetite for repeating the 1956 adventure. While Britain was openly sympathetic to Israel (having little to lose in an Egypt which had severed diplomatic relations earlier over the Rhodesian question), France proclaimed its "neutrality" and gave signs of reorienting its policy toward the Arabs.

But it was on the third, crucial point—that of superior armament—that Nasser's intelligence seems to have misled him, or his sense of realism deserted him. As the appalling havoc Israel wrought on his air and ground forces showed, he was not militarily ready to go over the brink. Yet there must have been confidence among the Arab general staffs that they could at least score some initial victories before the powers would step in and put an end to the fighting. Operational plans discovered by the Israelis in Egyptian, Syrian, and Jordanian command posts called for land attacks on peripheral points—the propaganda machine talked about a short walk to Tel Aviv. Nasser had apparently planned to cut off and occupy Eilat, thereby achieving by military means a goal he had once hoped to attain by diplomacy as a precondition for a settlement.

In general, the Arabs' propensity for announcing aims far beyond their military capacity to achieve had the effect of magnifying the danger in the eyes of Israeli public opinion. While the Israel army command never doubted the outcome of conflict, the public became increasingly anxious as the days wore on without any reaction beyond feverish diplomacy. There was fear that Nasser, seeing his boldness pay off, would not stop at closing the Straits and would extend his revisionism beyond 1956. Nasser himself told Britain's Christopher Mayhew in a television interview broadcast on 5 June that the problem was no longer just Tiran but "Israel as such." In Israel, comparisons with Hitler and Czechoslovakia, Munich and the Sudetenland, were found frequently even in the usually temperate press. And in Egypt, Husseinan Heikal, Nasser's trusted spokesman and editor of *Al Ahram* predicted that Israel could not keep silent in the face of

Egypt's challenge. "After Egypt closes the Gulf, Israel will be left with no alternative but to strike the first blow. . . . Then the death blow will be dealt by the United Arab Republic."

Differences and Parallels

Some of the salient differences in the circumstances surrounding the two campaigns have become clear from the foregoing. A significant overall departure from the 1956 precedent was that in 1967 Israel did not fight a preventive war.

A preventive war requires painstaking preparation—its launching is timed for optimum effect, both military and political. In Israel, the main spur to the concept was the Czech-Egyptian arms deal which took place more than a year before the Sinai Campaign. In 1967, Israel was reacting to Egyptian initiative rather than taking the initiative itself. The lead time from the closing of the Straits until 5 June was less than two weeks. But during that period, Israel's Foreign Minister pursued the quest for a diplomatic solution as diligently as had his predecessor in 1955–1956. The results, while not comparable in detail, were similar in essence: Israel saw no way out through diplomacy.

There are parallels, too, in the personalities of the two foreign ministers, each in his own way a Western-style, small-state diplomatist and accomplished linguist, conscious of the political limitations of military power and determined to exhaust the possibilities of negotiation before letting force be brought into play. Each of these two moderates had an activist faction to contend with on his home territory, ready to press for military action when the diplomatic efforts proved unavailing. While Ben-Gurion consistently embodied the hawk position in contrast to the dovelike Sharett, it was the Chief of Staff, Moshe Dayan, who urged the immediate opening of the Straits of Tiran in November 1955 even after the Cabinet demurred. Eban did not have a contrary-minded Prime Minister, but the same General Dayan, now Min-

229

ister of Defense in the Eshkol Cabinet, brought a counterweight to bear against the diplomatic camp. He attended his first Cabinet meeting on 3 June—on the fifth the Israel radio announced that Egyptian units had been detected moving toward Israel on land and in the air, and that as a countermove Israel's own forces had crossed the frontier. (Dayan has since taken the position—as did Eban in his speech to the U.N. General Assembly—that it was immaterial who fired the first shot on that day; it was Egypt's closing of the Straits which constituted aggression.)

Next to the parallels, there were striking differences in the political circumstances surrounding the two campaigns. One lay in the attitude of the great powers.

Without a doubt, the Soviet Union exerted the most forceful influence on events in the Arab-Israel area. Many observers felt that the hand of Russian policy-makers could be discerned behind Nasser's initial moves. The Soviets' role in passing on the report about Israeli troops concentrations has been mentioned, and the visit of Soviet Foreign Minister Andrei Gromyko to Cairo shortly before the crisis began would also lend support to this version. But even apart from such subsurface indicators, the Soviets made it clear enough that they were backing the "progressive" Arab states to the hilt. Soviet support of the Arab cause in the United Nations had become so automatic in the period since Sinai that Israel no longer felt it stood a chance in the Security Council. Military aid was so massive that both Syria and Egypt were led to believe that their armaments were a match for Israel's sophisticated war machine, and economic and technical help was given generously.

In a way, the two states suffered from the same drawback which dogged Israel in 1956: too much great-power support. Israel has since come to regret the meshing of its plans with the Anglo-French operation, and one result of these second thoughts was the determination this time to go it alone. Moshe Dayan's outstanding contributions to Israel's public relations abroad was his statement that Israel did not wish "American or British boys" to die for it. (Nasser paid Dayan the compliment of paraphrasing him in his speech commemorating the fifteenth anniversary of the revolution on 23 July; he said he had told Soviet President Podgorny that Egypt did not want Russian soldiers to die for her— "we have enough heroes of our own.")

Unlike in 1956, the United States was now wholly sympathetic to Israel's cause, though it did not offer Israel the kind of unconditional backing Russia granted to Syria and Egypt. The United States was not ready to abandon its interests in the Arab world and leave the field to the Soviets, nor did it wish to see Israel suffer defeat without a shot being fired and thereby confer victory upon the Soviets by proxy. But the United States also had an overriding interest in avoiding an armed confrontation with the Soviet Union, which might well have come about if either superpower had backed its side with armed intervention. Maneuvering in this complex of partly conflicting, partly compatible interests resulted in a policy of qualified American backing: President Johnson's assurance to Eban of political support; his plea that Israel abstain from the use of force while the United States tried by diplomatic means to open the Straits, followed by the abortive attempt (so reminiscent of the Dulles ploy in 1956) to set up a combination of "maritime nations" to test the blockade. In the end, Israel's decision to act on its own took the United States off the hook and indirectly served Western interests by checkmating Soviet ambitions.

A fundamental change had occurred, therefore, in the effect of the U.S.-Soviet relationship on the Arab-Israel confrontation. In the period when the Cold War was at its height, Israel found itself in a state of isolation as both powers vied for position in the Arab world. After Ben-Gurion ignored President Eisenhower's plea just before Sinai not to use force, the United States ranged itself with its Cold War foe in exerting every diplomatic pressure for the withdrawal of Israeli forces. This time, by contrast, the

United States not only tolerated the employment of power by Israel but also made unusual efforts to resist Soviet-Arab attempts at making Israel surrender its territorial gains without a prior commitment to peace. Although the Cold War had subsided in the intervening years, the continuing U.S.-Soviet tension over America's role in Vietnam doubtless played a part in the formulation of U.S. Middle East policy; in that sense, the contention that the two crises were interlinked had some substance.

There was another way in which Vietnam may have affected the course of events: just as Israel had assumed that the superpowers were busy elsewhere in 1956, so Egypt may well have concluded that the United States was too preoccupied in Vietnam to get involved in 1967 and to fulfill the pledge it had given in the United Nations ten years earlier. This belief may have been shared by Russia as well.

The role played earlier by President Eisenhower in seeking to restrain Israel was now taken over by President de Gaulle. When Eban stopped off in Paris for a hurriedly arranged interview on his way to Washington, de Gaulle opened the conversation with a lofty admonition to the Foreign Minister: "Above all, don't be the first ones to attack!" But the French President had nothing more helpful to suggest than a four-power meeting which the Soviets had already indicated they would not attend; nor did he go along with Israel's claim to innocent passage through the Straits. Small wonder his counsel had no decisive influence on Israeli policy.

France's interests now no longer coincided with Israel's. In effect, a cooling off in Franco-Israeli relations had been discernible to experienced observers for some time, as France attempted to regain at least part of its traditional role in the Arab world. However, Israeli public opinion kept clinging to the idyll of "friendship" long after the disappearance of the community of interests that existed before de Gaulle liquidated France's Algerian commitment. As a result, the new French attitude came as a sore disappointment. Nor did de Gaulle's proclaimed aim of seeking a general solution to the outstanding problems of the Middle East by four-power agreement strike a sympathetic chord: Israel was accustomed to interpreting "great-power agreement" as a euphemism for solutions at its own expense.

As the French stand progressively hardened until it manifestly aimed at easing Soviet hegemony in the area, Israel reacted first with incredulity, then with ill-concealed bitterness. At last there remained no doubt that the eleven-year French-Israeli honeymoon was over.

The situation was different with regard to Britain, whose attitude, while on the whole sympathetic, was nonetheless equivocal and influenced by both remorse over Suez and nostalgia for Britain's former role. However, Israel had long become used to viewing Britain as a waning power and did not expect much from the former mandatary in the way of support.

Israel's relations with the United Nations reached a nadir following U Thant's decision to order the withdrawal of the Emergency Force. A passage critical of U Thant in Eban's major General Assembly speech brought forth an angry rejoinder, and only a generously worded clarification from the Foreign Minister prevented an open rift.

Unable to obtain a decision in the Security Council (where only Bulgaria, Mali, and India supported its resolution) the Soviet Union had abandoned its long-standing opposition to the General Assembly as an alternate decision-making forum and called for the convening of a special session to deal with the crisis. But here too the Arab-Soviet coalition, in the face of vigorous American diplomacy, was incapable of mustering the required two-thirds for a vote demanding Israel's unconditional withdrawal from the occupied territories. As for the two Pakistani resolutions calling on Israel to rescind its annexation of Jerusalem which were adopted by overwhelming majorities, Israel contended that the Assembly was not competent to act in this matter.

Israel had once again presented the world community with a *fait accompli* regarding the status of the Holy City, but whereas the earlier moves were made after the U.N. internationalization decision was already on the books, now the Knesset enacted the enabling statutes and the annexation was consummated before a U.N. resolution was on the record.

Legal considerations apart, the consensus in Israel was that the United Nations, having twice shown itself unable to prevent the shelling of Jewish Jerusalem by the Arab side, was now bereft of the moral authority to legislate on the fate of the city.

Public Opinion

Sympathy for Israel in the United States and Britain was not confined to the level of government; in the entire English-speaking world and in Western Europe (France included) public opinion was single-mindedly on the side of Israel, whose image was initially that of a weak nation with a just cause being bullied by a clever and unscrupulous adversary. Israel's hesitation after Nasser closed the Straits caused mounting alarm among its friends who feared that it was being led into a trap. In contrast to 1956, Israel was the side under attack; its cause—the defense of innocent passage through an international waterway—was just, and even the subsequent controversy surrounding the actual opening of hostilities hardly affected this. The thesis that the blockade in itself constituted the initial act of aggression found wide acceptance. It was only when, following its stunning victories, Israel ceased being the underdog and the aftermath of the war brought forth a fresh victim deserving of compassion (namely the new wave of refugees) that a shift took place in world opinion.

The reaction among the Jewish population outside of Israel was also strikingly different from that in 1956. Then many Jews shared the dismay of the general public when Israel attacked, and Jewish opinion only gradually swung around to identification with

Israel. This time, anxiety among Jews for Israel's fate rose to a fever pitch almost immediately, and by the time the war began had expressed itself in an unprecedented outpouring of monetary contributions. Even Jews who had never publicly identified with Israel's cause suddenly showed their solidarity. The total collected and pledged in gifts and loans throughout the world was about $350 million, which made it likely that Israel, in spite of the drain caused by the war, would end the year with higher reserves in foreign currency than at the beginning. Thousands of young Jews in the Western countries volunteered for civilian tasks in Israel to replace men and women serving at the front. (Ironically, the short duration of the war and consequent rapid demobilization left Israel with the problem of what to do with superfluous volunteers.) At the same time, American Jews in particular had the comfortable feeling that their sentiments were in line with their government's policy rather than opposed to it, as in 1956. For the first time, the United States was giving Israel its broad political backing, and there was no need to apply organized pressure with a view to influencing policy. In sum, there is no doubt that the crisis and war greatly strengthened the bonds between Israel and diaspora Jewry, reversing the trend toward divergency that had been operative since the state was established.

The Inter-Arab Alignment

In 1956 the various alliances among the Arab states remained paper pacts. In 1967 mutual defense agreements were implemented, and for Israel the dread prospect of a three-front war became reality. But that reality turned out to be less somber than anticipated. It was Nasser's commitment to come to Syria's aid which got Egypt into the war, but the knockout blow Israel dealt to Egypt's forces in Sinai was so swift and so devastating that Israel was able to deploy its forces in time to cope with its remaining two foes. By the time serious fighting broke out on the Syrian front, Egypt was not only unable to assist, but was beyond assistance itself. As for Jordan's position, the fate that befell the Hashimite Kingdom as the result of Egypt's initiative is the stuff tragedy is made on. Hussein obviously miscalculated when he signed the pact with Nasser on 30 May, but his assumptions were reasonable: he must have been convinced that either Egypt was strong enough to defeat Israel in battle—in which case he would find himself isolated if he stood aside; or that Israel would accept the blockade without a fight, in which case Nassar would become irresistible. So he jumped on the bandwagon while there was still time. Having placed his army under Egyptian command, he may have had little choice but to fight once the war had started—or else he simply felt honor bound to live up to his commitment and open a second front.

Israel was genuinely taken aback when Jordanian guns began firing on the New City at 11:30 A.M. on 5 June and Jordanian troops simultaneously moved into the demilitarized zone to occupy U.N.T.S.O. headquarters in the former Government House. Through U.N. channels, Foreign Minister Eban urged King Hussein to desist, but the Jordanians not only kept up their shelling of the Israeli capital but also used long-range artillery against populated points on the coast. Israel rushed its crack troops to the lightly manned central front, and the battle for Jerusalem was under way. Of the 730 Israeli dead in the war, nearly 200 lost their lives in the heavy fighting for the Old City before it was taken. The rest of Jordan's West Bank was occupied in short order.

Of the other Arab states, Iraq's principal contribution, after stationing troops in Jordan, was to send a heavy bomber against Tel Aviv, but the pilot bombed the seaside resort of Natanya instead before his plane was downed. Algerian troops and planes arrived in Egypt after the cease-fire was signed; and the Lebanese Chief of Staff is said to have refused to obey an order to open hostilities.

236

Causes of the Victory

The swiftness with which Israel completed the conquest of the Sinai Peninsula—the first Israeli units reached the Suez Canal less than forty-eight hours after the fighting began—was the more astonishing as this time there was no surprise. The armies had been facing one another for at least two weeks, each intent on the other's every move. In a massive buildup, Nasser had poured 100,000 men and more than 900 tanks into the peninsula, in contrast to 1956 when he moved forces out to meet the Anglo-French invasion. In the intervening years, redoubtable defensive positions had been prepared under Soviet guidance.

Israel's victory was, of course, a composite of many factors. The lessons learned in the earlier test of strength on the same territory were applied in more sophisticated tactics the second time; the mistakes made in 1956 were avoided. But the most important ingredient was the attainment of absolute air superiority, which in turn made possible the nearly complete destruction of Egyptian armor in the peninsula. By 11 A.M. on 5 June, the Egyptian air force had become nonoperational, and by noon the air arms of Jordan and Syria too were out of action. The record of that "shortest day" added up to 451 enemy planes destroyed—391 of them on the ground at 17 different airfields, and 60 in air battles. The threat of aerial bombardment of Israel's cities was thus eliminated without outside assistance, and Israel's air force devoted its striking power to the destruction of enemy armor, transport, and artillery, and to other forms of ground support. The four main interrelated elements responsible for these results were the following:

(1) Impeccable air intelligence, supplying detailed knowledge of the disposition of enemy aircraft and installations. By contrast, Egypt's appreciation of Israel's capability was deficient in the extreme. Nasser's contention that Britain and the United States

sent carrier-based planes against Egypt was presumably based on the impression that Israel's air force could not have flown all the sorties counted. Yet achievement of minimum turnaround time, far below conventional standards, did make this possible.

(2) Planning of the initial operation with such precision that 99 per cent of the execution went according to plan.

(3) Superior operational capacity and control.

(4) Superior quality of the human element, as it found expression in flight crews capable of maximum utilization of their equipment, and imbued with uncommon fighting spirit.

This last feature doubtless played a decisive role in determining the outcome of the war, and it was here that the Egyptian intelligence failure was most glaring. Cut off from direct contact with Israel, the Arabs were unable to understand the powerful will to collective existence which created out of the entire able-bodied population a tightly coiled war machine whose striking power was extraordinary once it was unleashed. Together with this misjudgment, the Arabs overvalued the effect of the Russian armaments in their own hands. In effect, the Six-Day War proved again that a small state can overcome the limitations of its absolute power inventory if its population possesses the motivation and technological skills to achieve relative superiority; whereas numerical superiority and ample arms supplies are unavailing when the human factor is inadequate. (The conflict proved too, of course, that even in the atomic age small powers will resort to war as a means of policy: Egypt proved it by its misguided brinkmanship; Israel by taking up the challenge. But it also showed that the superpowers are less likely to become involved in the small states' struggles than earlier; that they may confine themselves to sitting on the sidelines and watching each other while the small states fight it out.)

Political Consequences

If the Israeli planning for the various military contingencies was meticulous, political planning for the new conditions created by the military victories was by no means comparable in efficacy. The speed and thoroughness of these victories astonished even the Israelis themselves: within less than a week Israel found itself transformed from potential victim to military juggernaut riding astride a large part of the region. The existing power relationship, called into question since 15 May, was basically altered as the Jordanian and Egyptian armies could be written off as offensive units; the superpowers neutralized each other's influence; while the United Nations itself, laboring under the same power constellation, could do little more than call for a cease-fire along lines which ratified the situation created by Israel's advance.

These cease-fire lines, extending from the Suez Canal in the south to the Jordan River in the east and up to the Golan Heights of Syria left Israel in control of territory three times larger than its own. They also confronted it with a host of problems, not only in the realms of administration and security, but also of an economic and psychological nature. Many of them were being handled skillfully and with the flair for improvisation characteristic of Israel's army; others—especially those of an economic nature —were proving rather more intractable for a country with considerable economic problems of its own. The initial assumption— or at least the hope—was that the Arab states concerned would find the loss of these territories incentive enough to modify their stance of nonrecognition and belligerency. When this did not come about, Israel saw no other course open to it but to hold on to the territories as its trump card for a future settlement, and as a gauge for its security.[3] The Sinai Peninsula should not again become a base for rocket, air, or ground attack, the Jordanian bulge for artillery bombardment, or the Syrian Heights for the shelling of settlements in the valley.

The inability of the Soviet-Arab bloc to have either the Security Council or the General Assembly adopt a resolution calling for unconditional withdrawal fortified Israel in its resolve.

Since the Sinai Campaign, Israel had refused to attend sessions of the Israeli-Egyptian Mixed Armistice Commission, regarding the armistice agreement as no longer in force on the ground that Egypt had violated its main provisions. Now Israel declared the agreements with Jordan and Syria invalid as well because of the armed attacks by the two countries. Relations with the defeated states, therefore, were based on the cease-fire agreements—indeed, Premier Eshkol announced that Israel would not again be content with armistice agreements on the 1949 model but would prefer the absence of any legal document whatsoever until peace was signed.

Alternative Solutions

As long as the government was unwilling to commit itself as to the ultimate fate of the territories being held, it was natural that public opinion in Israel should be preoccupied with the problem. The official policy of holding on "until peace do us part" was widely approved, but there was also a sizable body of opinion, especially on the right, favoring outright annexation. (With the establishment of a Government of National Unity during the crisis, the former right-wing opposition became a full-fledged partner to decision-making, and Herut's Menahem Begin for the first time occupied a Cabinet post.) Another group advocated that a Palestinian state be established on the West Bank and in the Gaza Strip, possibly tied to Israel in a federation of which Jerusalem would be the capital. Still another group, in which Mapam party members were prominent, felt that it would be better to have King Hussein as a neighbor again than an independent Republican Arab state which could easily turn Nasserist. These people acknowledged that Hussein had shown the capacity to rule and to maintain stability; they were willing to forgive him for betting on the wrong horse, particularly since his step should be understood in the light of the prolonged hesitation on Israel's part. Those opposing annexation were mindful that such a policy would add roughly a million Arabs to Israel's population, and thereby in effect make of it the kind of binational state which the majority had once so vehemently rejected as a solution to the Palestine problem. At the same time, they wished to utilize the opportunity for dealing directly with the Arabs of Palestine, most of whom were now under Israel suzerainty and no longer needed another Arab government as their spokesman. However, in the initial weeks it was too early for any meaningful dialogue: the West Bank and Gaza Arabs were still in the state of shock caused by the transition from talk about Israel's destruction on one day to living under Israel's flag on the next.

Since the West Bank and the Gaza Strip together held some twenty-five refugee camps, Israel now came face to face with this human problem. A strong conviction took hold that Israel should take the initiative in solving it, and the government set up a working party of forty experts under the direction of social scientists of the Hebrew University to produce a blueprint. However, the initial ground swell of opinion that called for doing something "right away" was soon replaced by the realization that the problem was too big for Israel to tackle alone, and that any radical solution would have to await regional cooperation and international financing.

In the anxious days before the war broke out and in the tense atmosphere of war itself, Israel had had no time to formulate specific goals beyond its determination not to let its victory be forfeited this time without the prize, peace. Aware that hostility can only be overcome by interest, Israel used its victory to create a situation where the Arab states' overwhelming interest—namely to regain the lost territory and, for Egypt the use of the Canal—would bring them to the peace table. By early August, Israel was still waiting for the Arabs' "telephone call" (in General Dayan's phrase) to begin direct talks, but the phone was not likely to ring for as long as the two extremist Arab states, Algeria and Syria, pressed for continued belligerency. Indeed, it was conceivable that the Arab position would harden further under this pressure, to which was added the renewed agitation of Ahmad Shuqairi. For Israel, on the other hand, prolonged occupation of the territories would tend to create new facts and a new *status quo* from which it would become increasingly difficult to retreat.

The question of what Israel's policy should seek first, peace or security, thus posed itself more sharply than ever: if peace was the primary goal, then there would have to be some measure of faith that security would flow from it. This would call for a balance between creating negative interest, the desire on the Arabs' part to relieve the pressure on them, and a positive interest which would make the prospect of an arrangement attractive, or at least palatable. If, on the other hand, maximum security was the first priority, if the main consideration was the operative depth offered by the Sinai Peninsula and the West Bank in case of another threat of armed attack, then the risk that peace will not be a natural concomitant would have to be taken.

In spite of these cautions, however, it would be rash to predict that Israel's attempt to pluck peace from victory need fail once more. In a situation at once static and volatile, bound in by old shibboleths and open to new initiatives, those stubborn, brave, and imaginative qualities which Israel had demonstrated so amply on the battlefield may yet prove themselves in a bold breakthrough for peace.

Notes

The following abbreviations are used in the notes.

A.J.I.L. = *American Journal of International Law*

D.B.G. = David Ben-Gurion

D.S.B. = *U.S. Department of State Bulletin*

DK = *Divrei ha-Knesset* (Israel Parliamentary Proceedings)

P.D.H.C. = *Parliamentary Debates, House of Commons*

J Post = *Jerusalem Post*

M.A.C. = Mixed Armistice Commission

R.I.I.A. = Royal Institute of International Affairs

O.R. = *Official Records*

U.N.G.A. = United Nations General Assembly

U.N.S.C. = United Nations Security Council

U.N.T.S.O. = United Nations Truce Supervision Organization

Introduction

1. In her pioneer work on small-state foreign policy, Annette Baker Fox describes small-state behavior as "anti-balance of power" (*The Power of Small States* [Chicago, 1959], p. 187).

2. Quincy Wright, "International Conflict and the U.N.," *World Politics*, X (October 1957), 34.

3. "Interests are what a nation feels to be necessary to its security and well-being; objectives are interests sharpened to meet particular international situations; policies are thought out ways of attaining objectives" (Stephen B. Jones, "The Power Inventory and National Strategy," *World Politics*, VI [July 1954], 421–52).

4. Implicitly by Secretary of State John Foster Dulles in his report

243

on his Middle East tour on 1 June 1953, and more explicitly by Prime Minister Sir Anthony Eden in his Guildhall Speech of 9 November 1955. Texts in J. C. Hurewitz, *Diplomacy in the Near and Middle East,* Vol. II (Princeton, 1956), pp. 337–42 and 413–15, respectively.

5. David Ben-Gurion, "Israel's Security and Her International Position before and after the Sinai Campaign," *Israel Government Year Book 5720* (1959–1960), p. 57.

6. Richard L. Rubenstein, "The Significance of Zionism," *Reconstructionist,* XXVI (29 April 1960), 6.

7. *Israel Government Year Book 5712* (1951–1952), p. ix, xii.

8. "Israel's Security," p. 22.

9. Ben-Gurion, *Rebirth and Destiny of Israel* (New York, 1954), p. 296.

10. Text in *Reshumot–Sefer ha-Huqim* (Official Publications—Book of Laws), No. 51, 6 July 1950, p. 159.

11. See Joseph B. Schechtman, "The Frozen Stampede," *Midstream,* VI (Summer 1960), 66.

12. "Himmlisches und Irdisches Israel," *Yediot Hadashot* (Tel Aviv), 6 Nov. 1953, p. 2.

13. "Israel's Security," p. 82.

14. Baruch Kurzweil, "The New 'Canaanism' in Israel," *Judaism* 2 (January 1953), p. 3. See also S. Ephraim, "The Canaanites," *Jewish Frontier* 19 (August 1952), 25–26. An Israeli observer wrote in 1961 of the Canaanites: "As an organized body they have since disbanded (though they turned up again in different guise for a while). There is no doubt, however, that some of their attitudes have penetrated far and wide, even though they may assume less articulate form. That it was found necessary to take active steps to promote 'Jewish awareness' in the schools is in itself partly a result of the prevalence of such attitudes." (Israel Schen, "B. G. and the Gallant Six Hundred," *Jewish Spectator,* XXVI [January 1961], 20).

15. Elie Kedourie, *Nationalism* (New York, 1960), p. 76.

16. "Poles" (pseud.), *Ha-Arez,* 29 April 1960, p. 2.

17. In connection with Israel's admission to the U.N., Moshe Sharett told the General Assembly unequivocally that Israel claims no allegiance from Jews outside its borders (*O.R.,* 3rd Session, 207th Mtg., 4 May 1949, p. 332). The most widely publicized such statement was Premier Ben-Gurion's declaration to Jacob Blaustein,

president of the American Jewish Committee, on 23 Aug. 1950 (*American Jewish Year Book* 53 [1952], p. 182).

18. An example is the statement by Meir Argov (Mapai) in 16 *DK* 2554 (30 Aug. 1954).

19. "The Jewish State and the Jewish People," Address to plenary session of World Jewish Congress, Stockholm, August 1959 (unpublished typescript obtained from World Jewish Congress, New York).

20. An account of the origins and development of these movements may be found in Feliks Gross and Basil J. Vlavianos (eds.), *Struggle for Tomorrow: Modern Political Ideologies of the Jewish People* (New York, 1954). See also Judd L. Teller, "The Making of the Ideals that Rule Israel," *Commentary,* XVIII (January–February 1954), 49–57, 157–62.

21. Israel's parliament consequently has its left, its center, and its right parties, and a group of religious parties in addition. Starting with the extreme left, the spectrum—in turns of percentage of votes received by the various parties in the elections of 26 July 1955— looked as follows (figures in parentheses indicate the number of seats held in the Knesset):

Communists, 4.5 (6)
Mapam, 7.3 (9)
Ahdut ha-Avodah, 8.2 (10)
Mapai, 32.2 (40)
Progressives, 4.4 (5)
General Zionists, 10.2 (13)
Herut, 12.6 (15)
National Religious, 9.1 (11)
Agudat Israel–Poalei Agudat Israel, 4.7 (6)
Arab "lists" affiliated with Mapai, 4.4 (5)

22. An example is Ya'qov Riftin's statement on 31 May 1950, in 5 *DK* 1572.

23. 19 *DK* 244–46 (3 Nov. 1955).

24. See Esco Foundation for Palestine, *Palestine: A Study of Jewish, Arab and British Policies,* 2 vols. (New Haven, 1947); J. C. Hurewitz, *The Struggle for Palestine* (New York, 1950); and Ben Halpern, *The Idea of the Jewish State* (Cambridge, 1961).

25. 14 *DK* 1588 (15 June 1953).

26. See Ernest Stock, "The Press of Israel," *Journalism Quarterly,* XXXI (Fall 1954), 481–94.

27. Ya'qov Hazan (Mapam), 1 *DK* 125 (10 March 1949); Arieh Altman (Herut), 14 *DK* 1588 (15 June 1953).

28. Frederick H. Hartmann, *The Relations of Nations* (New York, 1957), p. 5.

Chapter I

1. The most authoritative account in English of the military operations is Netanel Lorch, *The Edge of the Sword: Israel's War of Independence 1947–1949* (New York, 1961). Lt. Col. Lorch is a former Chief of the Military History Division of the Israeli General Staff.

2. D.B.G., "Israel's Security," p. 11.

3. 1 *DK* 53 (8 March 1949).

4. *Ibid.,* p. 68.

5. *Ibid.,* pp. 69–70.

6. 1 *DK* 757 (20 June 1949).

7. 5 *DK* 1589 (31 May 1950).

8. James G. McDonald, *My Mission to Israel* (New York, 1951), pp. 165–68.

9. Arthur Lourie, quoted in *The Jewish Chronicle* (London), 10 June 1960, p. 8.

10. Walter Eytan, *The First Ten Years: A Diplomatic History of Israel* (New York, 1958), p. 52.

11. Eytan relates that members of the individual Arab delegations at Lausanne sought direct contact with the Israelis at odd hours and out-of-the-way locations so as to avoid being detected by their colleagues. He concludes it would have been better for the Commission, or for the Israel delegation, to insist at once that the Conference not take place as long as the Arabs refused to sit at the same table with the Israelis, as they had done at Rhodes (*ibid.,* 53–54).

12. Rony E. Gabbay, *A Political Study of the Arab-Jewish Conflict* (Geneva, 1959), pp. 251, 322.

13. *Ibid.,* pp. 318–22.

14. For the Commission's progress reports, see U.N.G.A., A/819,

838, 927, 992, 1252, 1255, 1288, 1367/Rev. 1, 1793, 1985, 2121, 2216, 2216/Add.l, 2629, 2897, 3199. Analytical discussion of the proceedings may be found in Gabbay; in Don Peretz, *Israel and the Palestine Arabs* (Washington, 1958); and in Ben Halpern, *The Idea of the Jewish State* (Cambridge, 1961).

15. 1 *DK* 729 (15 June 1949).

16. Haim Ben-Asher, 1 *DK* 53 (8 March 1949).

17. Quoted in Jon Kimche, *Seven Fallen Pillars* (New York, 1953), p. 315.

18. 1 *DK* 721 (15 June 1949).

19. Mediator's Progress Report, U.N.G.A., A/648.

20. Resolution 194 (III/1); Sharett to Knesset, 1 *DK* 721 (15 June 1949).

21. 3 *DK* 851 (23 Jan. 1951).

22. Peretz, p. 44.

23. U.N.G.A., A/992, 22 Sept. 1949.

24. 8 *DK* 848 (23 Jan. 1951).

25. Eytan, p. 56.

26. Gabbay, p. 152.

27. U.N.G.A., A/992, p. 3.

28. *N.Y. Times,* 26 July 1949.

29. P.C.C. Report of 25 October 1950, A/1985. The same report to the Secretary General also called on the Arabs to adapt their policy to the new state of affairs; to integrate nonreturnees among refugees in their midst, and so on. But while Israel's policy was necessarily shaped in part by the attitude of the Arabs, this study is mainly concerned with analyzing the foreign policy of Israel and not that of the Arab states.

30. Gabbay, pp. 6–8.

31. Text of protocol in U.N.G.A., A/927, Annex C, 13 June 1949, p. 13.

32. Eytan, p. 61.

33. Hans J. Morgenthau, "Khrushchev's New Cold War Strategy," *Commentary,* XXVIII (Nov. 1959), 381.

34. *Ibid.*

35. See Hurewitz, *The Struggle for Palestine* (New York, 1950), p. 324.

36. Meir Grabovsky (Argov), 5 *DK* 1576 (31 May 1950).

37. Sharett, 8 *DK* 851 (23 Jan. 1951).

38. 1 *DK* 858, 861 (29 June 1949).

39. Y. Hazan, 1 *DK* 125 (10 March 1949).

40. Y. Meridor, 5 *DK* 1574 (31 May 1950).

41. 1 *DK* 861 (29 June 1949).

42. 5 *DK* 1580–81 (31 May 1950).

43. 8 *DK* 852 (23 Jan. 1951).

44. Y. Riftin, 5 *DK* 1572 (31 May 1950).

45. *Ibid.,* p. 1587.

46. 1 *DK* 719 (15 June 1949).

47. Michael S. Comay, "Five Years of Israel Diplomacy," *Zionist Newsletter* 5 (5 May 1953), p. 9.

48. 8 *DK* 855 (23 Jan. 1951).

49. *J Post,* 26 Jan. 1954.

50. 20 *DK* 1707 (23 April 1956).

51. Riley cable to Security Council 12 June 1951, S/2194.

52. S/2298/Rev. 1. Passage of the resolution pointed up still another dilemma for Israel's foreign policy: the more support Israel's position received in the West, the greater the hostility shown it in the Arab world. As Gabbay points out, the Security Council's action whipped up a wave of virulent anti-Israel propaganda in the Arab states (p. 327).

53. Text in Hurewitz, *Diplomacy in the Near and Middle East* (Princeton, 1956), Vol. II, p. 308.

54. *Ibid.,* pp. 309–10.

55. The count (unchecked by the author) was apparently made by Michael Foot and Mervyn Jones, who so state in their *Guilty Men* (New York, 1957), p. 78.

56. Anthony Eden, *Full Circle* (Boston, 1960), p. 372.

57. *N.Y. Times,* 10 April 1956.

58. *Full Circle,* p. 589.

59. 5 *DK* 1574 (31 May 1950).

60. *Ibid.,* p. 1576.

61. *Ibid.,* p. 1572.

62. Page 141.

63. A. A. Ben-Asher (pseud.), *Yahsei Huts shel Israel* (Israel's Foreign Relations) (Tel Aviv, 1955), p. 102.

64. *Ibid.,* p. 103.

65. Quoted by Y. Riftin in 5 *DK* 1572 (31 May 1950).

66. Text of four-power proposal to Egypt on Middle East Command in U.S. *Department of State Bulletin* 25 (22 Oct. 1951), p. 647.

67. Page 142.

68. 10 *DK* 277–81 (4 Nov. 1951).

69. 10 *DK* 327 (5 Nov. 1951).

70. *J Post,* 7 Nov. 1951.

71. 10 *DK* 284 (4 Nov. 51).

72. *J Post,* 23 Nov. 1951.

73. *N.Y. Times,* 23 Oct. 1951.

74. *D.S.B.* 25 (19 Nov. 1951), p. 817.

75. All quotes from Eytan, p. 143.

76. Hal Lehrman, "The Arabs, Israel, and Near East Defense," *Commentary,* XIV (Dec. 1952) 563, 567.

Chapter II

1. See J. C. Hurewitz, *The Struggle for Palestine* (New York, 1950), pp. 287, 305–07.

2. *Soviet News* (London), 17 April 1955.

3. See Oles Smolansky, "The Soviet Union and the Arab East, 1947–57: A Study in Diplomatic Relations" (unpublished Ph.D. dissertation, Columbia University, 1959); George Lenczowski, "Evolution of Soviet Policy Toward the Middle East," *Journal of Politics,* XX (Feb. 1958), 162–86; and Geoffrey Wheeler, "Russia and the Middle East," *Political Quarterly* (London), XXVIII (April–June 1957) 127–36; among others.

4. Walter Z. Laqueur, *Communism and Nationalism in the Middle East* (New York, 1956), p. 260.

5. Text in *J Post,* 30 April 1953.

6. For text of Dulles' speech, see note 4, Chapter I.

7. 14 *DK* 1581 ff. (15 and 16 June 1953).

8. 14 *DK* 1412 (27 May 1953).

9. 14 *DK* 1587 (15 June 1953).

10. *Ibid.*

11. *Ibid.*, p. 1588.

12. *Ibid.*, p. 1581.

13. *J. Post*, 18 Sept. 1953.

14. For a summary of the results of this analysis, see E. Stock, "The Press of Israel," *Journalism Quarterly*, XXXI (Fall 1954), 481–94.

15. My analysis of press content referred to in the preceding note was supplemented by interviews with some sixty leading Israelis in various walks of life.

16. *J Post*, 9 Oct. 1953.

17. 15 *DK* 314 (7 Dec. 1953).

18. See p. 78.

19. S/3122, Annex 1, 23 October 1953.

20. *D.S.B.* 29 (16 Nov. 1953), pp. 674–75.

21. *J Post*, 25 Oct. 1953.

22. 21 and 26 Oct. 1953.

23. Moshe Keren, "Israel's Isolation," *Ha-Arez*, 30 Oct. 1953.

24. *D.S.B.* 29 (26 Oct. 1953), p. 553.

25. Editorial in *J Post*, 15 April 1954.

26. *D.S.B.* 30 (26 April 1954), p. 628, and 32 (10 May 1954), p. 708.

27. 16 *DK* 1596 (12 May 1954).

28. The Israeli raiders on occasion left leaflets at the scene which explained the reason for the attack (Elmo H. Hutchison, *Violent Truce: A Military Observer Looks at the Arab-Israeli Conflict 1951– 1955* [New York, 1956], p. 15).

29. "Jordan Admits Breach of Armistice Agreement," *J Post*, 29 Nov. 1951, p. 1. On the same occasion, Israel also expressed regret over the killing of an Arab Legionnaire.

30. Hutchison, pp. 13–18.

31. S/3139/Rev. 2, 24 Nov. 1953.

32. *O.R.*, 637th Mtg., 12 Nov. 1953, pp. 1–41.

33. *J Post*, 24 March 1954. For Cmdr. Hutchison's own account of these events, see *Violent Truce*, 47 ff.

34. *Davar*, 1 April 1954.

35. *J Post*, 30 March 1954.

36. Eytan, p. 108.

37. *Ibid.*

38. Lt. Gen. E. L. M. Burns, *Between Arab and Israeli* (London, 1962), p. 47.

39. *J Post*, 25 Jan. 1955, p. 1.

40. U.N.S.C., *O.R.*, 688th Mtg., 13 Jan. 1955, p. 18.

41. *N.Y. Times*, 3 March 1955.

42. *Ibid.*, 4 March 1955.

43. S/3378, 29 March 1955.

44. *O.R.*, 694th Mtg., 23 March 1955, p. 17.

45. *O.R.*, 697th Mtg., 6 April 1955, pp. 7–10.

46. Burns's report to U.N.S.C., S/3390 & Add.1, 14 April 1955.

47. *O.R.*, 698th Mtg., 19 April 1955, p. 25.

48. Burns, *Between Arab and Israeli*, p. 77.

49. *Ibid.*, pp. 83–90.

50. S/3422, 8 Sept. 1955.

51. Burns, *Between Arab and Israeli*, p. 92.

52. *Ibid.*, 93 ff. See S/3101 for Egypt's complaint of 2 Oct. 1953 alleging that on 28 Sept. 1953 Israeli armed forces had occupied positions in the demilitarized zone.

Chapter III

1. *J Post*, 28 Dec. 1952, p. 1.

2. See editorials in *J Post*, 16 July 1953, and *Zmanim*, 11 Oct. 1953.

3. Text of U.S.–Iraq Military Assistance Agreement in Hurewitz, *Diplomacy in the Near and Middle East* (Princeton, 1956), Vol. II, pp. 346–48.

4. *J. Post*, 23 April 1954.

5. 16 *DK* 1599 (12 May 1954).

6. 16 *DK* 1655–56 (17 May 1954).

7. Text of treaty, which was signed on 3 Oct. 1954, in Royal Institute of International Affairs, *Documents 1955*, p. 248.

8. *J Post*, 21 Aug. 1954.

9. 16 *DK* 2551–70 (30 August 1954). Thus Mapam found that the "American policy of arming the Arabs" was linked to the re-

arming of Germany, and also used the same opportunity to polemicize against the acceptance of the U.S. grant-in-aid, which entailed "political and economic strangulation" and was a danger to sovereignty.

10. 16 *DK* 2610 (1 September 1954).

11. *The Times* (London), 17 September 1954.

12. See Inis L. Claude Jr., *Power and International Relations* (New York, 1962); Ernst B. Haas, "The Balance of Power: Prescription, Concept or Propaganda?" *World Politics,* V (July 1953), 442.

13. Leonard Binder, "The Middle East as a Subordinate International System," *World Politics,* X (April 1958), 410, 426.

14. The rivalry between the Nile power and Mesopotamia goes, of course, back to antiquity. For ancient Israel's efforts to influence this regional power balance, see E. Stock, "Egypt—Israel: Some Earlier Relations," *Reconstructionist,* XXV (20 March 1959), 19.

15. Haim Ben-Asher, 10 *DK* 314 (5 Nov. 1951).

16. Nicholas John Spykman, *America's Strategy in World Politics* (New York, 1952) pp. 21–25.

17. Yitzhak Oron, "The Revolutionary Regime and Egypt's Potential," *Ha-Mizrah he-Hadash* (Hebrew), VII (1960), 173–79.

18. Gen. Yigal Allon, writing after Sinai, goes so far as to imply that Israel's only possible defense lies in an "interceptive attack" aimed at making an Arab attack impossible. He declines to use the term "preventive war" on the ground that a state of war already exists. *Masakh shel Hol* (Curtain of Sand) (Tel Aviv, 1959), p. 76.

19. Netanel Lorch, *The Edge of the Sword: Israel's War of Independence 1947–1949* (New York, 1961), pp. 146–66, *passim.*

20. See John Bagot Glubb, *A Soldier with the Arabs* (London, 1957).

21. F. H. Harbison and Ibrahim Abdelkader Ibrahim, *Human Resources for Egyptian Enterprises* (New York, McGraw Hill, 1959) pp. 27, 29.

22. *Ibid.,* pp. 30–33.

23. See Council of Jewish Federations and Welfare Funds, *Ten Years of American Aid to Israel* (New York, mimeo, 1957).

24. Kurt R. Grossmann, *Germany's Moral Debt: The German-Israel Agreement* (Washington, 1954).

25. *Bank of Israel Report 1961,* p. 30.
26. *N.Y. Times,* 10 Nov. 1952, p. 10.
27. Oron, p. 172.

Chapter IV

1. Frederick H. Hartman, *The Relations of Nations* (New York, 1957), pp. 3–4.
2. See Albert Hourani, "The Middle East and the Crisis of 1956," *St. Antony's Papers No. 4* (London, 1958).
3. Page 35.
4. Don Peretz speaks of an "Arab diaspora" in his "Arab Refugee Report" to the Rockefeller Foundation (mimeo, 1962).
5. Hans J. Morgenthau, *Politics among Nations* (New York, 1954), p. 64.
6. Eytan says that Israel was always conscious of the loose wording in some of the clauses of the agreements, but let it go through on the assumption that they would last less than a year (*The First Ten Years: A Diplomatic History of Israel* [New York, 1958], p. 37).
7. U.N.S.C., *O.R.,* 549th Mtg., pp. 8–9.
8. *Ibid.,* pp. 17–18.
9. S/2322, 1 Sept. 1951.
10. 686th Mtg., 7 Dec. 1954, p. 20.
11. *Israel's Armistice Agreements with the Arab States* (Tel Aviv, 1951), p. 83.
12. Simcha Dinitz, "The Legal Aspects of the Egyptian Blockade of the Suez Canal," *Georgetown Law Journal,* XLV (Winter 1956–57), 186.
13. *A State of War After the Cessation of Hostilities* (Jerusalem, 1961), pp. 41–42, 75. Cf. also the chapter on "Truces and Armistices" in L. M. Bloomfield, *Egypt, Israel and the Gulf of Aqaba in International Law* (Toronto, 1957).
14. U.N.S.C., *O.R.,* 683rd Mtg., 3 Nov. 1954, p. 22.
15. An interesting precedent cited by him is the refusal of Lithuania in the 1920's to establish normal relations with Poland, aspiring instead to maintain "an intermediate state between war and peace."

16. Philip C. Jessup, "Should International Law Recognize an Intermediate Status Between Peace and War?" *A.J.I.L.,* XLVIII (1954), 100. Jessup had in mind primarily the Cold War.

17. The term unilateral initiative was coined by Charles Osgood to denote an action softening the military posture for the purpose of communicating a desire for peace to the other side. The context was, of course, the Cold War.

18. 16 *DK* 1598–99 (10 May 1954).

19. U.N.S.C., *O.R.,* 656th Mtg., 22 Jan. 1954, p. 6.

20. U.N.G.A., *O.R.,* 7th Session, Ad Hoc Pol. Comm., 1 Dec. 1952, 165–71.

21. "Israel Restates Her Peace Offers," *N.Y. Times,* 20 Dec. 1955.

22. A detailed account of the efforts of the P.C.C. to make progress on the compensation problem, and of the changing attitudes of the two sides, may be found in Don Peretz, *Israel and the Palestine Arabs* (Washington, 1958), chs. x, xi.

23. One such critic was Hedley V. Cooke, former American Consul in Jerusalem. See his *Israel: A Blessing and a Curse* (London, 1960), p. 215.

24. Eytan, p. 115.

25. Peretz, chs. ii, xii.

26. E. L. M. Burns, *Between Arab and Israeli* (London, 1962), p. 41.

27. Cmdr. Hutchison's book, *Violent Truce* (New York, 1956) is anti-Israel in tone, and Maj. Gen. Vagn Bennike gave an interview distinctly uncomplimentary to Israel after he left his post (*N.Y. Times,* 7 Nov. 1954, p. 30).

28. Page 5.

29. This highly condensed account of the dispute is based on the detailed exposition in J. C. Hurewitz, "The Israeli-Syrian Crisis in the Light of the Arab-Israel Armistice System," *International Organization,* V (Aug. 1951), 459–79. The article also describes the relationship of the armistice system to the U.N. Security Council in considerable detail.

30. Report of Chief of Staff to Security Council, 6 Nov. 1951 (S/2389).

31. S/3106, 12 Oct. 1953.

32. S/3122, 23 Oct. 1953.

33. *D.S.B.* 29 (26 Oct. 1953), 533.

34. Aranne (Mapai), 15 *DK* 281 (30 Nov. 1953).

35. "Lesson of the Deterrent," *Jewish Observer,* IX (7 Oct. 1960), 9. See also *Diary of the Sinai Campaign* (London, 1961), p. 9.

36. Abba Eban, *The Voice of Israel* (New York, 1957), p. 192.

37. Moshe Dayan, "Israel's Border and Security Problems," *Foreign Affairs,* XXXIII (Jan. 1955), 260.

38. Burns, p. 63.

39. John Bagot Glubb, "Violence on the Jordan-Israel Border: A Jordanian View," *Foreign Affairs,* XXXII (July 1954) 552–62.

40. *N.Y. Times,* 14 March 1955.

41. Burns, p. 59.

42. Gen. Glubb maintains that, in the five years following Rhodes, there had not been a single incursion into Israel planned, executed or connived at by the Arab Legion.

43. *J. Post,* 28 March 1954, p. 1.

44. 15 *DK* 268 ff. (30 Nov. 1953).

45. *Ibid.*

46. *Hakidmah* (Tel Aviv), 6 Nov. 1953.

47. Sir Anthony Eden states in his memoirs that "The Agreement's most serious weakness was not recognized by many at the time. Egypt still proclaimed herself at war with Israel and there was nothing in the clauses to limit or restrain future Egyptian ambitions, except a reaffirmation of the freedom of the Suez Canal" (*Full Circle* [Boston, 1960], p. 289). If there is a somewhat hollow ring to this admission, it is because the British had remained in the Canal base for nearly three years after the September 1951 resolution of the Security Council without having affected Egypt's policy of interference with Israel commerce through the Canal.

48. Ambassador Eban in press briefing, 13 October 1955 (mimeo release by Israel Embassy, Washington).

49. U.N.S.C., *O.R.,* 686th Mtg., 7 Dec. 1954, p. 20.

50. Eden, p. 281.

51. *N.Y. Times,* 1 Feb. 1955.

52. Speech to officer graduates, quoted by Burns, p. 63.

53. Interview in *N.Y. Times,* 6 Oct. 1955, p. 1.

54. See his Suez nationalization speech of 26 July 1956, in R.I.I.A., *Documents 1956*, pp. 77–113.

55. 4 April 1955.

56. "The Egyptian Revolution," *Foreign Affairs*, XXXIII (Jan. 1955), 199.

57. Lord Birdwood, *Nuri As-Said: A Study Arab Leadership* (London, 1959), p. 229.

58. Burns, p. 76.

59. 12 *DK* 2985 (18 Aug. 1952).

60. Reprinted in *Rebirth and Destiny of Israel* (New York, 1954), p. 483.

61. Reported in *Jewish Observer*, II (30 Jan. 1953).

62. 16 *DK* 2548 (30 Aug. 1954).

63. Riftin, 14 *DK* 1586 (15 June 1953).

64. "The Egyptian Revolution," p. 199.

65. Interview with the author.

66. International News Service Dispatch from Tel Aviv dated 7 July 1955, reprinted in *Ner* (Jerusalem), VI (July–Aug. 1955), 12–13.

67. "Israel's Security . . ." in *Israel Government Year Book 1959–60*, p. 56. Also in interview in *Look,* 15 April 1958, p. 95.

68. The essence of Cairo's version of the affair, first published in a series of articles in *Al-Ahram,* was reprinted in the *Jewish Chronicle* of London on 18 November 1960 ("Middle East Diary," p. 19). The pseudonymous author of the column comments that "it is the only coherent account of the affair to be issued." A more detailed account, featuring the names of the principals, was published in the 6 December 1964 issue of the *Jewish Observer* (London).

69. Eliahu Hasin and Dan Horowitz, *Haparasha* (Tel Aviv, 1961), p. 120. The same information is contained in the book-length manuscript prepared for David Ben-Gurion by Haggai Eshed. Publication of a censored version of this manuscript took place, in serialized form, in *Ha-Arez* during February of 1965, notwithstanding the Defense Ministry's prohibition on grounds of "copyright."

70. See J. C. Hurewitz, "The Role of the Military in Society and Government in Israel," in *The Military in the Middle East: Problems in Society and Government,* ed. Sydney N. Fisher (Columbus, Ohio,

1963). In discussing the Lavon affair, Hurewitz concludes: "The existing arrangement . . . poses a potential threat to Israel's security because of inadequate co-ordination of defense activities at the executive level. It also leaves unresolved the question of control over the framing of defense policy" (p. 103).

71. For a more general version, see Laqueur, "Israel and the Arab Blocs," *Commentary*, XXIV (Sept. 1957), 187–88.

72. Hasin and Horowitz, p. 12.

73. 17 *DK* 590, 592 (17 Jan. 1955). (The term "piracy"— *shod*—was used by Sharett in rebuttal of the Herut proposal for interfering with Egyptian shipping in retaliation against the detention of the Bat Galim.)

74. 17 *DK* 655–56 (25 Jan. 1955).

75. Hasin and Horowitz, pp. 67 ff.

76. 14 *DK* 1581 (15 June 1953).

77. 15 *DK* 313 (7 Dec. 1953).

78. 20 *DK* 2042 (18 June 1956).

79. 20 *DK* 2067 (19 June 1956).

Chapter V

1. *P.D.H.C.,* Vol. 515, col. 894, 11 May 1953. Calling himself a "faithful supporter of the Zionist cause ever since Balfour," Churchill said: "I earnestly pray that the great Zionist conception of a home for this historic people . . . may eventually receive its full fruition."

2. *P.D.H.C.,* Vol. 531, cols. 724–820.

3. As in the Tripartite Declaration of 25 May 1950. Another example is a speech by Byroade to the American Jewish Committee on 31 Jan. 1954.

4. Typical was the editorial in *Ha-Boker,* 24 Aug. 1953.

5. See Nathan Feinberg and Associates, *Israel and the United Nations* (New York, 1956), pp. 6–16.

6. See Arieh L. Plotkin, "Israel's Role in the United Nations: An Analytical Study" (unpublished Ph.D. dissertation, Princeton University, 1955).

7. U.N.S.C., *O.R.,* 664th Mtg., 29 March 1954, p. 12.

8. Page 38.

9. Altman in 14 *DK* 1588 (15 June 1953); Begin in 19 *DK* 90 (19 Oct. 1955).

10. Rimalt in 19 *DK* 92 (19 Oct. 1955).

11. Yona Kesseh (Mapai), 20 *DK* 1695 (22 April 1956).

12. James G. McDonald, *My Mission to Israel* (New York, 1951), p. 183.

13. *Rebirth and Destiny of Israel* (New York, 1954), p. 479.

14. 19 *DK* 87 (18 Oct. 1955)

15. "Israel's Security and Her International Position before and after the Sinai Campaign," *Israel Government Year Book 5720 (1959/60)*, p. 77.

16. An account of the origins and history of this group may be found in Samuel Halperin's chapter on "Zionist Counterpropaganda: The Case of the American Council for Judaism," in his *Political World of American Zionism* (Detroit, 1961), pp. 281–90.

17. J. C. Hurewitz, *Struggle for Palestine* (New York, 1950), p. 309. See also Frank E. Manuel, *The Realities of American-Palestine Relations* (Washington, 1949), pp. 300–61; and *The Forrestal Diaries* (New York, 1951), pp. 309, 322–23.

18. Rabbi Abba H. Silver, interviewed in *J Post,* 29 March 1963.

19. At the decisive moment, President Eisenhower showed himself unconcerned with the possible adverse effect of his actions on the Jewish vote in the presidential elections of 1956. He emphasized this in a warning to Ambassador Eban, through Secretary Dulles (transcript of 26 Jan. 1960 news conference in *N.Y. Times,* 27 Jan. 1960). Since Eisenhower carried New York by a comfortable margin, his discounting of the Jewish vote turned out to be justified, at least in this particular instance. It must be recalled, too, that the Sinai invasion was unpopular among American Jews in its initial stage.

20. 16 *DK* 2555–56 (30 Aug. 1954).

21. Cf. "Egypt Criticizes Zionists of U.S." *N.Y. Times,* 28 Oct. 1954.

22. Hal Lehrman, "American Policy and Arab-Israeli Peace," *Commentary,* XVII (June 1954) 546–56. Passage quoted on p. 549.

Chapter VI

1. 19 *DK* 85 (19 Oct. 1955).

2. Interview in *U.S. News and World Report,* 4 Nov. 1955, pp. 50–54.

3. 19 *DK* 677 (2 Jan. 1956).

4. *Ibid.,* p. 671.

5. "Israel's Security and Her International Position before and after the Sinai Campaign," *Israel Government Year Book 5720 (1959/60),* pp. 17, 25.

6. Interview with Israel army officer formerly on General Staff.

7. E. L. M. Burns, *Between Arab and Israeli* (London, 1962), p. 99.

8. Abba Eban, *Voice of Israel* (New York, 1957), p. 139.

9. Interview with Kennett Love in *N.Y. Times,* 5 Oct. 1955.

10. 19 *DK* 232 (2 Nov. 1955).

11. Background talk by Ambassador Eban to correspondents, 13 Oct. 1955.

12. *U.S. News and World Report,* 4 Nov. 1955.

13. 19 *DK* 229 (2 Nov. 1955).

14. D. Dishon, "The Foreign Policy of the Revolutionary Regime in Egypt," *Ha-Mizrah he-Hadash,* VII (1956), 180–84.

15. Israel Beer, *Der Nahe Osten—Schicksalsland zwischen Ost und West* (München, n.d.), pp. 180–81.

16. "Israel's Security," p. 15.

17. Oskar Morgenstern, *The Question of National Defense* (New York, 1961), pp. 12–13.

Chapter VII

1. Cf. Amitai Etzioni, "Alternative Ways to Democracy: The Example of Israel," *Political Science Quarterly,* LXXIV (June 1959) 208–09.

2. Dan Horowitz, "The Permanent and the Transitory in Foreign

Policy" (Hebrew), *Min ha-Yesod* (Tel Aviv, 1962)—a collection of essays on political matters (the title of the book means "From the Ground Up") published by the group by the same name which formed around Pinhas Lavon after his ouster.

3. Page 44.

4. 16 *DK* 2558 (30 August 1954).

5. 16 *DK* 2607 (1 Sept. 1954).

6. 19 *DK* 88 (18 Oct.) and 236 (2 Nov. 1955). Mrs. Esther Raziel-Naor of Herut used a similar argument on 24 Oct. p. 135.

7. 19 *DK* 240 (2 Nov. 1955).

8. 19 *DK* 107–08 (19 Oct. 1955).

9. *Ibid.*

10. *Ibid.,* p. 250.

11. *Ibid.,* p. 244.

12. 19 *DK* 690 (2 Jan. 1956).

13. *Ibid.,* p. 697.

14. 19 *DK* 722 (9 Jan. 1956).

15. *Ibid.,* 732.

16. 19 *DK* 733–34 (9 Jan. 1956).

17. 19 *DK* 232 (2 Nov. 1955).

18. *Ibid.,* 266–67.

19. On 15 October 1956, Ben-Gurion disclosed that some General Zionists had also pressed for preventive military action, though not from the public platform (*Ma'arekhet Sinai* [Tel Aviv, 1959], p. 193).

20. 19 *DK* 671 (2 Jan. 1956).

21. 20 *DK* 1689–91 (22 April 1956).

22. *N.Y. Times,* 4 Oct. 1955, p. 16.

23. 19 *DK* 232 (2 Nov. 1955).

24. *J Post,* 4 Nov. 1955.

25. 19 *DK* 236 (2 Nov. 1955).

26. *Ibid.,* p. 282.

27. Pp. 104–06. These emissaries included, in addition to U.S. Secretary of the Treasury Robert Anderson, Maltese Premier Dom Mintoff and Maurice Orbach, M.P.

28. Pages 118–19.

29. 19 *DK* 680–81 (2 Jan. 1956).

30. Address to National Press Club, Washington, 21 Nov. 1955 (text in *Israel Digest*, 25 Nov. 1955).

31. *P.D.H.C.*, Vol. 539, col. 899.

32. Text in *D.S.B.* 33 (5 Sept. 1955), 378–80.

33. Message read at Madison Square Garden rally on 15 Nov. 1955 (*J Post*, 17 Nov. 1955).

34. 19 *DK* 88 (19 Oct. 1955).

35. *Ibid.*, 85.

36. 16 Nov. 1955, p. 11.

37. 19 *DK* 235 (2 Nov. 1955).

38. *Ibid.*, pp. 235, 245.

39. 19 *DK* 696 (3 Jan. 1956).

40. *N.Y. Times*, 2 Feb. 1956, p. 4.

41. *P.D.H.C.*, Vol. 549, cols. 2116–21, 7 March 1956.

42. Actually, the U.S. had permitted Israel to purchase some categories of weapons on a limited scale.

43. *D.S.B.* 32 (4 April 1955), 546–49.

44. Background talk to correspondents, 13 Oct. 1955.

45. 19 *DK* 85 (18 Oct. 1955).

46. *J Post*, 1 Nov. 1955, p. 1.

47. Michel Bar-Zohar, *Suez Ultra-Secret* (Paris, 1964), pp. 110 and earlier. Bar-Zohar's book, written as a Ph.D. dissertation at the Sorbonne, is a largely undocumented account of Franco-Israel relations culminating in the Suez crisis.

48. 19 *DK* 678 (2 Jan. 1956).

49. *Ibid.*, p. 671.

50. D.B.G. in 19 *DK* 232 (2 Nov. 1955); Eban press statement 13 October 1955; Sharett interview, *U.S. News*, 4 Nov. 1955.

51. Y. Rafael in 19 *DK* 133 (24 Oct. 1955), among others.

52. *N.Y. Times*, 9 Oct., 18 Oct., and 13 Nov. 1955.

53. Text of Dulles letter in *D.S.B.* 34 (20 Feb. 1956) 285–86.

54. 19 *DK* 681 (2 Jan. 1956).

55. Page 289.

56. John C. Campbell, *Defense of the Middle East* (New York, 1958), pp. 87–88.

57. Department of State Press Release No. 517, 26 Aug. 1956.

58. 19 *DK* 678 (2 Jan. 1956).

59. *Ibid.*

60. Address to National Press Club, 21 Nov. 1955.

61. 19 *DK* 325–26 (15 Nov. 1955).

62. *The Times* (London), 14 Nov. 1955.

63. *O.R.,* 10th Session, 531st Mtg., p. 210.

64. Lord Birdwood, *Nuri As-Said: A Study in Arab Leadership* (London, 1959), p. 236.

65. "Arab-Israel Peace Held Possible as British Press Separate Talks," *N.Y. Times,* 29 Nov. 1955, p. 1.

66. *P.D.H.C.,* Vol. 547, cols. 838–39.

67. Page 368.

68. Yigal Allon, "Israel at Bay," *Midstream,* II (Spring 1956), 5–11.

69. 19 *DK* 684 (2 Jan. 1956).

70. 20 *DK* 2067 (19 June 1956).

71. E. L. M. Burns, *Between Arab and Israeli* (London, 1962), pp. 140–41.

72. *Idem.*

73. *Ibid.,* p. 142.

74. S/3562 corr. 1, 4 April 1956.

75. S/3587 and S/3596.

76. Burns, p. 143.

Chapter VIII

1. Erskine B. Childers, *The Road to Suez* (London, 1962), p. 183.

2. Moshe Dayan, *Diary of the Sinai Campaign* (London, 1966), pp. 12–13.

3. *Ibid.,* pp. 14–15.

4. *Ibid.,* p. 71.

5. E. Rimalt (Gen. Zionist), 20 *DK* 1691 (22 April 1956).

6. See Michel Bar-Zohar, *Suez Ultra-Secret* (Paris, 1964), pp. 110–21.

7. *J Post,* 15 April and 12 May 1956.

8. Ben-Gurion, "Israel's Security and Her International Position before and after the Sinai Campaign," *Israel Government Year Book 5720 (1959/60)*, pp. 26, 28.

9. *Ibid.*, p. 26.

10. *Ibid.*

11. *Ibid.*, p. 27 (English trans.).

12. The principle sources used in this account are: *United Nations Yearbook 1956;* U.S. Department of State, *The Suez Canal Problem, July 26–September 22, 1956: A Documentary Publication;* "Issues Before the Twelfth General Assembly," *International Conciliation,* Sept. 1956; Royal Institute of International Affairs, *Survey of International Affairs 1956–1958;* Anthony Eden, *Full Circle* (Boston, 1960). A detailed, if somewhat partisan, account of the American Secretary of State's role in the crisis is Herman Finer's *Dulles Over Suez: The Theory and Practice of his Diplomacy* (Chicago, 1964).

13. *D.S.B.* 35 (30 July 1956) 188.

14. *D.S.B.* 33 (10 Oct. 1955) 56.

15. Eden, p. 475.

16. *Ibid.*, pp. 487–88.

17. Characteristic of the United States' equivocal attitude was a statement by President Eisenhower on 8 August in which he declared that "every important question in the world . . . should be settled by negotiation," but added, "I don't mean to say that anyone has to surrender rights without using everything they can to preserve their rights" (*The Suez Canal Problem,* p. 40).

18. James E. Dougherty, "The Aswan Decision in Perspective," *Political Science Quarterly,* LXXIV (March 1959), 41.

19. The term was used by Dulles at the meeting of the American, French, and British foreign ministers in London on 1 August (Eden, p. 487).

20. Dean Acheson, *Power and Diplomacy* (Cambridge, 1958), p. 112.

21. *The Suez Canal Problem,* pp. 291–92.

22. *Survey of International Affairs 1956–1958,* pp. 39–40.

23. According to Finer (p. 261), Dulles felt he had been deliberately misled on this point by Eden and Lloyd, who had failed to in-

form him of their intention before Dulles left London on the previous day.

24. Text of resolution, S/3671, 13 Oct. 1956.

25. See editorial in *Davar*, 2 Aug. 1956.

26. "Hebrew Corner," Cairo Radio, 1 Aug. 1956. Quoted in *Jewish Agency Digest*, 10 Aug. 1956, p. 1503.

27. Between 1951 and 1954 Egypt had allowed more than 60 ships not owned by Israel but with Israel cargoes to transit the Canal. The arrangement was unsatisfactory both for Israel and the owners because Egypt reserved the right of inspection and seizure and exercised it from time to time.

28. Text in *Ma'arekhet Sinai* (Tel Aviv, 1959), pp. 148–49.

29. *J Post*, 21 Sept. 1956, p. 4.

30. Interview with senior army officer.

31. Edgar O'Ballance, *The Sinai Campaign* (New York, 1959), pp. 26–77, *passim*.

32. 30 *DK* 78–79.

33. O'Ballance, p. 68.

34. F. L. M. Burns, *Between Arab and Israeli* (London, 1962), p. 165.

35. Ten Israelis were killed in this attack (Ben-Gurion in *Ma'arekhet Sinai*, p. 210).

36. Burns, pp. 171–72.

37. *Ma'arekhet Sinai*, p. 211. Cf. also Moshe Dayan, *Diary of the Sinai Campaign* (London, 1961), pp. 43–57.

38. Yair Evron, *"Mediniut Huz ha-khefufa la-Zava"* (When The Army Makes Foreign Policy), *Ha-Arez*, 5 Nov. 1965.

39. *J Post*, 14 Oct. 1956. See also Dayan, p. 53.

40. *Ma'arekhet Sinai*, p. 214.

41. *Ibid.*

42. Dayan, p. 20.

43. *Ibid.*, p. 22. The entry of 17 September refers to a date about a week earlier.

44. *Ibid.*

45. *Ibid.*, p. 64.

46. *Ibid.*, pp. 30–32.

47. *Ibid.*, Appendix I.

264

48. Geoffrey Barraclough *et al., Survey of International Affairs 1956–1958* (London, 1962), p. 48.

49. Terence Robertson, *Crisis: The Inside Story of the Suez Conspiracy* (New York: 1965), p. 163.

50. Dayan, Appendix II.

51. "Israel's Security and Her International Position before and after the Sinai Campaign," *Israel Government Year Book 5720 (1959/60)*, p. 31.

52. In his speech to the Knesset on 7 November, the Prime Minister began by elaborating on this theme, as though the conquest of the peninsula had occurred as a fortuitous result of the Egyptian counterattack. But on the following day he listed occupation of Sinai as a prime aim (*Ma'arekhet Sinai,* p. 219).

53. Frontispiece to Lt. Col. Benzion Tehan, "The Sinai Campaign," in *Ma'arakhot* (Israel army publication), May 1958.

54. Interview with the writer.

55. Dayan, p. 163.

56. English text in *Jewish Observer* (London), 16 Nov. 1956, p. 17.

57. O'Ballance, p. 79.

58. Randolph Churchill, *The Rise and Fall of Sir Anthony Eden* (London, 1959), p. 267.

59. Pages 178, 179.

60. *J Post,* 29 Oct. 1956, p. 1.

Conclusion

1. "Israel's Security and Her International Position before and after the Sinai Campaign," *Israel Government Year Book 5720 (1959/60)*, p. 55.

2. English texts of the exchange of correspondence between Eisenhower, Bulganin and Ben-Gurion; of the 7 November Knesset speech by Ben-Gurion; and of his radio broadcast to the nation on 8 November may be found in the *Jewish Observer* for 16 November 1956, pp. 11–17. Hebrew texts in Ben-Gurion, *Ma'arekhet Sinai* (Tel Aviv, 1959), pp. 219–32.

The Sequel: 1967

1. Of the books that have so far appeared, the volume by Randolph and Winston Churchill, *The Six Day War* (London, 1967), has vivid and authoritative reports of Israeli strategy and tactics, based on interviews with top military and political figures.

2. Haim Herzog, "What Brought Abdul Nasser to the Abyss?" *Ha-Arez,* 2 June 1967, p. 3.

3. Resolution adopted by Knesset, 2 Aug. 1967.

≺≺≺≺

Bibliography

Public Documents

Great Britain. *Parliamentary Debates* (Commons), Vols. 531, 547, 549, 557.

Israel. *Bank of Israel Report,* 1961.

Israel. *Divrei ha-Kneset* (Parliamentary Records), 1949–1956.

Israel. *Government Year Book,* 1951–1952, 1953–1954, 1959–1960.

Israel. [*Reshumot*]- *Sefer ha-Huqim* (Laws of Israel), 1950.

United Nations. *Documents of the U.N. Conference on International Organization, San Francisco, 1945.*

United Nations, General Assembly. *Official Records,* 1948, 1949, 1950, 1952, 1955.

United Nations, Security Council. *Official Records,* 1951, 1953, 1954, 1955.

U.N. *Yearbook,* 1956.

UNESCO. *Compulsory Education in the Arab States.* Paris, 1956.

U.S. Department of State. *The Department of State Bulletin,* 1951, 1953, 1954, 1955, 1956.

U.S. Department of State. *Press Release* No. 517, 26 August 1956.

U.S. Department of State. *The Suez Canal Problem, July 26–September 22, 1956: A Documentary Publication.* Washington: G.P.O., Publication No. 6392, 1956.

U.S. Senate, Committee on Foreign Relations and Committee on Armed Services. *Hearings.* 85th Congress, 1st Session, January–February 1957.

267

Books

Akzin, Benjamin. *New States and International Organization.* Paris: UNESCO and International Political Science Association, 1953.

Allon, Yigal. *Masakh shel Hol.* Tel Aviv: Kibbutz Hameuhad Publishers Ltd., 1959.

American Jewish Year Book, 1952. New York: The American Jewish Committee.

Bar-Zohar, Michel. *Suez Ultra-Secret.* Paris: Fayard, 1964.

Beer, Israel. *Der Nahe Osten–Schicksalsland zwischen Ost und West.* München: Verlag Europäischer Wehrkunde, n.d.

Begin, Menahem. *The Revolt.* New York: Henry Schuman, 1951.

Ben Asher, A. A. [Katriel Katz]. *Yahsei Huts shel Israel.* Tel Aviv: Ayanot, 1955.

Ben-Gurion, David. *Ma'arekhet Sinai.* Tel Aviv: Am Oved, 1959.

———. *Rebirth and Destiny of Israel.* New York: Philosophical Library, 1954.

Bernadotte, Folke. *To Jerusalem.* London: Hodder & Stoughton, 1951.

Birdwood, Lord. *Nuri As-Said: A Study in Arab Leadership.* London: Cassell & Co., 1959.

Bloomfield, L. M. *Egypt, Israel and the Gulf of Aqaba in International Law.* Toronto: Carswell, 1957.

Bromberger, Merry and Serge. *Secrets of Suez.* London: Pan Books, 1957.

Burns, Lt. Gen. E. L. M. *Between Arab and Israeli.* London: Geo. G. Harrap & Co., 1962.

Campbell, John C. *Defense of the Middle East: Problems of American Policy.* New York: Harper, 1958.

Childers, Erskine. *The Road to Suez.* London: McGibbon & Kee, 1962.

Churchill, Randolph. *The Rise and Fall of Sir Anthony Eden.* London: McGibbon & Kee, 1959.

Claude, Inis L., Jr. *Power and International Relations.* New York: Random House, 1962.

Connell, John [Robertson, John Henry]. *The Most Important Country: The True Story of the Suez Crisis and the Events Leading to It.* London: Cassell & Co., 1957.

Cooke, Hedley V. *Israel: A Blessing and a Curse.* London: Stevens & Sons, 1960.

Crossman, R. H. S. *Palestine Mission.* New York and London: Harper, 1947.

Dayan, Moshe. *Diary of the Sinai Campaign.* London: Weidenfeld & Nicolson, 1966.

Eban, Abba. *Voice of Israel.* New York: Horizon Press, 1957.

Eden, Anthony. *Full Circle.* Boston: The Houghton Mifflin Co., 1960.

Elath, Eliahu. *Israel and Her Neighbors.* Cleveland: World Publishing Co., 1957.

Ellis, Harry B. *Challenge in the Middle East: Communist Influence and American Policy.* New York: The Ronald Press, 1960.

———. *Israel and the Middle East.* New York: The Ronald Press, 1957.

Eytan, Walter. *The First Ten Years: A Diplomatic History of Israel.* New York: Simon & Schuster, 1958.

Feinberg, Nathan. *A State of War after the Cessation of Hostilities.* Jerusalem: Magnes Press, 1961.

——— and Associates. *Israel and the United Nations.* New York: Carnegie Endowment for International Peace, 1956.

Finer, Herman. *Dulles Over Suez: The Theory and Practice of His Diplomacy.* Chicago: Quadrangle Books, 1964.

Foot, Michael, and Jones, Mervyn. *Guilty Men.* New York: Rinehart & Co., 1957.

Fox, Annette Baker. *The Power of Small States.* Chicago: University of Chicago Press, 1959.

Frankland, Noble (ed.) *Documents on International Affairs, 1955.* London: Oxford University Press for the Royal Institute of International Affairs, 1958.

——— (ed.) *Documents on International Affairs, 1956.* London:

269

Oxford University Press for the Royal Institute of International Affairs, 1959.

Gabbay, Rony E. *A Political Study of the Arab-Jewish Conflict.* Geneva: Librairie E. Droz, 1959.

Glubb, John Bagot. *A Soldier with the Arabs.* London: Hodder & Stoughton, 1957.

Granados, Jorge Garcia. *The Birth of Israel.* New York: Knopf, 1949.

Gross, Feliks, and Vlavianos, Basil (eds.) *Struggle for Tomorrow: Modern Political Ideologies of the Jewish People.* New York: Arts, Inc., 1954.

Grossmann, Kurt R. *Germany's Moral Debt: The German-Israel Agreement.* Washington: Public Affairs Press, 1954.

Haas, Ernest B., and Whiting, Allen S. *Dynamics of International Relations.* New York: McGraw Hill, 1956.

Halperin, Samuel. *The Political World of American Zionism.* Detroit: Wayne University Press, 1961.

Halpern, Ben. *The Idea of the Jewish State.* Cambridge: Harvard University Press, 1961.

Harbison, Frederick and Ibrahim, Abdelkader Ibrahim. *Human Resources for Egyptian Enterprise.* New York: McGraw Hill, 1959.

Hartmann, Frederick H. *The Relations of Nations.* New York: The Macmillan Co., 1957.

Hasin, Eliahu and Don Horowitz. *Ha-Parashah.* Tel Aviv: 'Am ha-Sefer, 1961.

Henriques, Robert. *One Hundred Hours to Suez.* New York: Viking, 1957.

Hertzberg, Arthur. *The Zionist Idea.* New York: Doubleday, 1959.

Horowitz, David. *State in the Making.* New York: Knopf, 1949.

Hurewitz, J. C. *Diplomacy in the Near and Middle East,* Vol. II. Princeton: Van Nostrand, 1956.

———. *The Struggle for Palestine.* New York: Norton, 1950.

Hutchison, Elmo H. *Violent Truce: A Military Observer Looks at the Arab-Israel Conflict 1951–1955.* New York: Devin-Adair, 1956.

Ionides, Michael. *Divide and Lose: The Arab Revolt 1955–1958.* London: Geoffrey Bles, 1960.

Issawi, Charles. *Egypt at Mid-Century*. New York: Oxford University Press, 1954.

Johnson, Paul. *The Suez War*. New York: Greenberg, 1957.

Joseph, Dov. *The Faithful City: The Siege of Jerusalem 1948*. New York: Simon & Schuster, 1960.

Kedourie, Elie. *Nationalism*. New York: Praeger, 1960.

Kimche, Jon. *Seven Fallen Pillars*. New York: Praeger, 1953.

Kimche, Jon and David. *Both Sides of the Hill: Britain and the Palestine War*. London: Secker & Warburg, 1960.

Kirk, George E. *A Short History of the Middle East* (6th ed.). New York: Praeger, 1960.

Knorr, Klaus. *The War Potential of Nations*. Princeton: Princeton University Press, 1956.

Laqueur, Walter Z. *Communism and Nationalism in the Middle East*. New York: Praeger, 1956.

Levin, Harry. *I Saw the Battle of Jerusalem*. New York: Scribner, 1950.

Lorch, Lt. Col. Netanel. *The Edge of the Sword: Israel's War of Independence 1947–1949*. New York: Putnam's, 1961.

McDonald, James G. *My Mission to Israel*. New York: Simon & Schuster, 1951.

Marshall, S. L. A. *Sinai Victory*. New York: Morrow, 1958.

Meyer, Albert J. *Middle Eastern Capitalism*. Cambridge: Harvard University Press, 1959.

Millis, Walter (ed.) *The Forrestal Diaries*. New York: Viking, 1951.

Morgenstern, Oskar. *The Question of National Defense*. New York: Vintage Books, 1961.

Morgenthau, Hans J. *Politics Among Nations* (2nd ed.) New York: Knopf, 1954.

O'Ballance, Edgar. *The Arab-Israel War of 1948*. London: Faber & Faber, 1951.

——. *The Sinai Campaign 1956*. New York: Praeger, 1959.

Palestine: A Study of Jewish, Arab and British Policies. 2 vols. New Haven: Yale University Press for Esco Foundation for Palestine, 1947.

Pearlman, Moshe. *The Army of Israel*. New York: Philosophical Library, 1950.

Peretz, Don. *Israel and the Palestine Arabs*. Washington: The Middle East Institute, 1958.

Robertson, Terence. *Crisis: The Inside Story of the Suez Conspiracy*. New York: Atheneum, 1965.

Rosenne, Shabtai. *Israel's Armistice Agreements with the Arab States*. Tel Aviv: Blumstein's Bookstore for Israel Law Association, 1951.

Sacher, Harry. *Israel—The Establishment of a State*. London: Weidenfeld & Nicolson, 1952.

Safran, Nadav. *The United States and Israel*. Cambridge: Harvard University Press, 1963.

Sayegh, Fayez A. *The Arab Israeli Conflict*. New York: Arab Information Center, 1956.

Spykman, Nicholas. *American Strategy in World Politics*. New York: Harcourt, 1942.

Survey of International Affairs 1956–1958, by Geoffrey Barraclough and others. London: Oxford for Royal Institute of International Affairs, 1962.

Tournoux, J-R. *Secrets d'Etat*. Paris: Librairie Plon, 1960.

Utley, T. E. *Not Guilty (The Conservative Reply)*. London: Macgibbon, 1957.

Wheelock, Keith. *Nasser's New Egypt*. London: Stevens & Sons, 1960.

Wint, Guy, and Calvocoressi, Peter. *Middle East Crisis*. Baltimore: Penguin Books, 1957.

Articles

Allon, Yigal. "Israel at Bay," *Midstream,* II (Spring 1956), 5–11.

Attwood, William. Interview with David Ben-Gurion, *Look,* 15 April 1958, pp. 92–96.

Badeau, John. "The Middle East: Conflicts in Priority," *Foreign Affairs,* XXXVI (Jan. 1958), 232–40.

Ben-Gurion, David. "Israel's Security and her International Position before and after the Sinai Campaign," *Israel Government Year Book 5720 (1959/60)*.

BIBLIOGRAPHY

Binder, Leonard. "The Middle East as a Subordinate International System," *World Politics,* X (April 1958), 408–29.

Brilliant, Moshe. "Israel's Policy of Reprisals," *Harper's,* March 1955, pp. 68–72.

Burns, A. A. "A New Balance of Power," *Journal of International Affairs,* XIV (January 1960), 61–69.

Bz'oza, Hanoch. "Two Truths in Conflict," *New Outlook,* I (June 1958), 23–28.

Childers, Erskine B. "The Ultimatum," *The Spectator,* 30 October 1959, p. 579.

Dayan, Moshe. "Israel's Border and Security Problems," *Foreign Affairs,* XXXIII (January 1955), 250–67.

Dinitz, Simcha. "The Legal Aspects of the Egyptian Blockade of the Suez Canal," *Georgetown Law Journal,* XLV (Winter 1956–1957), 169–99.

Dishon, D. "The Foreign Policy of the Revolutionary Regime in Egypt," *Ha-Mizrah he-Hadash,* VII (1956), 180–84.

Dougherty, James E. "The Aswan Decision in Perspective," *Political Science Quarterly,* LXXIV (March 1959), 21–45.

Ephraim, S. "The Canaanites," *Jewish Frontier,* XIX (August 1956), 25–26.

Etzioni, Amitai. "Alternative Ways to Democracy: The Example of Israel," *Political Science Quarterly,* LXXIV (June 1959), 196–214.

Eytan, Walter. "Israel's Foreign Policy and International Relations," *Middle Eastern Affairs,* II (May 1951), 155–60.

Flapan, Simha. "The Theory of Interceptive War," *New Outlook,* III (April 1960), 42–43 (Review of Allon).

Fox, William T. R. "The Super-Powers at San Francisco," *The Review of Politics,* VIII (January 1946), 115–27.

Glubb, John Bagot. "Violence on the Jordan-Israel Border, a Jordanian View," *Foreign Affairs,* XXXII (July 1954), 552–62.

Haas, Ernst B. "The Balance of Power: Prescription, Concept or Propaganda?" *World Politics,* IV (July 1953).

Henriques, Robert. "The Ultimatum: A Dissenting View," *The Spectator* (London), 6 November 1959, p. 623.

Horowitz, Dan. "The Permanent and the Transitory in Foreign

Policy" (Hebrew), *Min Hayesod* (Tel Aviv: Amikam, 1962), pp. 94–128.

Hourani, Albert. "The Middle East and the Crisis of 1956," *Middle Eastern Affairs,* St. Antony's Papers No. 4 (London: Chatto & Windus, 1958).

Hurewitz, J. C. "The Israeli-Syrian Crisis in the Light of the Arab-Israeli Armistice System," *International Organization,* V (1951), 459–479.

——. "The Role of the Military in Society and Government in Israel," *The Military in the Middle East: Problems in Society and Government,* ed. by Sydney N. Fisher (Columbus: Ohio State University Press, 1963).

Issawi, Charles. "The Bases of Arab Unity," *International Affairs,* XXXI (January 1955), 36–47.

Jessup, Philip C. "Should International Law Recognize an Intermediate State Between Peace and War?" *American Journal of International Law,* XLVIII (1954), 98–103.

Jones, Stephen B. "The Power Inventory and National Strategy," *World Politics,* VI (July 1954), 421–52.

Jordan, Amos A., Jr. "Basic Deterrence and the New Balance of Power," *Journal of International Affairs,* XIV (January 1960), 49–60.

Kirk, Grayson A. "In Search of the National Interest," *World Politics,* V (October 1952), 113.

Knorr, Klaus. "The Concept of Economic Potential for War," *World Politics,* X (October 1957), 49–62.

Kurzweil, Baruch. "The New 'Canaanism' in Israel," *Judaism,* II (Jan. 1953), 3–15.

Laqueur, Walter Z. "Israel and the Arab Blocs," *Commentary,* XXIV (September 1957).

Lehrman, Hal. "The Arabs, Israel, and Near East Defense," *Commentary,* XIV (December 1952), 563–74.

——. "American Policy and Arab-Israeli Peace," *Commentary,* XVII (June 1954), 546–56.

Lenczowski, George. "Evolution of Soviet Policy Toward the Middle East," *Journal of Politics,* XX (February 1958), 162–86.

Levie, Howard S. "The Nature and Scope of the Armistice Agreement," *AJIL,* L (October 1956), 880–906.

Meyer, Albert J. "Economic Thought and Its Application and Methodology in the Middle East," *Middle East Economic Papers* (1956), pp. 66–74.

Mohn, Paul. "Problems of Truce Supervision," *International Conciliation* 478 (February 1952).

Morgenthau, Hans J. "Khrushchev's New Cold War Strategy," *Commentary*, XXVIII (November 1959), 381–88.

Nasser, Gamal Abdel. "The Egyptian Revolution," *Foreign Affairs*, XXXIII (January 1955), 199–211.

Nolte, Richard H. "American Policy in the Middle East," *Journal of International Affairs* XIII (2 – 1959), 113–25.

Oron, Yitzhak. "The Revolutionary Regime and Egypt's Potential," *Ha-Mizrah he-Hadash*, VII (1956), 173–179. Hebrew.

Peretz, Don. "Development of the Jordan Valley Waters," *Middle East Journal*, IX (Autumn 1955), 397–410.

Rubenstein, Richard L. "The Significance of Zionism," *The Reconstructionist*, 29 April 1960.

Rubinstein, Aryeh, "German Reparations in Retrospect," *Midstream*, VIII (Winter 1962).

Schechtman, Joseph B. "The Frozen Stampede," *Midstream*, VI (Summer 1960).

Schen, Israel, "B. G. and the Gallant Six Hundred," *The Jewish Spectator*, XXVI (January 1961).

Simon, Herbert A. "Notes on the Observation and Measurement of Political Power," *Journal of Politics*, XV (November 1953), 500–16.

Smolansky, Oles. "Soviet Policy in the Arab East 1945–57," *Journal of International Affairs*, XIII (1959), 126–40.

Snyder, Glenn H. "Balance of Power in the Missile Age," *Journal of International Affairs*, XIV (1960), 21–34.

Stock, Ernest. "The Press of Israel," *Journalism Quarterly*, XXXI (Fall 1954), 481–94.

——. "Egypt-Israel: Some Earlier Relations," *The Reconstructionist*, 20 March 1959.

"Suez and Its Consequences: The Israel View," *The World Today*, XIII (May 1957), 152–61.

Teller, Judd L. "The Making of the Ideals that Rule Israel," *Commentary*, XVIII (January–February 1954), 49–57, 157–62.

Vagts, Alfred. "The Balance of Power: Growth of an Idea," *World Politics,* I (October 1948).

Wheeler, Geoffrey. "Russia and the Middle East," *Political Quarterly* (London), XXVIII (April–June 1957) 127–36.

Wolfers, Arnold. "In Defense of Small Countries," *Yale Review,* XXXIII (Winter 1944).

Wright, Quincy. "International Conflict and the United Nations," *World Politics,* X (October 1957) 24–48.

Newspapers and Periodicals

Al ha-Mishmar (Tel Aviv). Daily of Mapam party.

Davar (Tel Aviv). Daily of Histadrut.

Ha-Arez (Tel Aviv). Independent daily.

Ha-Kidmah (Tel Aviv). German-language weekly of Progressive party. Defunct.

Ha-Zofeh (Tel Aviv). Daily of National Religious party.

Israel Digest (formerly the *Jewish Agency's Digest of Press and Events*).

The Jerusalem Post. English-language daily.

The Jewish Chronicle (London). Weekly.

Jewish Observer and Middle East Review (London). Weekly.

Ma'ariv (Tel Aviv). Independent afternoon daily.

Ner (Jerusalem). Monthly of *Ihud* Association.

The New York Herald-Tribune.

The New York Times.

Orient (Paris).

Soviet News (London).

The Times (London).

U.S. News and World Report.

Yediot Ahronot (Tel Aviv). Independent afternoon daily.

Yediot Hadashot (Tel Aviv). Independent German-language daily.

Zionist Newsletter (Jerusalem). Published by the Information Department of the Jewish Agency and the World Zionist Organization. Defunct.

Zmanim (Tel Aviv). Progressive Party daily. Defunct.

Unpublished Material

American Zionist Committee for Public Affairs. "For Peace and Economic development in the Near East." Pamphlet issued in Washington, December 1954.

Council of Jewish Federations and Welfare Funds. "Ten Years of American Aid to Israel." New York, November 1957. Mimeo.

Eban, Abba. Transcript of Press Briefing, 13 October 1955. Washington: Embassy of Israel. Mimeo.

Nasir, Khalil Ahmad. "The Foreign Relations of Pakistan: The First Ten Years." Ph.D. Dissertation, American University, 1959.

Peretz, Don. "Report to the Rockefeller Foundation on the Arab Refugees." New York, 1962. Mimeo.

Plotkin, Arieh L. "Israel's Role in the United Nations: An Analytical Study." Ph.D. Dissertation, Princeton University, 1955.

Sharett, Moshe. "The Jewish State and the Jewish People." Address to Plenary Session of World Jewish Congress, Stockholm, August 1959. Typescript, obtained from World Jewish Congress, New York.

Smolansky, Oles. "The Soviet Union and the Arab East, 1947–57: A Study in Diplomatic Relations." Ph.D. Dissertation, Columbia University, 1959.

Terry, E. A. "An Analysis of the Power Inventory of States and National Strategy and their Relationship in the Context of International Politics." Ph.D. Dissertation, American University, 1949.

Index

INDEX